CRAIG

MW00323026

BROOKLYN'S
MOST WANTED

THE TOP 100 CRIMINALS,
CROOKS AND CREEPS FROM
THE COUNTY OF THE KINGS

"Never has anyone put together a look into so many of Brooklyn's worst. This is a great read I highly recommend." —Thomas Dades, retired NYPD Detective and Bestselling Author of "Friends of the Family"

WILDBLUE
PRESS

BROOKLYN'S MOST WANTED

published by:

WILDBLUE PRESS

P.O. Box 102440

Denver, Colorado 80250

ISBN 978-1-942266-96-9   Trade Paperback

ISBN 978-1-942266-97-6   eBook

Interior Formatting/Book Cover Design by Elijah Toten www. totencreative.com

BROOKLYN'S
MOST WANTED

Dear Chrissy
+ Jesus,
Thank you so much
for the support.

Craig M

BROOKLYN'S MOST WANTED
Official Walking Tour

LEGEND:

1 - 420 Graham Avenue (Williamsburg), site of The Motion Lounge, mob nightclub owned by Bonanno crime family caporegime Dominick Napolitano, one of the central locations in FBI agent Joseph D. Pistone's six-year undercover operation.

2 - 205 Knickerbocker Avenue (Bushwick), Joe and Mary's Italian-American Restaurant, scene of July 12, 1979, assassination of Carmine Galante, Bonanno Mafia Family boss.

3 - Brooklyn Bridge (DUMBO), scene of March 1, 1994, attack by Lebanese-born immigrant Rashid Baz who shot at a van of 15 Chabad-Lubavitch Orthodox Jewish students, murdering 1 and injuring three.

4 - The Atlantic Avenue Tunnel of the Long Island Rail Road (Cobble Hill), site of an abandoned railroad tunnel that may hide secret diary pages of assassin John Wilkes Booth.

5- 127 Palmetto Street (Bushwick), site of infamous 1900 "Nurse Girl Murder" when Alice O'Donnell, charged with the care of an eighteen-month-old baby boy, murdered the child while the unsuspecting parents were in the next room.

6 - 95 Navy Street (Downtown), site of childhood home of Alphonse "Scarface" Capone.

7 - 222 Brooklyn Avenue (Crown Heights), site of the "Brooklyn House of Evil," where for two decades Devernon "Doc" LeGrand headed one of the most notorious crime families / religious cults in New York City history.

8 - President Street near Utica Avenue (Crown Heights), intersection where two children of Guyanese immigrants were unintentionally struck by an automobile in the motorcade of rebbe Menachem Mendel Schneerson, sparking the Crown Heights Riots of 1991.

9 - 1000 Sutter Avenue (Crown Heights), the 75th New York City Police Precinct, site of massive police corruption scandal in the 1980s led by former NYPD Officer Mike Dowd.

10 - 1080 Liberty Avenue (East New York), scene of The Palm Sunday massacre, a 1984 mass-murder that resulted in the deaths of ten people: three women, a teenage girl, and six children, leaving a sole survivor, an infant girl.

11 - 152 20th Street (South Brooklyn), former location of The Adonis Club, site of epic 1925 Christmas Day shootings claiming the lives of White Hand gang boss Richard "Pegleg" Lonergan and several underlings, effectively crippling the Irish mob in Brooklyn.

12 - 779 Saratoga Avenue (Brownsville), former site of the Midnight Rose Candy Store, the headquarters of Murder Incorporated during the 1930s and 1940s.

13 - 834 Flatbush Avenue (Flatbush), location of the She-She Boutique, one of three crime scenes for serial killer Salvatore "Son of Sal" Perrone who murdered Brooklyn shopkeepers during in a 2012 spree.

14 - Fountain Avenue near Belt Parkway (East New York), location where the body of Imette Carmella St. Guillen was found in February 2006, after she was brutally raped and murdered, a crime that led to the passage of legislation to require background checks of bouncers in bars and a security plan for nightclubs.

15 - 57th Street near 9th Avenue (Sunset Park), scene of Sunset Park Massacre where 25-year-old transient from China slaughtered his cousin's wife and four children with a meat cleaver.

16 - 4305 10th Avenue (Borough Park), scene of infamous hostage siege in 1996, where crazed ex-boyfriend executed his pregnant teenage lover and wounded three of her relatives before killing himself.

17 - 44th Street Near 13th Avenue (Borough Park), location where Levi Aron, a.k.a. "The Butcher of Brooklyn," who kidnapped eight-year-old Leiby Kletzky in the summer of 2011.

18 - 450 Avenue P near East 3rd Street (Gravesend), former site of Chase Manhattan Bank that was the focus on the infamous "Dog Day Afternoon" robbery on August 22, 1972

19 - 477 82nd Street (Bay Ridge), former offices of The Leverage Group, run by Phillip Barry, known to many as the Bernie Madoff of Bay Ridge for bilking local residents out of $24 million in massive Ponzi scheme that ran for more than 30 years.

20 - 9216 7th Avenue (Dyker Heights), location of Poly Prep Country Day School, elite Brooklyn private school rocked by sex scandal when Phil Foglietta, the school's football coach, molested players for years.

21 - 7506 13th Avenue (Bensonhurst), former site of Wimpy Boys Social Club, mob hangout frequented by Greg "The Grim Reaper" Scarpa.

22 - 6205 18th Avenue (Bensonhurst), longtime hangout of Gambino underboss and infamous Mafia turncoat Salvatore (Sammy Bull) Gravano.

23 - 4021 Flatlands Avenue (Flatlands), former site of The Gemini Lounge, stronghold and murder scene for ultra-violent Gambino crew led by Roy DeMeo in the 1980s.

24 - 1814 81st Street (Bensonhurst), scene of slaying of Costabile "Gus" Farace, Jr., a low-level associate with the Bonanno crime family who was killed in 1989 by Mafia hit squad in retaliation on an unsanctioned murder of a federal Drug Enforcement Administration (DEA) agent in New York City.

25 - 20th Avenue and Bay Ridge Avenue (Bensonhurst), site of the 1989 slaying of Yusuf Hawkins by Joseph Fama during racial attack.

26 - 5945 Strickland Avenue (Mill Basin), El Caribe Country Club, one-time headquarters of Brighton Beach mob boss Evsei Agron.

27 - Shore Parkway (Bath Beach), site of the final murder of serial killer David "Son of Sam" Berkowitz.

28 - 1852 Bath Ave (Bath Beach), Daniel George and Son Funeral Home, one of several locations used by Michael Mastromarino, "The Brooklyn Body Snatcher," who made millions by illegally harvesting skin and bones from corpses for sale.

29 - 91 Bay 29th Street (Bath Beach), site where in 1991, Bartholomew Borriello, personal driver of Gambino boss John Gotti, was gunned down in the driveway of his three-story frame house in retaliation of previous assassination of Paul Castellano.

30 – Avenue X, East 1 Street (Gravesend), site of a 1982 racially motivated gang murder of Willie Turks, an innocent African-American male, at the hands of a white bat-wielding mob.

31 – Riegelmann Boardwalk at West 29th Street (Coney Island), former site of the Half Moon Hotel, where Abe Reles, informant for the FBI who brought down numerous members of Murder, Inc., either jumped, fell or was pushed to his death on November 12, 1941, while in protective custody of the NYPD, just hours before he was scheduled to testify against Albert Anastasia.

32 – 1113 Brighton Beach Avenue (Brighton Beach), former site of now shuttered Odessa Restaurant frequented by Brooklyn Russian Mafia, where gangster Vladimir Reznikov had put a gun to the head of Marat Balagula. When Reznikov left Odessa, he was shot six times by Lucchese gunmen.

TABLE OF CONTENTS

For Anna,

Forever Brooklyn's Most Wanted

INTRODUCTION

If Times Square is the crossroads of the world, then across the East River you'll find the crossroads of the underworld.

Welcome to Gangland, U.S.A. – A.K.A. the bloody, brutal killing grounds of Brooklyn, New York.

From crime bosses to career criminals to corrupt politicians, pedophile priests to Ponzi scammers to psychotic serial killers, this is not your usual crime chronicle.

Walk with me as I rip open the underbelly of Brooklyn, the broken land, to see what spills out on a tour that takes us from the South Brooklyn Boys to the Soviet thugs of Brighton Beach's "Little Odessa."

Want to know what Billy the Kid, John Wilkes Booth and the Son of Sam all have in common?

Brooklyn.

Anthony "Gaspipe" Casso, Al Capone, Frankie Yale, Paul Vario, Roy DeMeo and so many more mischievous malcontents and maniacs stalk these pages, as I rank a rogues' gallery of the best of the worst from Brooklyn's crime-ridden past and present.

Much more than Murder, Incorporated, "Brooklyn's Most Wanted" chronicles kingpins and lone wolves alike, including modern multi-ethnic mobs mimicking the original La Cosa Nostra – the Russian Mafia, the Albanian Mafia, the Polish Mafia, the Greek Mafia, in fact more Mafias than you can shake a bloody blackjack at.

You want labor racketeering, hijacking, murder, loan sharking, arson, illegal gambling, money laundering?

Fugetaboutit!

We've ranked them all, barreling through a guided tour of the New York City's most notorious criminal stomping grounds, where you'll learn that when they say "In Brooklyn They Don't Play" they really mean it. Seriously!

Welcome to the County of the Kings!

Now watch your back.

ABOUT THE RANKING SYSTEM

The primary objective of the proprietary "Brooklyn's Most Wanted Index Rankings" is to list the 100 most-*notorious* individuals produced by Kings County, U.S.A.

no·to·ri·e·ty (noun)

The state of being famous or well known for some bad quality or deed.

To compile such a list, I selected 34 individual indicators that each carry a different weighting when calculating the overall scores. Indicators range from type of criminal activity (i.e. murder, extortion, crimes against children) and type of criminal (i.e. white-collar criminal, pedophile priest, mob boss). While not revealing the actual weighting formula, the indicators are as follows:

Born or Lived in Brooklyn	Drug Dealer, Involvement in Narcotics in Brooklyn
Committed Major Crimes in Brooklyn	Dirty Police Officer or Federal Agent
Famous for Crimes Beyond Brooklyn	Corrupt Brooklyn Politician
Murderer	Pedophile Priest Preying on Children of Brooklyn
Contract Killer	Mentally Disturbed, Psychopathic Tendencies
Serial Killer	Government Witness, High Profile Informant

Mass Murderer	Made Local New York / Brooklyn Media
Rapist	Made National Media
Harmed Children	Featured Prominently in Book Treatment
Harmed Elderly	Featured Prominently in a Documentary
Thief of Historical Significance	Featured Prominently in a Hollywood Film
Con Artist	High Household Name Recognition
White-Collar Criminal, Embezzler	Did Prison Time
Lone-Wolf Criminal	Died While Incarcerated in Prison
Racketeer: Associate or Soldier	Died in Electric Chair, Other Capital Punishment
Racketeer: Captain or Consigliere	Died of Natural Causes
Racketeer: Don, Boss or Kingpin	Was Murdered

My formula takes into account elements of notoriety (i.e. media coverage, movie treatment, documentaries, household name recognition).

Lastly, I looked at the individual in relation to Brooklyn (i.e. born in Brooklyn, percentage of crimes committed in Brooklyn).

The indicators were based on objective facts and data, as well as subjective opinion of the author and a select committee of researchers and real crime fans.

As with all such systems, the "Brooklyn's Most Wanted Index Rankings" has its limits and these imperfections are certain to inspire criticism and heated debate. There is no perfect system, though I welcome your comments to improve my ranking methodology and expand this list.

You are encouraged to submit your comments, criticisms and candidates for this list at www.BrooklynsMostWanted.com.

Let the debate begin!

The media is always looking for latest Last Mohican.

In 2012, the *New York Daily News* heralded the end of an era when it christened Julius Bernstein "The Last Jewish Mobster," lowering the curtain on a storied chapter in Brooklyn crime lore.

Born in 1922, Bernstein was raised during the Great Depression in impoverished East New York, Brooklyn. This was the heyday of the Jewish Gangster, when Murder, Incorporated rose to prominence as the Italian Mafia's personal hit squad. (Dubbed "Murder, Incorporated" by the media, the organized crime group comprised mainly of Jewish and Italian-American gangsters from the Brooklyn neighborhoods of Brownsville, East New York, and Ocean Hill and terrorized the city in the 1930s and 1940s.)

Serving in the United States Army during World War II as an infantryman, Bernstein charged the beaches in Normandy as part of the D-Day invasion, before returning to Brooklyn for a long career as a low-level gangster.

While "Spike" Bernstein never earned the notoriety of such Jewish underworld luminaries as a Meyer Lansky or a Benjamin "Bugsy" Siegel, he was a solid earner for the Italian mob as an associate of the Genovese Crime Family. Forbidden from becoming a "Made" member of the Mafia, as he was not of Italian heritage, Bernstein formed a close relationship with Matthew "Matty the Horse" Ianniello, who reached the rung of acting boss of the Genovese clan in 1995 when Vincent Gigante was packed off to prison. Ianniello went on to serve more than just jail time, standing in as Spike's best man at his wedding.

Back in Brooklyn, fresh off the beaches of northern France,

Bernstein became what was known as a bagman, collecting extortion payments for more than four decades, including a bus union, the Sbarro Italian restaurant chain and other Brooklyn businesses bent backwards for shakedowns.

According to FBI records, by 1971 Bernstein was bumped up in the Brooklyn underworld, placed by the Genovese family in a leadership position in Amalgamated Transit Union Local 1181, a union for New York City school bus drivers and matrons. But Bernstein was no bus driver. His sole role was managing the Genovese family's shakedown for Ianniello. He held the post for 35 years, siphoning off thousands of dollars in hard-earned union dues and channeling it to the mob. Bernstein also ran a successful gambling book under the watch of notorious Brooklyn Genovese crime boss Frank "Funzi" Tieri.

Most notable of Bernstein's criminal exploits was his role in the extortion of the popular Sbarro restaurant chain. Gennaro Sbarro opened his first *salumeria* on the corner of 65th Street and 17th Avenue in Bensonhurst, Brooklyn, in 1956. Sbarro opened his first mall location in 1970 in the Kings Plaza Shopping Center on Flatbush Avenue in Marine Park, Brooklyn, and grew the business to become the fifth-largest pizza chain in America.

Taking a slice of the American Dream, Sbarro debuted its Initial Public Offering in 1977, and by the early 1990s was launching up to 100 stores per year. The company was brought private by the family in 1999 and sold for $450 million in 2006, though it has struggled in recent years, declaring bankruptcy in 2011 and again in 2014.

Based on Bernstein's testimony, the FBI learned that the mob's extortion of Sbarro began as far back as the 1960s. By 2004 the Genovese family was being passed $20,000 annually under the table. Bernstein personally collected the twice-annual $10,000 payments.

At the age of 82, Bernstein was caught up in an FBI probe of Sbarro and arrested in July 2005. Facing a lengthy prison term, Spike spilled the family secrets. Pleading guilty on multiple extortion counts, Bernstein began cooperating with the government in 2006.

Yet even after flipping for the feds, the wily Bernstein accepted a $20k payoff from a bus company owner inside a bathroom at the Staten Island Hilton, according to the *New York Daily News*.

Bernstein died on October 21, 2007. Though he provided damning evidence about his criminal career that implicated his cohorts, his death spared him the awkward humiliation of standing witness against them in open court.

When Bernstein's FBI papers became available in 2012 through a Freedom of Information Act request filed by *The New York Daily News*, in a subsequent article he earned that final distinction, dubbed the Last Jewish Gangster.

Yet in truth, that era had long since passed.

99
John Wilkes Booth – Lincoln Assassin

John Wilkes Booth 1865

Was John Wilkes Booth, dastardly assassin of U.S. President Abraham Lincoln, gunned down by a Union soldier?

Or did he escape to Europe via the Brooklyn waterfront? Oh, you never heard that one?

That little-known conspiracy theory lands Booth the rank of No. 99 on the "Brooklyn's Most Wanted" list.

Long before "The Grassy Knoll" entered our lexicon, multiple conspiracy theories shrouded the assassination of U.S. President Abraham Lincoln.

In fact, the Lincoln assassination's own version of the Zapruder film — missing pages torn from the diary of the villainous John Wilkes Booth — may be hidden in a 19th century subway tunnel located beneath the bustling streets of Downtown Brooklyn.

We know Booth murdered Lincoln in dramatic fashion, shooting the president in the head during a performance of the play "Our American Cousin" at Ford's Theater on the evening of April 14, 1865.

What we don't know is the full extent of the plot and its many tentacles. That's because after 12 days on the run, Booth was shot dead by Union Sergeant Boston Corbett.

In the aftermath of the killing of Booth, rumors of a cover-up bubbled up, speculating that Booth did not die on a farm in Virginia surrounded and gunned down by enraged Union forces, but rather he escaped to Europe through the Brooklyn docks.

A famous actor, Booth never served in the Confederate Army, yet was a staunch Southern sympathizer who interacted with members of the Confederacy's secret service. The theory follows that Booth was not a lone wolf, but a Confederate spy using his cover as a travelling thespian to journey throughout the Northern United States gathering and passing intelligence during and after the war. His role in the assassination was part of a larger conspiracy, or so the speculation goes.

Supposedly, Booth wrote down details of this nefarious plot in his diary, on pages now missing from the original manuscript, and possibly hidden in a locked box sealed in a bricked-up tunnel under Atlantic Avenue.

Records show Booth did perform on October 24th through October 26th in 1863 at the original site of the Brooklyn Academy of Music on Montague Street, between Court and Clinton streets. That puts him in close proximity to the tunnel.

At the time, there was a strong contingent of Southern sympathizers in New York, known as the Copperheads. The Copperheads, also known as Peace Democrats, lobbied for an end to the bloodshed and urged for negotiation with the South to end the conflict. The mayor of New York City at the time, Fernando Wood, suggested to the City Council that New York secede from the Union, to preserve its lucrative cotton trade with the South.

Did Booth slip out of New York through the bustling piers in Brooklyn, to live out his life in obscurity in some far-flung hamlet in rural Europe or remote Asia? The mystery may lie in the tunnel under Atlantic Avenue, a quest that captured the imagination of historian Bob Diamond.

The Atlantic Avenue tunnel itself is steeped in Brooklyn lore, as the oldest subway tunnel ever constructed in America, created as the final leg of an extension to connect the above-ground Long Island Railroad to Manhattan and then on to Boston. Beset by corruption and mismanagement, the project foundered and the tunnel was sealed at both ends.

Diamond accessed the tunnel in the 1980s, removing the first of two concrete walls to lead guided underground tunnel tours.

However, beyond the second, still-sealed concrete wall lays a train platform, and supposedly a vintage locomotive with a box containing Booth's long-lost diary pages. Diamond waged a campaign to unseal the tunnel. The National Geographic Channel was even involved for a time, investing in pre-production that included high-tech scan tests that identified an object about the size of a locomotive.

The story was featured in a *Newsweek* article and in an episode of the popular "Cities of the Underworld" series on The History Channel that delved into the tunnel's connection to the Freemasons (members helped finance the tunnel), its use as a hideout for bootleggers, and as a gangster graveyard where crime syndicate Murder, Inc. stashed the dead bodies of some of its victims.

Yet it was the Booth connection that draws the most sensational speculation. While there is no actual evidence supporting the theory, there is the nagging historical footnote that Booth's diary, recovered after the assassination, *is* missing 18 pages.

Was Booth a Southern spy?

Did he escape to Europe through Brooklyn?

Was the Lincoln assassination part of a larger conspiracy?

Are those lost diary pages in that Brooklyn tunnel, and if so, what do they contain?

Well, we likely will not know if that tunnel can answer these questions anytime soon. Diamond's tours have since been shut down, prompting him to bring a suit against New York City in federal court.

The New York City Department of Transportation has cited expense and safety concerns and declines further comment on the matter.

98
Mickey Cohen – West Coast Mob Kingpin

Ever since Brownsville's birth on the marshy flood plains of Eastern Brooklyn, it has been a perilous patch of earth. Early on it was too far from Manhattan to attract the well-heeled, instead drawing the starving huddled masses of the Lower East Side, mostly desperately impoverished Jewish immigrants yearning to breathe free.

Mickey Cohen
Mugshot 1961

By the turn of the 20th century, Brownsville was a violent slum, with thousands of poor souls packed into tenement housing in an area only a bit larger than a single square mile. From that cauldron of criminality gushed a generation of Jewish gangsters so fierce they transformed New York's underworld, while exporting their special brand of violence wholesale nationwide.

Mickey Cohen was one such product of Brownsville's criminal culture.

Cohen was a giant in the underworld, more known for his rise to dominate the West Coast rackets as a mob boss in the 1940s, hence why he does not rank more prominently on this list. Yet long before he succeeded his mentor, the infamous Benjamin "Bugsy" Siegel, as the reigning Jewish gangster in Los Angeles, Cohen was hustling on Brooklyn street corners.

"Mickey" entered this world on September 4, 1913, as Meyer Harris Cohen, born into an Orthodox Jewish family in a Brownsville steeped in poverty and overrun by crime, addiction, and desperation.

There were no childhoods for the children of Brownsville. Cohen's father passed away the year after he was born, leaving his mother, Fanny, alone to care for her brood. By the age of six, Cohen was chasing nickels on corners in the cut-throat world of the "newsies," a far more despairing existence than you'll find in any Broadway musical.

Desperate to escape the violent slums of Brooklyn, Fanny uprooted her family and fled far across the country, settling in the low-income area east of downtown Los Angeles called Boyle Heights. Different coasts, different corners, same path. Cohen picked up where he left off in Brooklyn, plunging into petty crime in Prohibition-era Los Angeles. Before turning 10, Cohen notched two stays in reform schools and had a hard-earned reputation for violence that grew by the beating.

A runaway by 15, Cohen took to boxing in the unforgiving fight clubs of the Cleveland underground, where his skill with his hands earned him recognition from top Jewish and Italian gangsters.

By his early 20s, Cohen was in deep in the Chicago underworld when the legendary Meyer Lansky ordered him to head back west with Ben "Bugsy" Siegel, already a major player in gangland. Siegel left a lasting imprint on the young brawler from Brownsville.

Cohen was at Siegel's side for the launch of the lavish Flamingo, a mob-funded casino that gave the Mafia its beachhead in the desert sands of Las Vegas. The hot-headed Siegel ran afoul of his mob associates and was assassinated in 1947. Cohen swept into the breach created by the rubout to seize control of the rackets in that romanticized sepia-soaked noir-era of Los Angeles.

From his humble roots in Brooklyn, Cohen rose to become one of the most notorious gangsters of that era, well earning a mention on this list. Cohen would not answer for the many murders he committed, nor for his gambling, extortion, drug dealing, labor racketeering and other crimes. Federal prosecutors locked him up on tax evasion charges.

Cohen was one of the high-profile crime figures questioned during the U.S. Senate hearings known as the Kefauver Committee. In January 1950, with U.S. Senator Joseph McCarthy targeting communist subversives and the FBI denying the existence of a national crime syndicate, Senator Estes Kefauver (Tennessee) launched a battery of hearings in 14 cities to investigate organized crime. With the advent of television, tens of millions of Americans watched raptly as a parade of arrogant gangsters like Cohen smugly invoked his Fifth Amendment right under the U.S. Constitution to refuse to give statements that could be used to incriminate himself in court. This was not a good look for Cohen and his criminal cronies, who much preferred to operate in the shadows. Among other things, the Kefauver Committee shined a harsh light on organized crime, compelling the FBI to divert resources to investigating the American Mafia.

Later Cohen found a nagging adversary in Robert F. Kennedy. During highly publicized U.S. Senate hearings in 1959 investigating corruption in labor unions, Kennedy grew incensed at Cohen's refusal to answer almost all questions. Then Kennedy asked, "What does it mean to have someone's lights put out?" Cohen replied, "Lookit, I dunno what you're talking about, I'm not an electrician... I got nuthin' to do with electricity." A frustrated Kennedy leapt forward as if to charge Cohen, and was restrained by his Senate colleagues.

Later, Cohen also did time in the infamous Alcatraz island prison and even had a *Time* magazine feature article written about him.

Cohen ultimately achieved something very few gang bosses were able to accomplish – he wasn't murdered, nor did he die in prison.

Mickey Cohen passed away in his sleep in 1976.

Posthumously, Cohen enjoys periodic cinematic reincarnations, played on the silver screen by such Hollywood heavyweights as Harvey Keitel (Bugsy, 1991), Paul Guilfoyle (LA Confidential, 1997) and Sean Penn (Gangster Squad, 2013).

97
Mendel Epstein – The Prodfather

The media often coins clever nicknames for criminals as a way to push papers, whether or not the offenders went by those names in real life.

Such was the case of Mendel Epstein, a corrupt Brooklyn rabbi who moonlighted as a violent extortionist. Epstein scammed a religious-specific style of shakedown, much in demand in the ultra-insular orthodox Jewish community of Brooklyn.

You see, Epstein had a knack for getting a *Get* from those who did not want a get got. Allow me to explain: In Jewish religious law, a *Get* is a divorce agreement that a husband presents to his wife. Among other things, it restores the wife's legal status. But until he signs that agreement, the husband retains those rights.

Traditional Jewish law does not recognize U.S. civil law, so a woman intending to continue to practice in the faith cannot initiate a divorce, own property, or serve her husband with a *Get*. The wife is trapped, unable to move forward with her life, especially from a financial perspective.

The husband?

Meh.

Even though a marriage may be emotionally over, if dissolution is not financially agreeable to the husband, he can prolong the union indefinitely.

As revealed in court testimony, several frustrated women in Brooklyn's Jewish community were more than eager to pay Epstein thousands of dollars to abduct and torture their husbands into signing a *Get*.

What does this have to do with media-manufactured nicknames?

Well, when Epstein's criminal ring was rounded up, *The New York Daily News* ran the following headline:

"The Prodfather: Rabbi used cattle zapper on hubbies till they granted divorces: feds."

That clever caption was in reference to Epstein's use of an electric cattle prod as an implement of torture to get those *Gets*. Investigators captured Epstein on a recording bragging how his ring of ruthless *Get*-getters beat and tortured their victims, holding them down while he zapped them with massive electric shocks intended to cow large animals.

The Federal Bureau of Investigation sent in undercover agents posing as weeping women desperate for divorces and willing to shell out up to $60,000 to make it happen.

Epstein was more than happy to oblige.

In October 2013, as Epstein and his henchmen descended on a location in Edison, New Jersey, ready to deliver another vicious beat-down, they were surprised by agents and taken into custody. Based on evidence and testimony, including the damning undercover recordings, the *Get*-getter got 10 years in federal prison when he was sentenced as ringmaster of the nefarious crew. In addition to Epstein, 10 accomplices were convicted of a range of crimes associated with the ring's activities.

While the FBI agents collected an extensive array of evidence, the infamous cattle prod was never recovered.

96
Walter O'Malley – The Man Who Murdered Baseball in Brooklyn

"Brooklyn's Most Wanted" is more than just a ranking of criminals, though there are plenty of convicted felons on this list.

This list also features some of the most despised, ruthless business men, who placed their personal interests above those of hard-working Brooklynites.

Walter O'Malley was not a criminal, despite the rants of our fathers and uncles.

Walter O'Malley did not assault, attack, maim or murder. Walter O'Malley was not a corrupt politician, a crooked ward boss, a caporegime or a consigliere. Walter O'Malley was not a serial killer, nor a mass murderer, not a Ponzi schemer, pedophile priest, dirty cop or drug trafficker.

For a generation of Brooklynites, though, Walter O'Malley was the most hated man in all of Kings County and beyond.

Why?

Following the 1957 Major League Baseball (MLB) season, Walter O'Malley did the unthinkable, relocating our beloved Brooklyn Dodgers west to Los Angeles.

They say baseball is a business.

They're wrong.

For the millions of hard-working men and women in the 1940s and 1950s, not to mention legions of young fans, the Dodgers *were* Brooklyn — a part of us that the greedy Walter O'Malley stole away to suck up more ticket sales and television revenue.

Sure Walter O'Malley had his reasons, business reasons. Like most owners of professional sports teams, O'Malley wanted more money than the rickety old Ebbets Field could pump out.

Walter O'Malley even had a plan, to tap into Title I of the 1949 Federal Housing Act — a U.S. government mandate furnishing funds for the development of downtrodden areas — to replace the stadium on Bedford Avenue in Flatbush, even if that meant a relocation to Queens. Revisionists argue that the true man who murdered baseball in Brooklyn was Robert Moses, the famed architect of urban planning who rejected O'Malley's bid.

Moses dismissed O'Malley's folly for constructing a $6 million domed-stadium downtown where Flatbush meets Atlantic avenues. (O'Malley's doomed dome was envisioned for the site of the current Atlantic Terminal Mall, just north of where the Barclays Center sits today.)

Did Moses push Walter O'Malley out of Brooklyn?

Did O'Malley let himself be run off?

Does it matter?

When a publicist for the Dodgers made the announcement on October 8, 1957 – that the team was decamping for Los Angeles – a million moans washed over the flat plains of Brooklyn. Adding insult to New York sports fans' injured psyches, the villainous O'Malley supposedly persuaded Horace Stoneham, owner of baseball's New York Giants, to join him in his slimy slink west. Stoneham moved that team to San Francisco.

O'Malley, O'Malley, O'Malley.

What did you do?

The Dodgers were the only National League team to make money from 1952 to 1956, yet still, that was not enough for you.

Brooklyn has since welcomed two new teams. Well, not actually *new*, but reborn franchises that abandoned their own broken-hearted fans when they moved for more money — the Brooklyn Nets (basketball), formerly the New Jersey Nets, and the New York Islanders (hockey), from Long Island (geographically speaking, Brooklyn is part of Long Island). They both play in the Barclays Center arena.

For those former Dodgers fans who could never drag themselves to root, root, root for the Yankees, we got an MLB expansion team, the New York Mets, in 1962, even if they did play in Queens. And Brooklyn even has a baseball team, the Brooklyn Cyclones, a Mets farm team that plays on the shores of Coney Island.

But Brooklyn was *never* the same after the Dodgers left.

Brooklyn is a different place now, a harder place.

Gone are the ghosts of Ebbets Field past, the echoes of "*Dem Bums,*" our bums, Jackie Robinson, Pee Wee Reese, Roy Campanella, Duke Snider, Gil Hodges, Carl Furillo, Don Newcombe and Carl

Erskine.

Gone even is Ebbets Field, razed to pave the way for massive public housing projects.

We no longer need nine men to carry our hopes and dreams and inspire us in the face of a fearsome world.

We no longer need a team to rally around, to conspire and inspire and incense.

Still, man, it would have been nice.

Damn you, Walter O'Malley.

95
Alphonse Capone - Scarface

Alphonse Gabriel "Al" Capone, the Babe Ruth of organized crime, may be better known for rising to rule the rackets in Prohibition-era Chicago, but he was a product of Brooklyn.

Al Capone Mugshot 1931

In fact, a brawl in a Brooklyn waterfront saloon where Capone was bouncing produced the ugly slashing that inspired the nickname everyone knew not to call him to his scarred face.

Long before Scarface seized the spotlight as the most notorious gangster of his era, he was born in Brooklyn on January 17, 1899, one of nine children of Italian immigrants from Salerno. His father was a barber in Downtown Brooklyn, his mother a seamstress.

The Capone family lived at 95 Navy Street, in the rough Navy Yard section of Downtown Brooklyn, rife with criminal activity fed by the nearby waterfront. Yet Capone's father was not a criminal, nor was his home life the kind you'd expect from the origin story of such a brutal gangster. Later, Capone's father Gabriele relocated his growing family to Park Slope, moving into a nicer home at 38 Garfield Place.

A bright student for the brief time he attended school, Capone's temper proved the undoing of his promising academic career. First attending Public School 7, Capone was later expelled from Public School 133 for striking a female teacher, after she belted him first. He never returned to complete his formal education.

Now unencumbered by school, Capone hit the streets hard, cycling through a mix of legitimate and illegal activities, drawing the eye of Brooklyn Italian mobster Johnny Torrio, who became Capone's early mentor. Capone joined Torrio's James Street Boys gang. His criminal development continued in his association with some of the premier gangs of the era, including the Brooklyn Rippers, the Bowery Boys and the Junior Forty Thieves.

Capone gained employment from Sicilian gang boss Frankie Yale, who ran the Black Hand mob, specialists in extortion, labor racketeering, gambling, prostitution and other criminal activities. Yale gave Capone a job in his raucous dance hall in Coney Island, The Harvard Club. While working as a bouncer at that establishment, Capone insulted the sister of Frank Gallucio, a neighborhood heavy, who gashed Capone's left cheek. Capone was ordered to apologize, and even gave Gallucio a job as muscle in later years. Yet ever after, the vain Capone hid the scar when sitting for photographs, at times lying that he received the wound overseas during the war.

In 1910, Capone followed Torrio to Chicago. Torrio had relocated to the Windy City a decade before at the request of James "Big Jim" Colosimo to help run the gang lord's brothel business. After the enactment of Prohibition in 1919, Torrio brought out Capone, recruiting reinforcements to backstop his burgeoning bootlegging operation.

The rest is mob history.

Those interested in taking a closer look can visit Public School 133 in Downtown Brooklyn on Butler Street where Capone attended school, as well as St. Mary Star of the Sea in Carroll Gardens where he was married.

94
William Bonney – Billy the Kid

When we think of the baby-faced outlaw Billy the Kid, we recall romantic images of the Wild West, desperate shootouts at corrals that are just OK, daring train robberies in tumble-weeded territories destined to become fly-over states.

We don't think of Brooklyn.

Yet long before Billy became *THE* kid he was just *A* kid pitching papers on a Brooklyn street corner.

True story.

Billy's mother, Catherine McCarty, fled Ireland

Portrait of American Outlaw Billy the Kid

when her immediate family fell to famine and disease. She landed in New York and headed for Brooklyn, seeking the safety of extended family members.

Upon arriving, Catherine was shocked to learn her New York relatives had also died from disease.

Homeless, alone, desperate to survive, to even eat, Katherine resorted to prostitution. Many historians suspect Catherine may have become pregnant from selling herself in the bars and taverns of 19th century Brooklyn, as she was not married when Billy was born. Others claim Catherine knew Billy's father and he passed away before the boy was four years old.

In any event, before he became the notorious outlaw "Billy the Kid," in fact before he was William Bonney, he was William Henry McCarty Jr., born right here in Brooklyn at 210 Greene Street in September 1859.

Henry the kid was christened on September 28, 1859, in the Church of St. Peter at 16 Barclay Street. Old St. Peter's is the oldest Roman Catholic parish in New York State.

Catherine soon took up with William Atrim, and followed him west with her son, arriving in Kansas by 1870. By 1875, Billy, still a kid at 16 years old, cut the first of many notches on his gun handle. "The Fastest Gun in the West" was a suspect in 21 murders. On July 14, 1881, Billy the Kid was killed in Fort Sumner, New Mexico, shot in the back by the cowardly Sheriff Pat Garrett.

Billy never lived to see his 22nd birthday. And buried in Fort Sumner, he never did return to Brooklyn.

93
Ludwig Lee – "Torso Parts Clues in Double Murder"

The mysterious case of Ludwig Lee offers many of the hallmarks of a sensational murder mystery, the kind the mainstream media cannot resist.

City editors know their readers love a good who-done-it, especially when the one it was done to is an innocent widow. Toss in a lurking fiend, dismembered body parts showing up in different locales, and clues leading authorities directly to the doorstep of the diabolical murderer, and you've got front-page news.

That's just what Ludwig Lee delivered back in 1927, with sensational headlines nationwide emanating from Brooklyn and screaming bloody murder. Consider this headline from *The Evening Independent* in St. Petersburg, Florida: "Torso Parts Clues in Double Murder - New York Has Dual Murder Mystery as Women's Dismembered Bodies Are Found."

If that wasn't dramatic enough, the article opened with: "Woman's Head Found."

On the Saturday morning of July 9th, 1927, the dismembered legs of a woman were discovered by a New York City policeman on foot patrol in Battery Park, rotting in the summer heat. July 11th a package containing more decomposing body parts was found in a Brooklyn churchyard. Later that week, a torso was found concealed under a fire escape in a motion-picture theater, also in Brooklyn.

Yet the limbs were not adding up. As the days progressed, the public gasped with each new newspaper article revealing more mysterious packages surfacing in and around Brooklyn, for not one, but now two female victims.

Curiously, the heads were missing.

The identity of the victims would not remain a mystery for long. Perceptive investigators noticed the packages were wrapped in a distinctive brown paper. They traced that paper to a Brooklyn outlet of the Great Atlantic and Pacific Tea Company grocery store chain, known today more commonly as A&P.

Meanwhile, intrepid investigators ran down a missing person's report filed in Brooklyn for a Mrs. Selma Bennett, wife of the local iceman and mother of four. Bennett was last seen entering a boarding house at 28 Prospect Place. Her husband, Alfred, reported her missing just days earlier, coinciding with the same time period when body parts began popping up around Brooklyn.

Police rushed to the boarding house, gaining access from Ludwig Lee, a 38-year-old Norwegian immigrant who said he performed handiwork for the building's owner.

Then, after a bit of poking around by authorities, the plot thickened.

The Bennetts lived in an apartment house on Lincoln Place, located directly behind the boarding house. The Bennetts had sold the property earlier that year to a Ms. Sarah Elizabeth Brownell. Bennett's son, John, told police he last saw his mother heading to the Brownell house to address Mrs. Brownell's complaints of a leak.

Upon further questioning, the police learned that no one had seen Brownell either in days.

A second missing female. When asked whether or not he had seen Brownell, Lee said she told him she was leaving the city to visit relatives far, far away.

Ludwig Lee was taken into custody, yet despite 12 hours of aggressive interrogation, he maintained his innocence. Lee protested that he had no motive for murder, as he was employed by the victim. He even added a twist. Ms. Brownell, Lee asserted, proposed marriage, though he declined.

The police arraigned Lee on a murder charge, he pled not guilty, and was held without bail. The authorities theorized that Lee had robbed, then killed Brownell, and was dismembering the corpse when Bennett stumbled across the crime scene and had to be dealt with by the murderer.

In the basement of the boarding house, investigators uncovered bone fragments and human tissue in ash cans, before finding Mrs. Bennett's head. They also found a massive axe that had been cleaned recently.

By questioning tenants and neighbors, investigators came across Cristian Jensen, an employee of the nearby Great Atlantic and Pacific Tea Company location. Jensen informed investigators that he provided Lee with a quantity of the same distinct brown paper used to package up the body parts. In fact, a closer look revealed Jensen's own handwriting was found on some of the paper used in the crime.

In a particularly gruesome scene recounted for readers in newspaper reports, the investigators pieced many of the body parts together on a table of the boarding house in an attempt to make identifications.

Police also found Brownell's savings book showing deposits totaling $4,000, all made out to Ludwig Lee.

When the investigators surprised Lee with Jensen and the brown paper evidence, he confessed. He admitted to killing Brownell, and then Bennett when she came across him in the basement trying to conceal the first crime.

"There was nothing to do but chop them into little pieces," Lee told investigators, adding, "It was a lot of work, doing all the running around."

During the trial, the case drew international attention due to charges of police brutality. Lee's defense attorney claimed his client was violently beaten by Brooklyn coppers to extract a confession. A formal protest issued by the Consul General of Norway made its way to the desk of U.S. Secretary of State Frank B. Kellogg, who requested that then-New York State Governor Alfred Smith launch a formal investigation. A grand jury found that Lee had not been assaulted while in custody.

Based on his confession and the extensive physical evidence, Lee was convicted in a short trial in October 1928, and then sentenced the following month to die in the electric chair. The sentence was carried out shortly thereafter at Sing Sing.

92
Gino Bova - The Murder of Willie Turks

Before there was Bensonhurst and Howard Beach, there was Gravesend.

The racially-motivated killings in those neighborhoods defined an era in New York, haunting images of bat-wielding mobs of white youths running down unsuspecting, innocent black men.

Gravesend is old Brooklyn, as foreboding as its name implies when the night comes down and the F train rumbles overhead on its way out to Coney Island. Gravesend is block after block of two-family brick homes, nondescript commercial buildings, auto body shops, train yards and warehouses fronted by massive roll-down gates.

Just the kind of place an innocent black man does not want to confront a mob of weapon-wielding white boys.

In 1982, Willie Turks was a 34-year-old maintenance worker for the New York City Transit Authority. After his shift ended, Willie was planning to return to the home he shared with his wife and 10-year-old daughter on Beach Channel Drive in Far Rockaway, Queens.

That would not be the case on the evening of June 22, 1982.

That night Willie Turks left work at approximately 11:30 p.m. with two co-workers, Dennis Dixon, 30, and Donald Cooper, 34. The men exited the train yards at Avenue X and McDonald Avenue in Gravesend. Following their usual routine, they drove to a nearby eatery, the Avenue X Bagel and Deli Shop.

A bit after midnight, the men exited the store and headed back to Dixon's vehicle, when they were approached by two young white men. One began shouting racial insults at them, ordering the men to leave, that they didn't belong in *their* neighborhood.

A frantic Dixon attempted to drive away.

Tragically, the vehicle stalled.

Imagine the dread that overcame Willie while he watched as a crew of more than a dozen white men, most in their early 20s, stormed out of nearby Public School 216 schoolyard, located off Avenue X on East 1st Street. They dragged Dixon from the station wagon first, kicking and beating him. He managed to get back to his feet and sprint away, waving down an ambulance a couple blocks away.

Cooper exited the vehicle next and was assaulted on the run. He too managed to escape the clutches of the mob. Waving his arms wildly, Cooper flagged down a passing police cruiser a short distance away.

Neither the ambulance nor the patrol car made it to the scene in time to save Willie.

Up to 20 men surrounded the vehicle, smashing in the windows with pipes and sticks. They dragged Willie from that car and they kicked and beat him mercilessly down to the Brooklyn blacktop. Some of the attackers struck him with bats under those dim streetlights.

Willie Turks died within hours from the injuries suffered during the gang beating, the result of brain injuries and a fractured skull.

Dixon and Cooper were treated for their wounds and released.

The unprovoked attack drew some media coverage, yet this was before the racial attacks in Bensonhurst and Howard Beach. Police Commissioner Robert McGuire assigned 25 police officers to the case. Investigators swarmed the neighborhood, interviewing more than 100 people. Before long they had a name.

Gino Bova.

Gravesend is a quiet, blue-collar section of Brooklyn, though anyone from the area could attest to its undercurrent of racial tension. That summer, residents complained of the crowds of young men regularly drinking, fighting and making a nuisance late into the night.

This wasn't a high-crime area, though a group of white youths assaulted an off-duty housing police officer the previous May. Like Willie Turks, that victim was a black man. And less than a month before the attack on Turks, police broke up a street brawl on nearby Kings Highway between opposing groups of white and black students from James Madison High School.

At trial, witnesses claimed Gino Bova, the 18-year-old ringleader of the mob attack, repeatedly struck Turks in the head with a wooden stick.

Bova wept in court, offering his feeble apology before being convicted on a second-degree manslaughter count, but not on the second-degree murder charge that carried a much harsher penalty. He was sentenced to five-to-15 years for the crime, the maximum sentence State Supreme Court Judge Sybil Hart Kooper could impose.

In her comments, Kooper lamented how the entire neighborhood of Gravesend was stained by the racially motivated actions of Bova and his crew.

Little did she know this was an early crest in waves of racial violence that would wash over Brooklyn in the coming years.

91
Ostap Kapelioujnyj - The Greenpoint Crew

Any crime beat reporter will tell you, not all capers are created equal.

To bounce the story from the police blotter to the front page, headline writers need some unusual aspect of the crime or the criminal.

Like a Ukrainian-trained gynecologist-turned-gang-boss trying to pawn off a stolen Stradivarius.

Say what?

Not quite the Gambinos, The Greenpoint Crew was a gang that gained notoriety in the early aughts, based out of that predominantly Polish and northernmost neighborhood in Brooklyn and led by Ostap Kapelioujnyj.

As headline-writers highlighted, Kapelioujnyj was so much more than your regular, run-of-the-mill ruthless gang boss, but actually a "Ukrainian-trained" gynecologist. That unusual professional distinction was repeated in media accounts of his crimes. Not sure if the "Ukrainian" method of gynecological training is much different from that here in America, but it sure conjures up an odd image of a gangster.

In 2006, the NYPD swept up 21 members of the crew, which according to investigators trafficked in everything from drugs to guns to stolen goods. The case had all the hallmarks of a high-profile take-down, including a well-placed informant. Supposedly, the gang's plant in the NYPD would run plates for them.

This Brooklyn North bust also had the distinction of being the first-ever racketeering case brought against a criminal enterprise from Eastern Europe operating on American soil. That alone is enough notoriety to make this list.

Ukrainian gynecology aside, it was one particular crime that newspaper writers had the most fun with, leading to an absolutely awesome headline in a March 9, 2006, article by *The New York Daily News* crime beat reporter John Marzulli: "The Stringfellas. Cops bust Euro gang in drug and violin capers."

Amidst a litany of crimes compiled to support the RICO case against gang members was a scheme to sell an 18th-century Stradivarius violin, initially stolen in Europe. For its safe return, the gang sought $750,000.

Now there's something you don't read every day on the crime blotter.

Even then-NYPD Commissioner Raymond Kelly got in on all the *pun*, quoted in *The New York Daily News* as saying: "This case was a virtuoso performance played by New York City police officers, FBI agents and federal prosecutors."

Gang member Lukasz Zalewski first brought the criminal caper to the attention of the crew's leadership, including Kapelioujnyj and Krzysztof Sprysak. An informant later told police that Kapelioujnyj suggested a double-cross, to rob a potential buyer *and* keep the precious violin for another illegal re-sale.

Kapelioujnyj never got his chance at the double-cross, as the gang was rounded up and the violin recovered, and subsequently determined to be a fake, much to the chagrin of all criminals and former gynecologists involved with the doomed caper.

Kapelioujnyj, Sprysak and other gang members were convicted of multiple crimes, from illegal gun sales and drug trafficking to armed robbery and car theft. Kapelioujnyj was even caught on video threatening to smash in the head of a debtor with a golf club.

Media accounts, though, failed to report the impact on his future career in Ukrainian gynecology.

90
Joanna Pimentel - the Brooklyn Godmother

Today, the Sunset Park section of western Brooklyn is a story of urban renewal success, a neighborhood continually redefined over the years by waves of immigration.

In 2016 *The New York Times'* Real Estate section heralded Sunset Park as one of "New York's Next Hot Neighborhoods." That distinction followed more than 100 years of demographic turnover. Sold by the Canarsee Indians to the Dutch hundreds of years ago, the neighborhood now known as Sunset Park evolved into a shipping center by the 19th century, attracting Irish, Polish and Scandinavians, and was even dubbed "Little Norway" for a time.

Subsequent colonies of more Irish, Italians, Polish, Greeks, and, more recently, Hispanic, Chinese, Korean and Middle Eastern peoples continue to transform the area. The neighborhood today brims with more than 100 nationalities mingling within its boundaries, remnants of something old, something new. This is what Brooklyn is all about, the metaphor of the melting pot made true, for better and for worse.

Decades of decay that set in during the Depression, when jobs dried up along the Industry City waterfront corridor, have been reversed and the area is now on the rise.

Yet not too long ago, circa 1990s, rolling off a devastating crack-cocaine epidemic, Sunset Park was the center of a gangland power struggle for the leadership of the violent Asociación Ñeta, a street crew that first coalesced in the penal system of Puerto Rico before spreading to American shores. In Brooklyn the majority of its gang members are ex-convicts, according to court records.

By this period, Sunset Park was a major stronghold for the gang in the United States, its members immersed in a wide range of criminal activities including narcotics trafficking, extortion, robbery, assaults and homicides.

Then in the 1990s, an unusual phenomenon occurred in the traditionally patriarchal structure of the Ñetas, when Joanna Pimentel, a female gang member dubbed "La Madrina" or "the godmother," vied for power. In her role with the gang, Pimentel coordinated with prison officials on behalf of convicted gang members, supporting them while they were incarcerated, to help steer them onto the right path upon release.

According to court transcripts, in 1994, Pimentel organized the "Junta Central," a consolidated administrative core established for the gang, intended to bring some needed leadership to the loose confederacy of Ñeta chapters throughout the New York Tristate region. This marked a dramatic departure, in terms of the roles women play historically in gangland. Female associates usually served as aiders and abettors, but not direct participants in crimes and certainly not in leadership roles.

In 1994, Pimentel heard rumors that Galiat Santiago, the gang boss of the Sunset Park-based Ñetas, had raped a number of female members. This was serious business. For the Ñetas, rape is punishable by death.

Pimentel put Santiago on "trial," to face a jury made up of the presidents of various Ñeta chapters. Though found guilty, Santiago eluded a death sentence, and instead was punished with a vicious beat down. Blaming Pimentel, Santiago swore revenge. Responding to the threats, Pimentel launched a preemptive strike, allegedly orchestrating the shooting death of Santiago.

A female gang leader is just the kind of underworld plot twist the media foams at the mouth for, and true to form the investigation and prosecution of "La Madrina" made local and international headline news.

Publicly, Pimentel portrayed herself to the media as a community activist, not a criminal black widow. The Ñetas has a legacy for advocacy on behalf of convicts in Puerto Rican prisons, and later the United States when it spread into New York and elsewhere. Behind the scenes, though, Ñetas' members are heavily involved in drug trafficking, arms dealing, extortion, armed robbery and other serious criminal activities.

Following a lengthy investigation involving undercover operatives and gang turncoats, federal investigators and local law enforcement agents descended on multiple locations throughout Brooklyn and beyond, rounding up nearly 30 gang members, booking them on an assortment of crimes, from gun running to drug dealing.

The sweeps corralled members of two gangs, Pimentel's chapter and The Hard Pack. Both gangs had flooded the streets of Sunset Park with drugs and weapons. In fact, undercover agents bought at least 14 guns and plastic explosives from this network of gangs during the undercover operation that lasted more than two years.

Despite her insistence that she was a neighborhood activist trying to make a difference, prosecutors had enough evidence, including eyewitness testimony, to secure a conviction for violations of several federal laws, including conspiracy in the Santiago murder. Federal prosecutors pursued Pimentel under the Violent Crimes in Aid of Racketeering (VCAR) statute that provides for prosecution "when those allegedly responsible participated in the violent crime in order to gain, maintain, or increase a position in an enterprise engaged in racketeering activity."

In February 2001, in the United States District Court for the Eastern District of New York, La Madrina was handed a life sentence.

Since this book is called "Brooklyn's Most Wanted," it had to include the crew called "Brooklyn's Most Wanted," (BMW) a Flatbush gang that plagued the East 50s, until it was dismantled in 2013.

As the holiday season approached in 2013, members of the NYPD gang unit swept into East Flatbush to round up nine members of the hierarchy of the crew, including gang boss Shamar "Smirk" Brooks.

The gang sprang to the top of the Brooklyn South Gang Unit's most-wanted list following a high-profile shooting in 2011, under the control of gang-leader Brooks. This included a Labor Day strafing at a party on East 54th Street. Turned away at the door, several BMW gangsters responded with gunfire, the opening barrage in a battle with the rival G Stone Crips that led to several more shootings between the two sets. Crips leader Tyrese Gary was killed in that initial hail of gunfire, and Brooks was wounded in future gun battles on at least two occasions.

In those pre-dawn raids in 2013, the NYPD's gang unit captured nine members of BMW and brought them up on an assortment of charges, from conspiracy to gun possession, basically eliminating BMW as a significant gang presence in East New York. Several high-power automatic weapons were also recovered during the arrests. Police forensics investigators traced DNA on a number of those guns, linking multiple gang members with crimes, including several open homicides. The conspiracy case was bolstered by the appearance of gang members in YouTube videos, with provocative titles like "Beamas Gettin Fetty" and "Fistful of Bullets."

The shootings continued, including one ambush outside the Kings County Supreme Court Building in Brooklyn, and another one on

July 12th, when a 22-year-old woman was caught in the crossfire, catching a bullet meant for BMW, prompting New York City Police Commissioner William Bratton to quip: "Talk about a gang that couldn't shoot straight."

By 2014, the NYPD had rounded up 15 members of the G Stone Crips, bringing a 75-count indictment in 2015 against gang members, a takedown snaring rising rap star Bobby Shmurda, who profiled the gang's exploits in his music. (On October 19, 2016, Shmurda, born Ackquille Pollard, was formally sentenced in Manhattan Supreme Court on a weapons charge and received seven years in prison.)

Despite these murders and numerous arrests, the violence between violent gang sets infesting bloody East New York continues to this day.

88
Barney Wolfson – Brooklyn's Own St. Valentine's Day Massacre

Sometimes in the Brooklyn underworld, being in the wrong place at the wrong time can cost you your life.

Take the 1931 gangland slaying of Anthony Ferrara.

Ferrara, along with chums Angelo Ciurrani and Murray Leonardi, were kidnapped by a Brooklyn armed-robbery crew led by ex-marine Barney Wolfson.

Initially, Wolfson's underlings mistakenly snatched up Ferrara, a low-level street thug who was not the intended target. They were supposed to abduct Ciurrani, a former member of Wolfson's gang who was blabbing around Brooklyn, badmouthing his former boss.

So Wolfson's goons went back and kidnapped Ciurrani and Leonardi, then took all three captives to a deserted lumber yard in Brooklyn and forced them to face a wall.

This was literally the gang who could not shoot straight. In the ensuing barrage, only Wolfson connected with his target, shooting Ferrara in the back of the head, killing him instantly. The other gangsters shot wide. Ciurrani and Leonardi scampered away to live to tell their twisted gangland tale.

Less than a week later, an anonymous tip led the police to the gang's hideout in Bushwick. Armed police stormed the apartment building, blew a gaping hole right through the door of a second-story room and apprehended the surprised gang.

As profiled in "Chronicles of Historic Brooklyn," a fantastic read by John B. Manbeck, the Brooklyn Borough Historian from 1993 to 2002, the "copycat crime suggested by Chicago's St. Valentine's Day Massacre" was featured in an August 31, 1931, article in *The New York Times* entitled "Gang Firing Squad Surrenders in Raid."

All of the arrested gang members folded under questioning and were packed off to prison.

Wolfson, only 22 years old at the time, was paroled after a long prison stint and escaped into obscurity in Florida.

87
Elizabeth "Lizzie" Lloyd King & Mary Ann Dwyer – "Two Insane Women."

Sometimes circumstance swings us into the oncoming path of history.

Such were the colliding cases of Elizabeth "Lizzie" Lloyd King and Mary Ann Dwyer, two desperate, disconnected women from Brooklyn with nothing in common but fate and a converging news cycle.

Oh yeah, and murder.

In the early 1870s, King and Dwyer were linked in the media due to a remarkable coincidence in courtroom scheduling.

King thrust herself into the spotlight first after depositing three bullets into the head of Charles Goodrich, on March 20, 1873. Jilted by Goodrich following a stormy relationship, the unbalanced King was outraged at his attempt to evict her from a DeGraw Street home Goodrich owned in Downtown Brooklyn. Goodrich's corpse was found by his brother, William, along with the murder weapon and a suicide note.

William suspected foul play immediately and summoned the authorities, who concurred once realizing Goodrich's face had been washed and his shirt changed *after* he had been shot.

Questioning neighbors, police focused on a mystery woman linked to Goodrich, issuing a description of an attractive, pale, 23-year-old female of slender build and average height. Little did they know that Kate Stoddard, a.k.a. Elizabeth "Lizzie" Lloyd King, was already in the wind, taking flight after the killing to avoid arrest.

Lizzie King was a deeply troubled soul. Earlier committed, then released, from the Taunton Lunatic Asylum in New England, she relocated to New York City for a fresh start, finding employment as a teacher and milliner (someone who sells and/or makes hats for women). King met the widower Charles Goodrich through a personal ad he placed seeking a wife. She responded using the alias Kate Stoddard. A romance flourished and, based on letters recovered by investigators, the two were married in 1872. However, the marriage was never validated, neither civilly nor religiously, as the man presiding was not a member of the clergy or court.

The following year, Goodrich convinced King to get an illegal abortion after she became pregnant. The relationship soon soured. Goodrich then took up with Adeline Pabor, and the two lovers were engaged. King, however, was not ready to move on.

As a gentleman of means, Goodrich offered King financial support, as long as she would stop referring to herself as his wife. King declined the offer and dug in her heels, accusing Goodrich of cruelty and abuse, pining for a reconciliation. When the exasperated Goodrich delivered an ultimatum, attempting to toss King from an investment property he was developing in Downtown Brooklyn with his brother, King responded with three bullets to his head.

Eluding authorities for months, King was captured on July 8, 1873, arrested exiting the Fulton Ferry after she was spotted by former roommate Mary Handley. She was booked at the Second Precinct on York Street.

Following months of man hunting and media mania surrounding "The Goodrich Horror," authorities presented King before a judge in Brooklyn to answer for her crimes. Play-by-play news of her steady slog to justice captivated the city and her inquest attracted hordes of curious onlookers, eager to catch a glimpse of the murderous King.

That's when the timing of that inquest pulled King into the colliding orbit of Mary Ann Dwyer, a despicable wretch who one-upped King by murdering her three children.

Talk about a crowded news cycle.

The inquests for King and Dwyer were not only scheduled for the same day, but held in the same Kings Country courtroom down on Livingston Street.

Headline writers across the country could barely contain their glee, including *The New York Times* that ran a front-page piece the day following the dueling inquests with the headline: "TWO INSANE WOMEN."

King was a wild-eyed, muttering, disheveled disaster, much to the delight of onlookers. During a pre-trial hearing, a court-appointed psychologist deemed her mentally unfit to stand trial. She was packed away to the State Lunatic Asylum in Auburn. This was an institution built in upstate New York alongside Auburn State Prison to appease the reform movement advocating better treatment for mentally ill inmates by separating them from more dangerous inmates. King spent the rest of her days locked away in that cold institution.

The notoriety of King's case lingered for years, prompting local residents to successfully petition New York City to rename DeGraw Street between 5th and 6th avenues Lincoln Place to throw off the invasive crowds of true-crime curiosity seekers.

As for Mary Anne Dwyer, she was an Irish immigrant forced to flee her home country by the famine, arriving in New York at the age of 17. A mother of four, Dwyer nearly murdered her husband in their North 8th Street tenement apartment in Williamsburg, before killing three of her children.

For a time during the epic proceedings, King and Dwyer sat beside each other in the crowded, poorly ventilated courtroom, and even shared some small talk.

Dr. MacDonald, the former head of the Flatbush Insane Asylum testified that Dwyer was insane at the time of the murders, and that insanity ran in her family.

86
John Pappa - Brooklyn Mafia Renegade

By dropping the final body in the bloody Colombo Family War, John Pappa felt he deserved more out of *the life.*

Instead he got life.

In prison.

Throughout his childhood in Brooklyn and Staten Island, John Pappa revered the memory of his father. That's all he had left of him. Gerard Pappa, a soldier in the Genovese Crime Family, was murdered when John was five years old.

Following the murder of her husband, Pappa's mother moved her family to Holmdel, New Jersey. She wanted a better life for her son, to keep him away from the deadly lure of Brooklyn's streets. Over the years, like many Northern New Jersey communities, Holmdel attracted a sizable transplant population of Italian Americans that were former residents of Kings County. Without traffic, Holmdel was less than an hour car ride through Staten Island and across the Verrazano Narrows Bridge back into the heart of Brooklyn.

She should have moved further west.

For a time John flourished in New Jersey in school and on the soccer field, but his obsession with his father and organized crime drew him back to Bensonhurst, that Brooklyn bastion of mob brutality. Soon enough, Pappa was spending most of his time on the streets of Brooklyn as a low-level drug dealer with a mean streak.

Aligned to the struggling Colombo Family, a criminal organization beleaguered under the leadership of the incarcerated Carmine "The Snake" Persico and beset with an internal revolt, Pappa embarked on a killing spree that included Colombo Capo Joseph Scopo, a close personal confidante of acting-boss Vic Orena. That murder, on October 20, 1993, in Ozone Park, Queens, was the shot that ended the internecine Colombo Family War, ignited when the rebellious Orena attempted to wrest control of the organization from the imprisoned Persico.

By then a full-blown killer with a violent temper and a hair-trigger, Pappa's ego proved his undoing. He bragged constantly to his cohorts about his murders, evidence captured on wiretaps and recounted in court by eye witnesses.

Growing increasingly murderous and paranoid with every body he dropped, Pappa gunned down three associates, previously his accomplices on the Scopo murder. Angered that they were bragging about their roles in the rubout, Pappa felt he was setting the record straight. As Pappa saw it, he had single-handedly won the Colombo Family War with that one hit, though the war ending had more to do with Orena being sentenced to life in prison than one single act of violence.

As his murder-count mounted, Pappa grew bolder, a reckless criminal "cowboy" with a total depraved indifference for human life.

NYPD Detective Thomas Dades and his partner, Detective Mike Galletta, received chilling death-threat phone calls at the 68th Precinct, warning them to stay away from 13th Avenue, a center of the crew's mob activity.

Three years later, Detective Dades got his man on September 26, 1997, arresting John Pappa at St. Ann's Church on Staten Island. In a sick Brooklyn mob twist, Pappa was attending the wedding rehearsal for a friend, Salvatore Sparacino, the brother of a man Pappa murdered.

"*Police*, John," Detective Dades shouted at Pappa, surprising him as he walked up the front stairs of the church with his girlfriend. Pappa ducked inside while pulling out a loaded 9-mm. gun.

"Here you had John Pappa actually in the church for a wedding rehearsal of the brother of a man he murdered, able to act like nothing happened," Dades said. "Fortunately, we arrested him in the church, near the altar, without any further violence."

Pappa was convicted of four murders and is suspected in six other homicides.

Pappa received four life-without-parole prison terms plus an additional 45 years for drug dealing and other assorted criminal charges. Investigators suspected Pappa had a hand in other slayings, including the tragic murder of Carmine Gargano, Jr., an innocent Pace University student who went missing in 1994 and was later found in an unmarked mob burial ground in East Farmingdale, Long Island, in 2008.

With Pappa tucked away in federal prison, guaranteed to never see the light of day, the other investigations did not move forward.

When he was sent away for the rest of his life in 1999, John Pappa was 24 years old.

He never did get his "button" in the Brooklyn Mafia.

85
Clarence Norman Jr. - Corrupt Democratic Party Leader

What could have been?

Clarence Norman Jr. was a force in Brooklyn politics for years.

He is the son of Clarence Norman, head pastor of the First Baptist Church of Crown Heights, both spiritual and political leader for that large Brooklyn congregation. Attending college at Howard University, earning a law degree from St. John's University, the preacher's son was positioned to capitalize on the Norman name when he dove into politics.

With law degree in hand, Norman Jr. landed his first stint in state government as a general counsel to the New York State Assembly Subcommittee on Probation and Parole. After a tour in Albany, he went downstate to accept a position in the felony bureau of the Kings County District Attorney's office in Brooklyn.

Norman Jr. won his first election in 1982, securing a seat in Albany to represent the 43rd Assembly District in Central Brooklyn, covering his family's home base in Crown Heights and parts of Flatbush and Prospect Heights. He enjoyed a lengthy incumbency, holding that seat from 1983 through 2005.

Norman sank deeper into the swirling cauldron of Brooklyn politics, as the first-ever African American elected chairman of the Executive Committee of the Kings County Democratic County Committee. He was the youngest Democrat to hold that post. With control of one of the largest Democratic clubhouses in the nation, while a ranking member in New York State government and a beloved representative back in Brooklyn, Norman Jr. had it all.

And then came the fall.

That was when he tried to sell a judgeship.

On February 24, 2007, Norman Jr., already removed as Democratic assemblyman and Brooklyn party leader, was convicted on extortion charges for shaking down judicial prospects in exchange for peddling his influence. It marked the third conviction on corruption charges for Norman Jr. in less than 17 months.

The preacher's son came undone, at the time the latest political perp walking in a long parade of corrupt Albany powerbrokers, disgracing his family, betraying his people.

For many, Norman Jr. *was* Brooklyn politics, a prominent African American champion who was a regular presence in the community and the media. Yet after the scandal broke, Norman Jr. appeared on nightly news reports for other reasons. Prosecutors piled on the indictments, including for violating state election laws, faking business records, hiding funds, soliciting illegal contributions and other charges related to mishandling campaign monies.

The indictments included Norman Jr.'s solicitation of bribes from two candidates for judgeships in 2002. The candidates were told by Norman Jr. that they must either pony up bribes or lose the support of the Democratic Party machine in Brooklyn, a death knell for any hopes of securing those judicial seats.

For his crimes, Norman Jr. lost the chairmanship of the Kings County Democratic Party, had to resign his long-held New York State Assembly seat in disgrace, was disbarred and then sent to prison.

In 2008, Norman Jr. caught a break and was sent to a work-release program in Manhattan. He was paroled in 2011.

While Norman Jr. is out of Kings County politics, at least for now, he is active in the First Baptist Church of Crown Heights and several charities.

84
Luis Blanco – King Humble & The Latin Kings

On the streets of Brooklyn, the more violent you are, the greater your street cred.

Attempting to scalp someone not only elicits fear, it vaults you right off the crime blotter and onto the front pages of New York's tabloids.

You read right: Scalping. Not as in the illegal sale of event tickets, but the act of physically peeling off the skull skin of a fellow human being with a razor-sharp blade.

That was just one of a slew of crimes compiled by investigators when they took down a vicious Latin Kings set operating in Brooklyn in 2014, led by Luis Blanco, a.k.a., King Humble. In the fall of that year, investigators arrested 14 gang members from the Brooklyn faction of the Latin King Nation, charging them with crimes stemming from a series of incidents, many of which were boasted about on social media, gaining substantial notoriety at the time.

The Almighty Latin King and Queen Nation is a particularly notorious, predominantly Hispanic street gang founded in 1954 in Chicago. Boasting tens of thousands of members and chapters in dozens of U.S. cities, the Nation is cascaded under two factions — Motherland, also known as KMC (King Manifesto and Constitution) that follows the Southside Chicago philosophy, and Bloodline (New York City) founded in 1986 in prison by Luis "King Blood" Felipe.

The Outlaw Tribe, as the set was known on the street, was led by "First Crown" Blanco from a Brooklyn power base spanning Bushwick and East New York. Investigators were drawn by community outcry over a series of violent assaults during a running street war between Blanco's set and rival gangs in Park Slope and Queens.

When they finally collared Blanco in a sweep rounding up 14 members of the Outlaws, investigators charged the crew with gang assault, weapons possession, witness intimidation, conspiracy to commit murder, and multiple assault counts – stabbings, shootings and the aforementioned scalping.

Yet of all these crimes it was the near-scalping that bubbled up to the front page. That heinous act achieved substantial attention not only for the novelty of its depravity, but for the fact that it occurred a block away from the gentrified Park Slope corner where New York City Mayor Bill De Blasio owns a home.

The scalping occurred during a September 27, 2013, pre-arranged rumble near 5th Avenue and 12th Street, when an Outlaw initiated a gang fight literally steps from De Blasio's steps. The confrontation pitted the invading Outlaws against the Hardbodys, a Latin King set based in Park Slope. The brief but bloody altercation left behind a gruesome crime scene.

The next day, Blanco ridiculed the Hardbodys on Facebook: "Guess ____ bodies aren't so hard after all. F____ with a real lion and get eaten ... Shout outs to the surgeons making that overtime pay . . . Ur welcome." Needless to say, the anything-but-humble King Humble incriminating himself on social media was a boon to investigators.

Likely oblivious he was making law enforcement's job that much easier, Blanco doubled-down on his Facebook taunts, further implicating himself by revealing rivalries with the Jamaican Mayas, the Woodhaven Mayas and the Loyalty Shadows, all Latin King factions from neighboring Queens.

In one incident, a faux Facebook profile was used to lure a rival gang member to Bushwick, where he was stabbed and shot.

Blanco currently faces 25 years in prison if convicted.

83
Vito Lopez - Democratic Party Kingpin

Supporters say Vito Joseph Lopez did plenty of good for his Brooklyn community as a member of the New York State Assembly and chairman of the powerful Democratic Party of Kings County.

They will remind you that Lopez pushed through affordable housing and helped expand community services that made a dramatic impact on the people of Bushwick, a long-underserved section of Brooklyn.

Yet the legacy of Vito Lopez is marred by a series of high-profile scandals that toppled the powerful Brooklyn politico, rocked by charges of sexual harassment and corruption.

From the streets of Bushwick to the halls of New York State's capital in Albany, Lopez ruled with a firm hand. It is true he created hundreds of units of affordable housing and pushed back some of the urban blight plaguing Bushwick.

First elected in 1985, Lopez rose to a number of senior posts, including the powerful chairmanship of the New York State Assembly Housing Committee.

Lopez, though, was not toppled by a single indiscretion, but charges of a pattern of sexual harassment. The lawmaker from Brooklyn saw the writing on the legislative wall, resigning in the wake of a New York State ethics investigation that identified no less than eight victims – including young staffers he preyed upon.

During the investigation a backroom deal came to light, where the New York State Assembly paid hundreds of thousands of dollars in hush money to quiet Lopez' accusers. These were tax-payer dollars quietly funneled to cover-up Lopez' crimes, indiscretions he publicly denied. The payoffs were approved by none other than Assembly Speaker Sheldon Silver, another corrupt Albany politician sentenced to more than a decade in prison in 2016 on unrelated charges.

By 2012, Lopez, the Brooklyn Democratic leader since 2006, opted to not seek another run for the post.

The following year, a New York State ethics commission published a report itemizing his actions sexually harassing the young women. In one disgusting passage, Lopez instructed one staffer to feel the tumors on his neck. Following months of withering media coverage, fined $330,000 and facing expulsion from the New York State Assembly, Lopez resigned in disgrace.

His reputation shredded, Lopez attempted a political comeback, but failed to even muster enough support to swing a New York City Council seat.

Within two years he was dead.

On November 9, 2015, broken, disgraced and succumbing to leukemia, Lopez slipped away into the night at approximately 10 p.m. at Memorial Sloan-Kettering Hospital in Manhattan.

82
Thomas McFarland – The Sex Killer of Brooklyn

In the early morning hours of April Fool's Day in 1935, the body of Nora Kelly was discovered by one of her tenants in her two-story Brooklyn home on Marine Avenue at the edge of Bay Ridge.

Patrick Murray, Kelly's boarder, returned home from his work as a subway conductor on the Brooklyn-Manhattan Transit lines. Investigating the howls of Kelly's dog, Murray discovered the elderly widow hanged from a rafter in the cellar of the building. Murray fled the home and brought back Brooklyn beat cops patrolling nearby.

Investigators were puzzled as to why Mrs. Kelly took her own life. Though struggling financially, friends and family said she did not seem suicidal. She received $30 a month in rent from Murray. Combined with financial support from a granddaughter, she made ends meet, if barely. Mrs. Kelly was particularly close to this granddaughter, Florence McVey, a live-in maid employed within walking distance in a home on Fort Hamilton Parkway.

As dawn broke and investigators combed the crime scene, suicide seemed less likely by the moment.

Then, the plot thickened.

As police moved through the home searching for clues, they found the cold, lifeless body of 18-year-old McVey. Curiously, investigators estimated the timeline of when both deaths occurred to be when Patrick Murray's wife, Helen, was at home with their young daughter. But upon questioning, Mrs. Murray swore that she could not recall anything unusual, nor had Mrs. Kelly's dog made a ruckus until long after the death supposedly occurred.

Very unusual circumstances, indeed.

With no evidence to indicate foul play other than dead bodies, the initial suspicion was that Kelly hanged herself and McVey died of natural causes, albeit a bit far-fetched for investigators to accept. Maybe McVey died from shock upon discovering the body of her dead grandmother. Or, perhaps Kelly killed herself, overcome in a fit of grief after discovering her lifeless, beloved granddaughter.

Still, no wailing or disturbance had been heard by the nearby tenant?

Suicide was ruled out once the coroner's report came back from the King's County Morgue. McVey had been sexually assaulted. The cause of death was determined to be asphyxiation, due to deprivation of oxygen from smothering.

A double-murder mystery was afoot, served with a side-order of sex-assault.

Forensics specialists ascertained that Mrs. Kelly was dead well before someone wrapped a noose around her neck and hoisted her up, in an attempt to disguise her murder.

Detectives interrogated neighbors, family and friends of the two victims, canvasing the Bay Ridge area near the crime scene, while the sensational news hit the local media.

The initial investigation yielded few suspects until Eleanor Meyers, a friend of Mrs. Kelly, walked into the local police station to volunteer information. Myers revealed that she visited the scene of the crime at around 9 p.m. on the evening of the murders. Receiving no answer, Meyers was turning to leave, when Mrs.

Kelly's door flew open.

Out stumbled Thomas McFarland, Mrs. Kelly's son-in-law, husband to her deceased daughter Anna and father to three grandchildren. McFarland was on the list of family members for police to interview, though they'd yet to speak with him.

Married in Bay Ridge's St. Patrick's Church, the couple had three children. Wife Anna died giving birth to their twins. Mrs. Kelly raised the children for a time, but as of late McFarland had moved to a rental on Humboldt Street with his motherless brood.

McFarland had to know something, investigators surmised, intensifying their search.

Police tracked him down to the varnish factory where he worked at in Long Island City and took him in for questioning. By then it was a bit more than 12 hours since the bodies were discovered.

Arresting officers noticed flecks of what appeared to be blood on the suit McFarland was wearing.

During questioning, McFarland revealed that after dining with his daughters the evening before the murders he headed to the home of Mrs. Kelly. He stopped off in the saloons in Brooklyn, before taking the train to the 95th Street station. He then walked the rest of the way to Mrs. Kelly's home for a visit, where he met her and McVey just after sundown.

By then McFarland was drunk, he freely admitted to police. In the presence of Mrs. Kelly, he continued to drink from a bottle of sherry he'd purchased, much to the consternation of his former mother-in-law.

An argument ensued.

The frightened McFarland then claimed to police that he must have blacked out and could recall nothing else from the evening. However, he did say he *may* have choked Mrs. Kelly, and then he *may* have choked McVey when she came into the room, fearing she was going to grab a knife that was on the table.

McFarland also mentioned that it was probably a mistake to answer the doorbell when Mrs. Meyers came calling.

McFarland was indicted for the murders and held over for a sensational trial the following year. During the court proceedings, McFarland's attorneys mounted what today would be akin to a Post-Traumatic Stress Disorder (PTSD) defense, claiming the defendant suffered from psychological damage related to his service during World War I. One of his daughters testified of his alarming behavior and frequent blackouts.

The jury didn't buy the defense and in 1936 they found McFarland guilty of first-degree murder and related charges. The judge sentenced him to the death penalty and on August 30th that year he went to the electric chair at Sing Sing.

81
Ismaaiyl Abdullah Brinsley - Cop Killer

In the winter of 2014, tensions ran high in minority communities throughout America following incidents where African-American men were killed by police officers in several U.S. cities, including Eric Garner (Staten Island, New York), Michael Brown (Ferguson, Missouri), and Freddie Gray (Baltimore, Maryland).

Controversy over the use of force by police within minority communities is not a new phenomenon in America, though 2014 did seem like a flashpoint. News stations nationwide ran troubling images of chaotic protest marches erupting into violence.

Ismaaiyl Abdullah Brinsley, a troubled 28-year Maryland resident, originally from Brooklyn, was furious at the cascade of coverage and became bent on taking action. We don't know what set Brinsley off on his bloody rampage at the height of the holiday season in 2014. When he was done, he turned his gun on himself, but not before perpetrating the cowardly sneak-attack-assassination of two on-duty New York City Police Department officers in the Bedford–Stuyvesant section of Brooklyn.

New York City was simmering in rage, as just weeks prior to the Brinsley shooting a grand jury declined to indict NYPD Officer Daniel Pantaleo for the choke-hold he placed on Eric Garner in Staten Island the previous July. Garner had been peddling street-side-single-sale "loosie" cigarettes not far from the Staten Island Ferry terminal when he resisted arrest, collapsing from Pantaleo's illegal choke-hold. CPR was not administered in time. Garner died at the hospital one hour later.

When news of the grand jury's decision hit the street, it sparked days of protest in New York, including a storming of the Brooklyn Bridge. Meanwhile, down in Ferguson, Missouri, a similar scenario played out when a grand jury declined to indict Darren Wilson, a police officer who shot and killed Michael Brown. That decision also ignited days of unrest.

Born in 1986 in Brooklyn into a Muslim African-American family, Brinsley was a lost soul by the time he was a young man. On December 20, 2014, Brinsley left Owning Mills, Maryland, on the outskirts of Baltimore, boarding a bus bound for New York City. Earlier in the day he was talked out of committing suicide by Shaneka Nicole Thompson, his ex-girlfriend. Following an argument, Brinsley then shot and wounded Thompson, before fleeing. She survived.

As he headed to New York, Brinsley posted a disturbing message on Instagram, indicating that he intended to kill police officers to avenge the deaths of Garner and Brown, specifically: "I'm putting Wings on Pigs Today ... They Take 1 of Ours ... Lets [sic] Take 2 of Theirs."

The Baltimore Police Department was already investigating

Brinsley, and sent a fax to its law-enforcement counterpart in New York.

The message did not avert the tragedy.

When Brinsley hit New York, he made his way to Brooklyn. Brinsley followed his fate to the busy intersection of Myrtle and Tompkins avenues in Bedford-Stuyvesant where he came across an NYPD cruiser idling at the corner.

Inside the vehicle sat Wenjian Liu and Rafael Ramos, two police officers assigned to the nearby 84th Precinct.

Brinsley drew his semiautomatic weapon, snuck up on the patrol car and opened fire, striking the officers with multiple rounds to their heads and torsos, killing them both.

Passersby alerted police patrolling nearby and a foot chase ensued. Brinsley fled into the Myrtle-Willoughby Avenues subway, where he was cornered. He committed suicide rather than be taken into custody.

The only son of Chinese immigrants, Wenjian Liu was a seven-year-veteran of the NYPD, who married his sweetheart two months prior to his murder. During Liu's wake at Ralph Aievoli & Son Funeral Home in Dyker Heights, Brooklyn, police officers turned their back on a screen playing while Mayor Bill de Blasio expressed his condolences, in response to ongoing enmity between the mayor and the police union.

While Liu left behind no children, his partner, Rafael Ramos, was survived by his grieving widow and two sons. The Silver Shield Foundation, a charity founded by former New York Yankees' owner George Steinbrenner, announced a pledge to pay for the college education of the younger Ramos boy, while Bowdoin College kicked in full-financial support for the elder son, who was already enrolled as a sophomore.

Days later, on December 27th, the funeral service for Ramos would be the largest in New York City's history, attended by more than 100,000 mourners. Broadcast around the world during the same news cycles as the ongoing protests, the funeral was depicted as a counter balance to scenes of angry marchers. Many of the police in attendance at the Ramos funeral also turned their backs on Mayor de Blasio as he again spoke, this time in person.

At the time of the shooting, Brinsley was estranged from family and friends. A career criminal with 19 arrests ranging from armed robbery to criminal possession of a weapon, Brinsley supposedly had ties to the Black Guerilla Family, a prison gang — an affiliation touted in the media. The conspiracy theory that the gang orchestrated the Brooklyn killings as revenge for the earlier police shootings was never confirmed, but it did help keep the case in the headlines.

In the weeks that followed, politicians, pundits and personalities across the country chimed in on the Brooklyn police murders, salting wounds that to this day have yet to heal. Yet back in Brooklyn, the true heartbreak lay with the families, captured so painfully by Ramos' son, Jaden, in his post on Facebook:

"Today I had to say bye to my father. He was [there] for me every day of my life, he was the best father I could ask for. It's horrible that someone gets shot dead just for being a police officer. Everyone says they hate cops but they are the people that they call for help. I will always love you and I will never forget you. RIP Dad."

Burn in hell. Brinsley.

Burn in hell.

80
Alice O'Donnell - The Nurse Girl Murder

The news of the sudden loss of life is something we deal with in our own little ways; a click of the tongue, a shake of the head, the sign of the cross.

Then there are the senseless murders of victims most innocent that really cause us to pause.

On December 7, 1900, after dinner in the early evening, Mr. and Mrs. James Jones of Palmetto Court in Downtown Brooklyn were relaxing on the patio of their cozy home. Little did they suspect within moments their lives would be harshly disrupted, thrusting them into the national spotlight as the subject of widespread sympathy and a parent's worst dread.

Mr. Jones had just finished singing a gentle ballad to his beloved wife after they had dined. In the next room, the family's nursemaid, Alice O'Donnell, was tending to their eighteen-month-old son, James Arthur. The 20-something O'Donnell had taken the nanny position two months prior. O'Donnell was later reported to have said, ""Let me take him ma am, I'll quiet him."

Sure, she quieted the child.

Mrs. Jones remarked later to investigators that in those subsequent moments, she was surprised how O'Donnell had so quickly silenced the boy.

Up until those moments, there was no indication of the demons tormenting O'Donnell's troubled soul.

Within earshot, the Joneses unwound the day in bliss, unaware as just steps away O'Donnell calmly, quietly held the infant down, drew out a sharp razor, slit the baby-soft skin of his delicate throat, splashing herself with blood as she felt the final moments of his life drain beneath her grasp.

When the deed was done, O'Donnell changed her clothes quickly before slipping away from the crime scene, returning to her home in Jersey City across the Hudson River.

Imagine the horror the young parents felt later that evening, when at approximately 11PM they walked into that blood-spattered room, discovering the mutilated remains of their only child. Mrs. Jones collapsed while neighbors rushed to the scene, drawn by the awful shrieks of the young couple.

There was not much more to this dreadful story, not a complicated mystery or prolonged pursuit and investigation. Perhaps it was the crime's senselessness that so inflamed mortified readers of all the New York tabloids the next morning, swearing to each other over breakfast tables from Coney Island to Crown Heights what they'd do if someone harmed one of their own, one so innocent, so vulnerable.

O'Donnell was not hard to find. Mr. Jones led police to the boarding house where she was staying in Jersey City. Soon after her arrest, the remorseless O'Donnell confessed.

The story shocked not just the good people of Brooklyn, but made the papers nationwide, such as this account in *The Indianapolis Journal* from December 9, 1900:

"She admitted killing the child, saying that her own baby, which was born eight months ago, was in an institution and she did not see why another woman should be able to have her child with her when the privilege was denied to her own child."

At the time, there were far fewer social services available to support young single mothers. Investigators confirmed that the destitute Alice, barely able to fend for herself, was forced to relinquish her newborn son less than a year prior.

The separation left a damning wound on the psyche of young Alice that she hid well when she arrived at the home of the unsuspecting Jones family. Investigators surmised O'Donnell was unable to cope with the ideal setting of her employers, spinning her off into a seething state of insane jealousy as she quietly tended to the innocent child.

The parents angrily dismissed the insanity angle, incensed that there could be any clinical excuse to explain the unexplainable. Alice, they argued vehemently, was calm and in her right state of mind, displaying no outward signs of insanity. Though, Mrs. Jones did acknowledge Alice was likely jealous of her precious, perfect child, due to the loss of her own babe. Yet she should be punished, locked away for the rest of her days in an institution for the criminally insane.

79
Benjamin "Bugsy" Siegel – The Father of Las Vegas

Long before John "the Teflon Don" Gotti grabbed headlines, there was Benjamin "Bugsy" Siegel, the original national celebrity gangster.

In the annals of outlaws from "The Broken Land" perhaps none is as mythologized as Siegel. After all, the self-made Jewish American mobster from Brooklyn is credited with founding the ultimate Sin City, that garish gambling mecca in the desert: Las Vegas.

As photogenic as Siegel was, though, he was every bit the psychopath – such a violent, runaway train that his own partners put him down like a mad dog. They assassinated Siegel at a home in Beverly Hills, slinging slugs through the front window, the kill-shot obliterating his eye socket, captured in an iconic crime-scene photograph.

Siegel's success convincing stingy mobsters to plow millions in ill-gotten pension funds, ripped off from Teamsters, to fund his dream of the Sunset Strip alone ranks him high on this list. But there are so many more layers to the man no one called Bugsy, at least not to his face. (In fact, had he done more of his dirt within the confines of Kings County, he most certainly would have ranked higher on this list.)

Long before Siegel was a top racketeer, gangster, casino developer and all-around menace to society, he was a rough-and-tumble street urchin scrapping to survive on the means streets of Brooklyn in the early days of the 20th century.

Born into desperate poverty in Williamsburg in 1906, the son of Russian Jewish immigrants, Siegel dropped out of school at a young age. His threw himself into the underworld with wingman Moe Sedway at his side, starting with a scam extorting pushcart vendors. Either they paid up, or the Siegel-Sedway combination torched their carts.

I imagine they all paid.

As he grew into a teenager, Siegel's rap sheet swelled with arrests for robbery, assault, attempted rape, even murder. Like many psychopaths, Siegel was charming and maniuplative, masking a violent temper simmering below the surface.

Siegel's brutality earned him a reputation for excessive violence that attracted Meyer Lansky, another rising Jewish gangster of the era, who became a close confederate for most of Siegel's life. Add to Siegel's resume an early stint as a hired gun for the Murder, Inc., outfit out of Brownsville, and you had the makings of one of the most notorious gangsters Brooklyn ever produced.

A prominent bootlegger during Prohibition, Siegel set his sights on expanding his gambling portfolio once the Volstead Act was repealed in 1933. Siegel left New York in 1936, heading west, much to the relief of his many Brooklyn rivals.

Storming the West Coast, Siegel's reputation made him a much-feared enforcer, leading him to Las Vegas, then little more than a run-down stop-over on the way to California. When developer

William Wilkerson ran out of funds to finish the Flamingo Hotel, Siegel swept into the breach, convincing his Italian and Jewish gangster partners back east to fund an expanded rennovation.

The Pink Flamingo Hotel & Casino opened on December 26, 1946, though soon closed for additional renovations, infuriating Siegel's silent partners.

That beachhead anchored the mob's wildly successful entrance into Las Vegas that threw off millions in illegal skim for decades to come. At the time, though, Siegel's extensive overruns, not to mention rumours Bugsy was pocketing mob money, sealed his fate.

On June 20, 1947, Siegel was shot to death through the window of the Beverly Hills home of his paramour, the legendary mob moll Virginia Hill.

Brooklyn's own Bugsy Siegel never did get to appreciate what he helped create.

Then again, neither did his many victims.

78
Anthony Weiner – A.K.A. Carlos Danger

Ripped from the files of fantastic flameouts we find now-infamous Brooklyn politician Anthony Weiner, once poised to make a serious run at the mayoralty of New York City in 2011.

Growing up in the Park Slope section of Brooklyn, Weiner was a proud product of the New York City public school system, attending Brooklyn Tech High School before going on to the State University of New York at Plattsburgh. A congressional aide to Charles Schumer when the Brooklyn Democratic dynamo was in the United States House of Representatives, Weiner then served in the New York City Council from 1992 to 1998, before winning Schumer's seat in New York's 9th congressional district in 1999. (Schumer has since gone on to be one of the highest-ranking members of the United States Senate and a national force in politics.)

Weiner made his first unsuccessful run at Gracie Mansion in 2005, bested by Fernando Ferrer in the Democratic primary. (Ferrer fell to incumbent Michael Bloomberg in the general election.)

Yet 2013 was supposed to be another story, with Weiner, the political darling of Brooklyn, leading a yipping pack of Democratic hopefuls.

And then something, shall we say, *came up*.

That's when the notorious Carlos Danger emerged from his secret lair.

Just who was Carlos Danger, this international man of mystery with a cartoony noir-ish nickname?

Well, Carlos Danger was Anthony Weiner's self-inflicted social media handle that he used when sexting pictures of his, uh, wiener, to women not named Mrs. Weiner.

In 2011, the scandal known as Weinergate burst all over the tabloid media, starting when the U.S. House member sent a link to a selfie of his erect member in tight boxer shorts to a 21-year-old college student in Seattle. Initially denying he sent the link, Weiner backpedaled away from the lie that someone hacked his account. He admitted later to sending the link, and other links, to more women, both before and during his marriage to Huma Abedin, a senior political advisor to Hillary Clinton.

The wilting Weiner resigned from Congress.

Imagine the glib glee that consumed smug headline writers in newsrooms across America.

"Weiner's Rise & Fall."

"Weiner: I'll Stick It Out."

"Same Old Schlong & Dance."

"Hide the Weiner."

Wait, it gets better, or worse, depending on how you feel about the double entendres of disgraced politicians.

In an even more hilarious/disastrous turn of events (dubbed "Weiner's Second Coming" by *The New York Post*), in 2013 he mounted another bid for New York City's mayoralty, only to have it prematurely deteriorate in the wake of yet another sexting scandal.

Really, Anthony?

The website "The Dirty" released the pictures sent by the mysterious "Carlos Danger" to a 22-year-old woman, supposedly in 2012 and 2013, well after Weiner resigned his seat in the U.S. Congress from the previous scandal. With every new detail the media whipped out clever headlines.

When Weiner withdrew himself from consideration for the mayoral race, it was: "Weiner Pulls Out."

When he was denying that he tweeted the photo, it was: "Weiner Gets Grilled."

When news emerged that wife Huma Abedin was pregnant, it was: "Little Weiner in the Oven."

When he started to drop in popularity polls, it was: "Weiner is Shrinking."

When the media caught him in an emotional moment, it was: "Naked Truth: Weiner Bawls."

When the President chimed in suggesting he resign, it was "Obama

Beats Weiner."

When the governor followed suit, it was "Cuomo Spanks Weiner."

Yes, we saw "Weiner Exposed," "Weiner's Schnitzel," and "Weiner's Pickle."

I could keep going, in fact I could probably fill this book with more Weinerisms. Needless to say, the serial-sexting scandal sunk Weiner's multiple election bids.

The former world beater was relegated to the role of baby-stroller-schlepping Mr. Mom, taking a backseat to the successful political career of his wife.

Yet every time Weiner poked his head into public life, headline writers were standing at attention, pens poised to spurt out quips clever enough to one-up one another on the next morning's front pages.

By 2017, with Weiner fighting yet another round of sexting allegations, this time with an underage girl, the couple were headed for divorce.

77
Sean Erez - The Holy Rollers

To succeed at international drug smuggling, you must carefully select those concealing your narcotics to minimize detection.

Take Sean Erez, a prolific Israeli-Canadian smuggler who masterminded an ingenious method for manning his international Ecstasy ring. He used Hasidic teenagers from Brooklyn as the mules who carried thousands of his little white pills in false-bottom bags from Europe to New York's John F. Kennedy International Airport.

The lucrative scheme netted millions of dollars in profit and became the subject of a Hollywood movie.

Erez rose rapidly in the drug trade in the mid-1990s as the demand for the club-drug Ecstasy exploded in the American subculture, fueling the party-rave phenomenon.

According to investigators, Erez recruited his pill jockeys from the Orthodox communities of Williamsburg and Borough Park, in Brooklyn, and Monsey, in upstate New York. The teens took $1,500 each to take the European round trip, with Erez misleading them to believe they'd be smuggling diamonds, not drugs.

You'd think ultra-religious Hasidic teens would be reluctant smugglers. Not so. Erez enticed them with the opportunity to visit Amsterdam and experience the types of entertainment rare in places like Borough Park and Monsey. That is, as long as the smuggling did not require traveling on Saturdays, the Sabbath, or traditional day of religious observance in the Jewish faith prohibiting any form of labor.

Running the largest international Ecstasy smuggling ring up to that point, Erez split his time between New York and Amsterdam, the originating point of the shipments. Before the ring ran its course, Erez and his band of black-clad dope mules smuggled more than one million pills into the United States, and they did it in less than a year.

In 1999, authorities rounded up Erez and many members of the ring. Not exactly hardened criminals, 18 confederates pled guilty to an assortment of crimes. To avoid harsher penalties, Erez took a plea in 2001, admitting his guilt to drug conspiracy charges in Brooklyn federal court. Sentenced to 15 years in prison, Erez was transferred to a facility in Ottawa in 2005, where his sentence was reduced to 10 years, as per Canadian-sentencing limits. He was released two months later in the summer of 2005.

Then this tale took on a life of its own.

The story was too bizarre to resist for Hollywood. Borrowing heavily from the Erez case, "Holy Rollers" debuted in 2010, starred popular actor Jesse Eisenberg as a young Hassid who gets swept up in a smuggling scheme. The movie poster ran with the tagline: "In 1998, 1 million ecstasy pills were smuggled into the USA by a group of Hasidic Jews."

Much of the shooting for the film took place in Williamsburg, Brooklyn.

76
Damion "World" Hardy – Brooklyn Drug Lord

The rap game and the underworld in Brooklyn have a mutually sycophantic relationship. That symbiotic swirling of artists and arch criminals lends the street cred that sells downloads.

Damion "World" Hardy was one who walked that line between both worlds.

A drug-dealer from the Brooklyn streets, Hardy led a violent drug gang dubbed Cash Money Brothers (CMB), biting the name for his crew off the classic gangster film "New Jack City," starring Wesley Snipes, Ice-T, and Chris Rock. Like the drug ring in that fictional depiction, Hardy's gang was responsible for commandeering a New York City public housing project, in this instance Lafayette Gardens in Bedford-Stuyvesant, Brooklyn. They lay siege to entire buildings, running a complex, large-scale narcotics operation out of multiple units. The captive residents either participated or turned a blind eye, under the very real threat of extreme violence.

At the end of his bloody decade, including fighting a running drug war that claimed his brother, CMB co-founder Myron "Wise"

Hardy, Hardy was nailed with a life sentence for six murders.

Hardy was an especially dangerous criminal, diagnosed with schizophrenia. It took more than a dozen years to drag him to trial, as his defense lobbied hard that he was not mentally competent to be prosecuted. Ultimately the government prevailed and Hardy, along with several underlings, were brought up on multiple counts of murder, assault, narcotics trafficking, racketeering and other charges.

Hardy was initially arrested in 2004, but due to his illness avoided trial for years. It took that long for federal prosecutors to get federal Judge Frederic Block to mandate he be forcefully administered medication to be able to submit to judgment. After a decade he was finally brought to trial.

During his ruthless reign Hardy achieved even more notoriety based on his short-lived romance with rap superstar Lil' Kim, who also grew up in Bedford-Stuyvesant, Brooklyn. The couple began dating in 2002 and were supposedly engaged, but the relationship fell apart by 2003, with Kim accusing Hardy of physical abuse in an article that ran in *The Source* magazine. Ever since, whenever Hardy was mentioned in the media, he was usually referred to as "Lil' Kim's ex."

Hardy gained further press coverage for a rumor that he put out a contract hit on heavyweight boxer Mike Tyson, who also has roots in the Brooklyn housing projects of "Do-or-Die Bed-Stuy." Adding to his street cred, Hardy was also involved in an altercation with rap-star 50 Cent.

Aside from drug-related homicides, Hardy was convicted of ordering henchmen to shoot to death a security guard at a Brooklyn roller rink where he had been bounced, as well the owner of a medical facility after an incident where Hardy felt slighted. At trial, Hardy received a life sentence in prison.

Convicted alongside Hardy, following a four-week trial, was

Aaron Granton, dubbed Hardy's "personal hitman." Granton was also handed a life sentence.

As several of the victims' family members lambasted the two in court while delivering their victim-impact statements, the two appeared disinterested and aloof, entirely lacking in empathy and remorse for the damage they wrought on the streets of Brooklyn.

75
Ronald Herron – Ra Diggs

Hip Hop genre Gangster Rap glorifies the darker side of street life, from drug dealing to murder. Yet its aficionados claim it's mostly an act to generate attention and drive street sales.

Not everyone thinks it's an act.

Ronald "Ra Diggs" Herron was a ruthless criminal affiliated with the New York Bloods loose-knit confederacy of gangs that rose to power in the 1990s, holding sway for years over the drug-ridden Gowanus and Wyckoff Houses in the Boerum Hill neighborhood of Brooklyn.

When not running drugs into Brooklyn housing projects, Ra Diggs ran his mouth as a rising rap star boasting of murder and mayhem. Yet Herron hid himself behind a cloak of creativity, claiming it was all an act.

Federal prosecutors disagreed.

Streaming his braggadocio in bold online videos posted on social media didn't help Herron's cause when he was indicted on numerous counts, including robbery, assault, racketeering, drug trafficking, and murder.

In those online clips, Herron heralded himself as top dog in the Murderous Mad Dogs, a set of the Bloods street gang in Brooklyn, while waving his guns in the air like he just didn't care.

But you know who did care?

The NYPD and federal investigator who were watching intently, especially when he boasted that he "beat a body." Artistic expression? Or did Ra Diggs get away with murder, as he claimed in verse.

Herron's tirade continued on Twitter, where he chirped how he "beat a stabbing," essentially repeating his "beat a body" claim.

Prosecutors alleged that Herron was referencing the murder of Frederick Brooks, an indictment he escaped in a 2002 trial, when he was acquitted due to witnesses refusing to testify out of fear of retribution from the Bloods' drug-gang leader and his murderous minions.

It would be many bloody years in those Brooklyn housing projects before Herron was brought to justice.

In 2015, Herron was brought to trial again. Throughout the dramatic high-profile trial, Herron drew a large, animated following of fans holding him up as an inner-city hero of the housing projects. They attended court daily, staring down the witnesses from the visitors' gallery with vicious glares.

The intimidation didn't work. Herron went down hard, convicted on 23 counts, including everything from robbery and drug trafficking to three murders.

Herron was handed 12 life sentences, plus an additional 105 years in prison, as well as a scolding from federal judge Nicholas G. Garafis for his courtroom outbursts and lack of empathy for the victims' families.

In addition to the Brooks' murder, Herron was convicted for the killings of Richard Russo in 2008 and Victor Zapata the following year.

Unlike in previous failed trials where Herron frightened witnesses, dozens of brave Brooklynites refused to be terrorized, providing the testimony necessary to rid Kings County of Herron once and for all, sending him away for the rest of his days.

74
Philip Barry - The Bernie Madoff of Bay Ridge

White collar crimes are not victimless.

Nor are they painless.

When it comes to white-collar-crime, there's bad, there's worse, and then there's being compared to Bernie Madoff, the Babe Ruth of ruthless fraud.

In 2015, thirty devastated victims of corrupt financial manager Philip Barry brought a $36 million suit in Brooklyn Supreme Court against JPMorgan Chase, M&T Bank, HSBC and TD Bank. The suit accused those institutions of facilitating Barry's long-running Ponzi scheme.

Newspapers dubbed Barry the "Bernie Madoff of Bay Ridge," likening the Brooklyn native to the now-infamous Wall Street villain who bilked thousands of investors out of more than $60 billion in what is likely the largest financial fraud in history.

Though Barry's scam was nowhere near as large in scope as Madoff, it was still cited as the longest-running Ponzi scheme of all time, by Loretta Lynch, United States Attorney for the Eastern District of New York.

Basically, a Ponzi scheme is a fraud where an individual or organization invests funds, usually on the promise of a lucrative return. Instead of investing responsibly and managing that money to generate profits, the crook running the scheme simply redistributes the new money raised from additional investors, while pocketing as much as he can.

Eventually the scheme collapses under its own weight. Barry's victims blamed not only him, but also the financial institutions with which he was associated. The victims maintained that these banks were sophisticated and so they must have known Barry was running the multi-million-dollar scheme over the course of 30 years, yet turned a blind eye as they raked in thousands in bank fees, according to the suit filed in Brooklyn Supreme Court.

Barry was no modern-day Robin Hood. Quite the opposite, he stole from more than 800 people, mostly Brooklyn blue-collar workers and elderly retirees, for more than three decades. One victim invested $2.3 million, as he was so convinced in Barry's ability to outperform the market.

Barry tried to turn a profit, so he says, though he was a less-than-spectacular investor. He elicited such trust and his fraud ran for so long mainly because he was one of Bay Ridge's own favorite sons. A regular fixture in the neighborhood, Barry lived in Bay Ridge since high school, and later opened his financial advisory firm from an office on 82nd Street. He didn't even have to advertise to attract a sizable clientele.

Hundreds of Brooklynites lost homes, retirement funds, college tuitions, nest eggs. They were ruined financially, emotionally, even physically. For many of his elderly victims, the loss of their savings is a life sentence of misery.

For Barry's victims, there was no meaningful recourse for recovery. The money was squandered, so any return will be pennies on the dollar, regardless the empty remorse he now professes. When he was arrested, Barry had $550,000 left of the fortune he embezzled.

Declaring bankruptcy in October 2008, Barry testified that he owed investors a staggering $60 million. Authorities arrested him the following year in the wake of a year-long investigation.

The crime was profiled in 2013 on CNBC's popular *America Greed* television program, in a segment billing Barry as "Brooklyn's Madoff."

As for Barry's victims suing the banks, insisting that these institutions should have seen the signs of financial fraud and made efforts to protect them. That's pretty difficult to prove in a court of law, especially to the tune of tens of millions of dollars. An initial suit, brought in 2011, was denied in federal court. The judge punted, ruling there were no grounds for it in the Federal Securities Litigation Uniform Standards Act law.

The current suit, brought in 2015, is now winding its way through the courts.

Barry was sentenced in 2011 to 20 years in prison, a fraction of the 150 years Bernie Madoff received. Addressing the victims at sentencing, Barry apologized.

And he promised to pay them back.

73
William "Wild Bill" Lovett
– The White Hand

It should be no surprise there are two entries on this list for Brooklyn bad boys that went by "Wild Bill" – one a turn-of-the-century Irish gangster, the other a Colombo Family War veteran.

Aside from similar career paths, it's likely if these two maniacs met in a dark alley, they'd try to kill each other.

William J. "Wild Bill" Lovett despised Italians, at a time when the Irish still held sway over large chunks of the Brooklyn waterfront.

Lovett was born into desperate poverty in County Kerry, Ireland, before his family fled to New York. He quickly assimilated with the young Irish thugs that played and preyed along the docks.

At the outbreak of World War I, like thousands of young Brooklyn Irish, Lovett enlisted in the United States Army, joining Company C, 13th Machine Gun Battalion, 77th Infantry Division. He plunged recklessly into the fierce fighting along the bloody Western Front in Europe, representing the slums of Brooklyn admirably, receiving the Distinguished Service Cross for courage under fire.

Such wartime bona fides translated well back on the streets of Brooklyn, lending Lovett a reputation for violence that only grew in the gang wars that lay ahead.

Lovett was not some low-level brute. He was educated and well-spoken, albeit headstrong, obstinate and notoriously prone to violence, especially when drinking, which was often, but not unusual for Brooklyn waterfront Irish. It was Bill's penchant for extreme violence while drunk that led to his nickname.

Returning from the killing fields of Europe, Lovett assumed the leadership of the rough-and-tumble Jay Street Gang, Irish boyos locked in a power struggle for the dock rackets against rival Dinny Meehan and his White Hand Gang.

Under Meehan's leadership, The White Hand coalesced drawing together a smattering of Irish gangs in Red Hook and surrounding areas that flourished around the turn of the century up through the Prohibition years. Meehan convinced Lovett to fold the Jay Street gang under his larger organization, and the two maintained a wary partnership for a time, though Wild Bill chafed under Meehan's yolk.

For interested readers, this period in Brooklyn's notorious waterfront history is captured very effectively by novelist Eamon Loingsigh in a trilogy of books that launched in 2014 with the debut of "Light of the Diddicoy," which I highly recommend.

The term "The White Hand" is sort of a backhand aimed at the "The Black Hand," (in Italian, Le Mano Nera) or the Sicilian gangs that specialized in extorting their own people. Each side along the ethnic divide hated the other fiercely, violently churning through the thousands of immigrants that landed in the area in the early 20th century.

In his rivalry with Meehan, Lovett prevailed, though the circumstances of Meehan's demise remain murky. We know Meehan was shot to death in bed with his wife Sadie on March 31, 1920 at their home at 452 Warren Street in Red Hook. Who did the deed, though, is up for debate.

Meehan, like most leaders of criminal enterprises, had many enemies. Police suspected Lovett, but never made it stick. Frankie Yale, the top Italian gangster on the Brooklyn waterfront at the time, was a prime suspect as well.

With Meehan eliminated, Lovett further consolidated the Irish gangs and rose to be the most prominent Irish gang boss of the era. With the advent of Prohibition, there was opportunity to move into the highly lucrative black-market business for bootleg liquor, but the short-sighted Lovett focused on extorting tribute from dockworkers and businesses along the waterfront, as well as demanding a cut from armed robberies, burglaries and other crimes committed in his territories.

When not running his rackets, Lovett was stamping out insurrections from upstart Irish brawlers and trading blows with the Italians. Suspected of either ordering or participating in multiple gangland slayings throughout the teens and twenties, Lovett himself narrowly sidestepped bullets in a 1921 assassination attempt, then caught three in the chest in 1923, surviving.

The assailants in both incidents were found dead in back alleys on the streets of Downtown Brooklyn.

Like many gangsters that came before and after, Lovett tired of *the life*, especially the part about ducking assassins and dodging bullets. Yet it took the love of a fine lass to convince him to call it a career.

Lovett fell hard for Anna Lonergan, the much-younger attractive sister of Peg Leg Lonergan, one of his top captains, and was willing to trade the White Hand for her hand in marriage. Famed for her beauty, the Irish Rose of the Waterfront tentatively accepted the marriage proposal of the brash Lovett, on condition that he leave *the life* and put down the drink.

Married in July 1923, Lovett resigned his leadership in the White Hand and decamped for a charming new cottage in Ridgefield Park, New Jersey. Peg Leg Lonergan, now Lovett's brother-in-law, assumed the gang's leadership.

I'd like to say this gangster fairy tale had an uplifting ending, but in the Brooklyn rackets, no one lives happily ever after. Least alone a brutal gangster like Lovett with a long list of scores unsettled.

In October 1923, Lovett was supposed to be in Manhattan for a job interview for a position as a factory foreman. Instead, he ducked out to Brooklyn to embark on a drinking binge with some of his old mates, sort of a victory lap around the old neighborhood.

Two days later, the body of Wild Bill Lovett was found in the back of a grocery store located at 25 Bridge Street. He'd been beaten and shot to death.

While Frankie Yale and the Italians were prime suspects, the murderers were never identified. It just as well could have been any number of Irish factions, due to past indiscretions. Lovett had more than his share of blood enemies.

Wild Bill almost escaped *the life*.

Almost.

During the early 20th century, ethnic gangs tried to steal and extort every last scrap of the millions of dollars in goods flowing through the bustling Brooklyn waterfront.

Dozens of ethnic dock gangs fought wild running battles for control of these lucrative rackets.

The Italians, mainly Sicilian thugs led by the vicious Frankie Yale, were pitted against the White Handers, primarily Irish, led by William "Wild Bill" Lovett, before that gang leader's murder in 1923.

Control of the Irish rackets fell to Lovett's brother-in-law, Richard "Peg Leg" Lonergan, so nick-named after he lost his limb in an awful trolley-car accident as a child.

Lonergan led a two-year campaign against Yale's forces that ended in defeat, marking him as the last-in-line of the Irish White Handers. Sure the Irish continued to have a profound footprint throughout Kings County, and their echo resounds today in popular watering holes like The Wicked Monk out on the edge of Bay Ridge. But all that pales in comparison to wild heydays of Peg Leg Lonergan.

When it comes to the demise of Irish gangsterism in Brooklyn, think of Peg Leg Lonergan as General Custer, and the infamous "Adonis Club Incident" as his Little Big Horn.

"The Adonis Club Incident" is sort of Brooklyn's answer to Chicago's "St. Valentine's Day Massacre," a mass murder. But instead of a cold, calculating pre-meditated hit, the "Incident" in Brooklyn was an impromptu execution sparked by a drunken, racist-ranting Lonergan.

Like many shanty Irish of the day, Lonergan held a deep-seeded animosity for anything Italian. Stuck on the same socio-economic rung, the Irish and Italians competed for every last scrap of opportunity in Brooklyn, legal and illegal. Beyond rivalry, this was hatred that often exploded into open hostility between the two factions. The fact that many Italians, especially Sicilians, had darker, olive-skinned complexions than the more-fair Irish, and spoke another language, deepened that divide.

Lonergan took his loathing to an entirely different level. One of 15 children born to Irish prize fighter and bare-knuckle boxer John Lonergan, Peg Leg came up rough in the hardscrabble Irishtown. No longer mentioned on modern maps, Irishtown was a destitute gutter enclave along the Brooklyn waterfront, with a sister settlement on the Manhattan side of the East River. It drew the poorest of the poor, the so-called Black 47 Famine Irish and their descendants, who left Ireland with rags on their backs, and kept coming throughout the late 19th century. The infamous slums of Brooklyn's Irishtown, once rife with crime and poverty, are now plush pockets of affluent gentrification called DUMBO, Vinegar Hill and the Brooklyn Navy Yard.

Even with a wooden limb, Peg Leg Lonergan was a feared gangster with a reputation for violence, enhanced when he beat a Sicilian drug dealer to death with his bare hands. Suspected in more than a dozen murders, Lonergan assumed the reins of the White Hand when Lovett gave up the rackets to marry Peg Leg's sister. (Rivals murdered Lovett when he returned to the old neighborhood for a bar crawl in October 1923.)

It was Christmas Day in 1925, and Peg Leg and five of his White Hand heavies dropped in on the Adonis Social Club in South Brooklyn, already tipsy and looking to tangle. Lonergan spewed racial insults at several Italian men present, at one point chasing out three who arrived with Irish dates. (Though there was strong animosity among many Irish and Italians, there was frequent intermingling and marrying between the two groups.)

Suddenly, the lights were cut.

Screams and shouts rang out.

Gunfire erupted.

The Adonis Club emptied.

When the police arrived, they found Peg Leg's White Hand right hand Aaron Harms shot dead in the street.

Inside, they discovered the bodies of Lonergan and Cornelius Ferry, killed with gun shots to the backs of their heads. Another White Hand member made it out alive, James Hart, and was found several blocks away stumbling along after taking two parting shots to the leg. Irish gang members Joseph "Ragtime Joe" Howard and Patrick "Happy" Maloney escaped unscathed.

The authorities rounded up the usual Italian suspects from Frankie Yale's crew that included a young Al Capone, in his pre-Chicago Brooklyn days.

No one was ever indicted for the killings.

Leaderless, the White Hand fragmented under internal bickering and soon dwindled in power along a waterfront now dominated by Italian gangsters, the forerunners to the more-organized New York Mafia families.

71
Salvatore Perrone –
The Son of Sal

In the annals of serial killers, Salvatore Perrone pales beside Berkowitz, Dahmer and Ramirez.

Yet during his short-lived murder spree in 2012, "The Son of Sal" sure inspired plenty of Brooklyn shopkeepers from Bensonhurst to Bay Ridge to close early.

Salvatore never called himself "The Son of Sal." That was a media invention, a clever hi-jacking of David "Son of Sam" Berkowitz serial-killer sobriquet, who a generation prior struck less than a mile from the scene of one of Perrone's murders.

Calling the "Son of Sal" the son of the "Son of Sam" is a stretch. Aside from the locale and the fact they murdered innocent people in sequence, there are few similarities between the two cases. But at the corner of sensationalism and journalism, appropriating the nickname worked and newspapers nationwide ran with "The Son of Sal."

Salvatore Perrone of Sunnyside, Staten Island, struck first in the summer of 2012, shooting 65-year-old Mohamed Gebeli, 65, in the neck in the store-owner's Valentino Fashion, located at 7718 Fifth Avenue in Bay Ridge, Brooklyn. Gebeli did not survive that July 6th shooting.

Police investigators began to suspect they had a serial killer on their hands following a similar shooting weeks later on August 2nd. This time the scene of the crime was in neighboring Bensonhurst at Amazing 99 Cent Deals, located at 1877 86th Street, in the middle of a bustling shopping corridor. Perrone shot Isaac Kadare, 59, in the head, then slit his throat. Kadare died at the scene from his wounds.

After a brief pause, Perrone struck for a third and final time, using the same hunting rifle from the previous murders to shoot Rahmattollah Vahidipour, 78, at his store, the She-She Boutique, at 834 Flatbush Avenue. Again, the victim died at the scene from his gunshot wounds.

By now media reports that the M.O. matched in all three attacks had shoppers and shopkeepers alike looking over their shoulders. In each crime, the owner was attacked right before closing time.

Before fleeing the scene, the murderer covered up the bodies with clothes and other store merchandise.

Solid police work and community outreach helped crack the case. Police retrieved street-side surveillance video near the Flatbush crime scene that revealed a suspect lugging a large black duffle bag. By circulating that video and still photographs through the media, police fielded numerous leads. One tip led them to the Sunnyside home of Sal Perrone.

Perrone was arrested in November 20, 2012, right before the holiday season and the panic in Brooklyn subsided.

A court-ordered search of Perrone's home turned up the rifle. Ballistics tests indicated it was the same weapon used in all three attacks. The police also recovered the knife used to cut Kadare's throat, based on DNA evidence drawn from the blade.

If that wasn't enough evidence, cell-phone records placed Perrone near two of the crime scenes at the time of the attacks.

But why?

Perrone feigned innocence, even as investigators shoveled on the evidence, cherry-topped with a compelling motive. Less than a year prior to the attacks, Perrone saw his once-successful clothing shop slide into bankruptcy, leaving him broken, frustrated and resentful.

Angry enough, it seemed, to kill.

Court-ordered psychologists reported Perrone had a personality disorder, though fell short of diagnosing a mental defect, allowing the case to proceed. At trial, Perrone raged about his innocence in irrational outbursts, blaming unnamed Middle Eastern mystery murderers, even claiming he was working with representatives of the Palestinian section of the CIA.

What a scene. Judge Alan Marrus sanctioned Perrone during one of his frequent, frothing outbursts. Family members of the victims, exasperated by Perrone's outrageous antics, added their shouts to the cacophony resounding throughout Brooklyn Supreme Court.

Perrone was convicted on all three counts of second-degree murder, as well as weapons charges. On March 4, 2016, the 67-year-old Perrone was sentenced to the maximum sentence allowed by law: 75-years-to-life in prison.

And sighs of relief could be heard that holiday season all along the shopping strip of 86th Street.

70
Michael Mastromarino – The Brooklyn Body Snatcher

In 2005, police arrested longtime Brooklyn resident and oral surgeon Michael Mastromarino for masterminding a scheme to illegally harvest bones, tissue and other body parts from the deceased. He resold the material for millions of dollars in blood money.

The body count in the indictment exceeded 1,200 corpses.

Mastromarino's company, Biomedical Tissue Services, supplied researchers, surgeons, transplant units, and other medical-field sources with the human remains. The body parts were used in thousands of procedures, from dental implant surgeries to knee replacements. A single body could yield material for multiple patients, bringing in thousands of dollars in fees.

Harvesting human material for the benefit of science has long been challenging. Grieving family members often cannot bear to think of their loved ones being dissected for medical science, regardless the benefits to mankind.

Not a problem for Mastromarino.

Starting in 2001, Mastromarino colluded with crooked funeral home directors throughout Brooklyn and beyond to harvest the human material without informing the families. This included the since-shuttered Daniel George and Son Funeral Home on Bath Avenue in Bensonhurst.

Among the victims in the scam was Alistair Cooke, the deceased former British journalist, best known to American audiences as the beloved television personality who hosted "Masterpiece Theatre" on PBS.

As reports on the ghastly scheme unfolded on nightly newscasts, Brooklynites were outraged at images of PVC plastic piping placed inside the corpses to conceal.

Yet this was more than a violation of trust. You see, Mastromarino did not screen for diseases.

When *The New York Daily News* broke the story that some of the corpses died from cancer, AIDS and other contagious diseases, it set off a panic among a population of recipients possibly topping 10,000 patients.

In a much-watched, though relatively brief trial in 2008, Mastromarino – now known in the media as "The Brooklyn Body Snatcher" – pled guilty to charges of corruption, reckless endangerment, forgery, grand larceny, and, of course, body stealing. He was sentenced to 18-to-54 years in prison. As part of his plea, he agreed to pay the families of his victims $4.6 million in restitution.

In perhaps the most appropriate instance of poetic justice in all of Brooklyn criminal lore, while incarcerated, Mastromarino died a painful death, succumbing to bone cancer that spread throughout his body.

Talk about karma.

69
Martin Shkreli - The Most Hated Man in America

Is Martin Shkreli guilty of the securities fraud he is alleged to have perpetrated — the focus of a federal investigation at the time this book hits bookstores and online booksellers?

It doesn't matter.

Those alleged infractions are not what made Martin Shkreli infamous. Nope, that's not it, not by far.

It's what he did before, and that was perfectly legal.

The Brooklyn-born Shkreli should have been celebrated as another example of the American Dream fulfilled. Shkreli was born to Albanian and Croatian immigrants who worked as janitors. He grew up in Sheepshead Bay, Brooklyn, and was a bright student. Shkreli attended Hunter College, later donating $1 million to that institution, and then earned a bachelor's degree in business administration from Baruch College.

A wildly successful entrepreneur and pharmaceutical executive, Shkreli founded the hedge fund MSMB Capital Management, was co-founder and former chief executive officer of the biotechnology firm Retrophin, and founder and former chief executive of Turing Pharmaceuticals.

It was his cut-throat pricing strategy at Turing that turned heads.

Shkreli founded Turing Pharmaceuticals in February 2015, setting the company on a course to secure licenses on out-of-patent medicines and re-adjust pricing schemes to exploit opportunities.

And patients.

As distribution of these drugs is usually limited to smaller populations, they often do not have generic alternatives. By limiting distribution and jacking up prices, Shkreli knew he could profit greatly.

But at what cost?

Turing acquired Daraprim (pyrimethamine) in 2015, an FDA-approved therapeutic drug in use since 1953. Among the drug's various applications, it is used to treat AIDS patients.

When news hit that Turing raised the price of the drug by 5,556 percent, or $750 per tablet, from $13.50, the reaction was immediate. Overnight Shkreli was crowned "The Most Hated Man in America" on dozens of media outlets and websites.

Seriously.

Go Google "The Most Hated Man in America" and see what returns in the search results.

From medical associations and presidential candidates to news anchors and national radio hosts, everyone with a platform or a podium slammed the young Brooklyn billionaire who acquired a life-saving drug and made a fortune with it exploiting the simple laws of supply and demand.

In December 2015, Shkreli was arrested by the FBI after being indicted on federal charges of securities fraud.

He is free on bail pending trial.

In an interesting postscript to this story, Shkreli drew even more consternation when he took $2 million of his ill-gotten gains and used it to purchase rap mega-group Wu-Tang Clan's infamous unreleased one-of-a-kind album "Once Upon A Time In Shaolin."

In early 2017, a listening party orchestrated by Shkreli for Webster Hall in Manhattan was canceled due to threats. On social media Shkreli promoted the event as "An Evening with Martin Shkreli," featuring lecturing on politics, healthcare, investing and other topics.

William Miller - The Original Ponzi Schemer

A Ponzi scheme is simple.

It is a fraudulent misrepresentation of a business opportunity. Gullible investors are promised irresistible returns for making up-front investments. On the back-end, where it counts, the "returns" are not actually profits from business ventures. Instead, the investors are paid with their own money and the money of other investors.

A Ponzi scheme requires one key ingredient to succeed – greed.

In recent history, Bernard Madoff's stunning fraud, exposed in December 2008, was an elaborate Ponzi scheme he kept afloat for decades, duping more than 4,800 clients. Yet nearly 90 years before Madoff made off with an estimated $64 billion, Charles Ponzi was peddling postal coupons in Boston in 1920, promising to double an investor's outlay inside of 90 days.

The problem with Ponzi schemes is that they all have a fundamental flaw. Sooner or later, someone wants their money back. To keep the scam going and pay out returns, a constant stream of new investors need to be lured into the pool. As the scam grows and grows and grows, the likelihood more will push the panic button to bail out becomes greater.

All it takes is for some of the sheep in the herd to get spooked to start the stampede.

For that to happen to Madoff, that took decades and an epic financial crisis in the U.S. economy.

For Charles Ponzi, it was seven months, though that was enough time for him to amass $8 million from more than 30,000 investors. And that's in 1920 dollars. Ponzi was convicted of fraud and packed off to prison for five years.

By now you must be wondering what a Wall Street psychopath and a 1920s postal-coupon peddler have in common?

What if I told you the original Ponzi schemer wasn't Charles Ponzi? In fact, Ponzi, Madoff and multitudes of others since actually swiped their scam from the original swindler, William "520 Percent" Miller, who launched "The Franklin Syndicate" in 1899 in none other than Brooklyn, New York.

Miller didn't make his pitch too good to be true; just too good to pass up. Not promising to double their money, Miller offered a return of 10 percent, per week, on the initial investment, a whopping 530 percent annual rate of return.

Miller and his two partners knew the scheme relied on greed. Yet they also knew that avarice needed evidence of the remarkable returns to keep the con humming along. When he paid his investors, more often than not they'd be willing to reinvest to increase their future "returns." They also referred to Miller a steady stream of friends and family.

Miller was a despicable man, preying on victims with little financial savvy. He wolfed down his first chunk of the con by fleecing the flock at the Christian Endeavor Society, a Brooklyn charity where he served as president. It started in March 1899, when Miller offered his scam to three members of the Society, falsely claiming he had access to inside information on Wall Street. Miller also offered a five-percent commission fee for referrals.

Expanding the scope of operations beyond Brooklyn, Miller placed advertisements in newspapers across the country, decades before truth-in-advertising statutes were even a concern.

Realizing such advertising unlocked a steady stream of out-of-town investors, Miller spent $32,000 alone in the summer of 1899 to place ads in more than 800 newspapers across America, a massive sum at the time. That investment paid off handsomely.

Before The Franklin Syndicate scam collapsed, Miller collected more than $1 million from thousands of investors, from Brooklyn and beyond, mostly poor and middle-class people trying to see some daylight.

Miller took the brunt of the legal blow, sentenced to 10 years in prison, serving six before he was pardoned.

Years later, Miller was contacted by The *Boston Post* doing an expose on Charles Ponzi, in the wake of the spectacular collapse of his scheme.

So then why don't we call it a "Miller Scheme?"

Simple.

Scale.

Ponzi raked in far more money, duping many more investors, leading to bigger headlines and greater notoriety.

When he was released from prison, persona no grata in Brooklyn, Miller wisely pulled up stakes and decamped for Long Island, where he lived out his days in relative obscurity minding a small local grocery store.

67
Joseph Profaci – Don Pepinno

Following New York's bloody Sicilian gang wars of the early 20th century, the Italian American Mafia was formally restructured into the "Five Families" in the summer of 1931. In Brooklyn Mafia genealogy, on this Five Family Tree, long before they were the Colombos, they were the Profacis, founded on the broad shoulders of a ruthless gangster.

Born in 1897 in Villabate, Sicily, Giuseppe Profaci rose to the upper echelons of organized crime, founding one of the first "New York Five Families" in 1928 that would bear his name for the three decades he ruled.

Unlike the low-key style of fellow don Carlo Gambino, Profaci lived life large, every bit the loud Runyonesque gangster.

In his early 20s, Profaci notched his first prison stint back in Palermo, Sicily, on a burglary charge. Profaci was released in 1921 after serving one year. He left Sicily behind and headed to America. After an unsuccessful run as a baker in Chicago, he moved again in 1925, this time to Brooklyn where he launched what would become a lucrative olive oil business. Behind the scenes, though, Profaci was more than a simple olive-oil peddler.

It was 1928 and Brooklyn was hotly contested by opposing Sicilian factions when Profaci entered the fray. Brooklyn gang boss Salvatore D'Aquila had been gunned down, destabilizing the already fragile underworld. To help smooth out the conflict, Profaci was anointed to succeed D'Aquila during a pow-wow in Cleveland that year. It was a curious selection. Profaci was not a senior, seasoned gangster at that point. His selection had as much to do with his familial connections in the underworld back home in Sicily.

Whatever the reason for his ascension, Profaci assumed control of the gang and its criminal interests, including gambling, extortion, loan sharking, hijacking, prostitution and more.

Following the epic Castellammarese War of the early 1930s, which saw the young Turks led by Charles "Lucky" Luciano oust the old-guard Sicilian "Mustache Petes," Luciano created the Mafia commission. Profaci assumed a seat on the ruling board as head of one of the founding five families.

Many gangsters of that era faced a new weapon from law enforcement: investigation on suspicion of tax evasion. Profaci shielded himself from such prosecution thanks to his wildly successful "Mama Mia Importing Company" and was now known as the "Olive Oil King." The U.S. Internal Revenue Service did pursue Profaci for more than $1 million in unpaid taxes, but was never able to prosecute him successfully.

Profaci was present at the infamous Appalachian Conference of 1957, at the upstate New York farmhouse of gangster Joseph Barbara. When the pow-wow was raided, he was one of the 61 mobsters rounded up by state troopers, while also among the 21 convicted of conspiracy. His sentence of five years was overturned on appeal.

Profaci was an old-time gangster who demanded complete complicity, ruthlessly meting out punishment for those who disobeyed his edicts. His tight-fistedness when it came to sharing the family's ill-gotten gains led to dissention in the ranks, manifested in a running battle with one of his captains in the 1950s, the aptly nick-named Joseph "Crazy Joe" Gallo.

Profaci reneged on a promise to hand Gallo the lucrative gambling interests of a bookie Gallo bumped off, a murder committed at Profaci's request. Gallo retaliated by kidnapping Profaci's underboss and several captains, including future family boss, Joseph Colombo. Profaci was furious and humiliated, as he himself narrowly evaded capture in the kidnapping, fleeing in his pajamas. The war raged on until Profaci's death.

There are many fascinating gangland stories that swirl around Profaci including one about a beautiful church in Bensonhurst, built in 1948 following World War II, on 65th Street and 12th Avenue. The Regina Pacis Votive Shrine was constructed in the style of the Italian Renaissance.

To help fund the project, families from the congregation of St. Rosalie in Bensonhurst and nearby Borough Park donated family gems. Many of these jewels not sold to pay for the construction were used to form two crowns, one for the statue of the Virgin

Mary and one for the baby Jesus. The crowns were taken to Rome to be blessed by Pope Pius and set on display in the church when it opened.

One morning in 1952, mortified Father James Russo noticed the crowns had been pilfered. The congregation was shocked and the story ran in *The New York Times*, among other media outlets. The story took on a life of its own beyond religious connotations, as the parishioners of St. Rosalia had pledged to build the church should America emerge victorious from World War II.

Eight days later, the jewels were recovered, arriving in neat packages delivered to the church rectory.

The mystery of who stole the crowns and who returned them was never solved. However, shortly before their return, Ralph Emmino, a low-level Mafia associate and jewel thief was found shot to death in Bath Beach, Brooklyn. Rumor has it that Joseph Profaci personally ordered the search and execution of the thief when he became incensed upon learning of the theft, and that before he was shot, Emmino was strangled with rosary beads.

Those rumors were never proven and the murder remains unsolved.

By 1962, in failing health, Profaci rebuffed a request to step aside made by rival family bosses Tommy Lucchese and Carlo Gambino. Profaci was dead set against retirement and the war with the Gallo faction in South Brooklyn raged on until his death later that year, when he succumbed to liver cancer.

While Joseph Magliocco ascended to become boss for a brief period, the Mafia Commission set him aside in 1963 and named Joseph Colombo to lead the family that then took his name.

66
Thomas Pitera - Tommy Karate

Thomas Pitera took pride in his craft as a crime-family contract killer, dropping bodies for the Brooklyn Bonannos at a gruesome clip throughout the 1970s and 1980s.

Pitera was a nightmare on the same Gravesend streets where he grew up, though no longer the victim of cruel bullies. Undersized as a youth with a falsetto voice some said was a cross between Michael Jackson and Mickey Mouse, Pitera was an easy target for local toughs.

Like many Brooklyn boys coming up in the 1960s, Pitera enjoyed Bruce Lee movies, sparking a lifelong interest in martial arts. Pitera took his obsession to the next level, studying martial arts in Japan for more than two years on a special scholarship.

Returning to the old neighborhood in 1974, Pitera put his training to good use as a street solider for the Bonanno crime family. That's when he earned a new nickname.

Tommy Karate.

The bullied became the bully.

Mafia thugs are by nature cruel and intimidating. Pitera, however, was a special breed of menace: an up-and-coming gangster with something to prove, and the muscle and martial-arts training to inflict exceptionally cruel and unusual punishment.

Pitera was assigned to the wing of the Bonannos led by "The Three Captains" of Alphonse "Sonny Red" Indelicato, Dominick "Big Trin" Trinchera and Philip "Phil Lucky" Giaccone. These three goons were unhappy with how boss Philip "Rusty" Rastelli ran the family through rival captains Dominick "Sonny Black" Napolitano and Joseph Massino.

Little did the gangsters know federal agent Joseph Pistone had infiltrated Napolitano's crew as thief Donnie Brasco, yet at the time Pistone was years from crippling the Bonannos. Later in

1981, the same three captains were assassinated in a group hit set up by Napolitano and Massino, gunned down at a Brooklyn bar owned by none other than Sammy the Bull Gravano from the Gambinos.

When the smoke cleared, Pitera was among those reassigned to a new captain and crew, and he was formally inducted into the Bonanno Family.

In August of 1988, as a favor to Gambino gangster John Gotti, Pitera murdered Wilfred "Willie Boy" Johnson. Gotti learned Johnson, his former driver and close friend, was cooperating with federal investigators since as early as the mid-1960s. Pitera was acquitted at trial of the Johnson murder.

Bonanno consigliere Anthony "The Old Man" Spero, who led the ultra-violent Bath Beach crew for the family, drew Pitera into his orbit. To carry out Spero's bidding, Pitera formed a squad of ferocious killers, which he also put to good use in a lucrative sideline robbing drug dealers. The thing about drug dealers is that once you rob them, they never run to the police. If they resisted, Pitera murdered them, burying them out in Staten Island, before selling their stashes. Investigators later dug up half a dozen of Pitera's victims in a makeshift mob graveyard in the William T. Davis Wildlife Refuge on Staten Island.

Pitera obsessed over the dismemberment and disposal of his victims. Diligently studying and perfecting his process, wrapping the bodies in plastic and burying them deep enough to throw off the cadaver dogs, Tommy Karate earned yet another, more fearsome nickname.

Tommy the Butcher.

By the time Pitera was indicted on seven murders and numerous racketeering charges, investigators suspected he may have been involved in more than 50 killings. Pitera murdered not only contract targets and low-life drug dealers, but members of his own crew he suspected of cooperating with police.

Searching his home in Gravesend, police hauled away a horde of weapons, not just firearms, but ornate swords and exotic knives, as well as hundreds of books on torture and dismemberment, including "The Hitman's Handbook." They also found a horde of mementos Pitera kept from his many victims, a telltale trait of a psychopathic killer.

At trial, Frank Gangi, a former member of Pitera's crew and nephew of Genovese crime-family captain Rosario Gangi, testified against Tommy Karate to get out from under his own legal problems. In chilling detail on the witness stand, Gangi recounted how Pitera murdered and disposed of his victims. Gangi escaped into the federal-witness-protection program. Though prosecutors pushed for the ultimate sentence for Pitera, four of the murders preceded the re-enactment of the death penalty in New York.

In the summer of 1992, Pitera was convicted on drug charges and six of the seven murders, but acquitted on the Johnson killing.

Pitera is currently high-kicking his way through a life sentence, incarcerated at the federal penitentiary in Allenwood, Pennsylvania.

65
Irving Nitzberg - Knadles

"Knadles" is not a fearsome nickname.

It is a German potato-dumpling dish.

Sort of funny, in a way.

But Irving "Knadles" Nitzberg was no joke.

Nitzberg was not an especially successful gangster, never rising to more than a button man. Yet he did achieve notoriety in Brooklyn in the late 1930s for a sensational murder.

Nitzberg was Bronx muscle, brought in as a triggerman on a contract killing by the Murder, Inc. crew from Brownsville, mainly because Knadles' mug was not well known in Brooklyn.

It was one of those murders that draw national media attention, not so much for the crime itself, but because it epitomizes a phenomenon in our culture. In this case, the rise of the Jewish gangster run amok. It was this widespread coverage and resounding condemnation that earns Knadles his notch on this list.

The target was certainly not sympathetic, Albert "The Plug" Shuman, an unsavory underworld character. According to the morning edition of *The Milwaukee Journal* on January 11, 1939, "Shuman was credited with originating the expression 'Shoot 'em twice in the back of the neck and they won't wiggle'."

And that's exactly how it went down.

Seated behind Shuman in a stolen vehicle, Knadles plugged "the Plug" with multiple slugs to the back of his head while they were riding together in a car through the streets of Downtown Brooklyn.

Shuman was a hood helping authorities build a racketeering case against gang lord Louis "Lepke" Buchalter. When Shuman got into the front seat of that stolen car, driven by henchman Albert Tannenbaum, he was convinced they were heading to pull a score. Instead he caught two bullets to the back of the head fired by Knadles Nitzberg.

Knadles was later arrested and put on trial for the murder, ratted out by former Murder, Inc. mainstay Abe "Kid Twist" Reles who was cooperating with federal authorities to escape a death sentence. By the time it came to try Knadles, testimony provided by Reles had already sent several other Murder, Inc. contract killers to the electric chair at Sing Sing.

Knadles was now on deck, with prosecutors eager to try and fry him. However, Nitzberg received a brief reprieve, and not the kind signed by the New York State governor.

Convicted of first-degree murder on May 23, 1941, Knadles was sentenced to die in the electric chair. However, the New York State Court of Appeals overturned the conviction when testimony used by non-accomplices, who were promised leniency, was brought into question.

In a second trial, the testimony from star-witness Reles had to be read back to the jury, for a very good reason. Reles had flown the coop, literally. Stashed away at the Half Moon Hotel in Coney Island, Reles mysteriously *"fell"* out a window in an attempted *"escape."*

At least that was the story given by the five policemen guarding Reles.

No one was ever held accountable for Reles' death. But there were rumors. Not that Knadles had anything to do with Reles' emergency ejection from the Half Moon. He didn't have that kind of pull. The most plausible explanation is that the Reles *"escape attempt"* was orchestrated by Albert "Lord High Executioner" Anastasia, when the Murder, Inc. mob boss realized it was only a matter of time before the government sicced their rat Reles on him.

So Knadles beat the case and was unleashed onto the streets of Brooklyn, where he fell right back into a life of low-level crime, mostly petty loansharking and thievery before disappearing from the public record.

64
Delroy Edwards – Uzi

In a federal courtroom in Brooklyn in 1984, before the jury

foreman delivered the verdict in the racketeering trial of Delroy Edwards, he passed the presiding judge a disturbing note.

''After rendering our verdict, will any precautionary measures be taken on our behalf?''

Following five days of deliberations, the jury had good cause to be alarmed of potential harm.

They'd just weathered six weeks of appalling murder and mayhem, cringing at blood-curdling testimony chronicling 42 counts including no less than six murders, 17 assaults, and a deep dossier of other criminal acts.

Delroy Edwards was the leader of one of the most violent drug gangs Brooklyn has ever seen. He was a narcotics-trafficking trailblazer credited with unleashing crack cocaine on the streets of Bedford-Stuyvesant.

The judge assured the nervous jurors that their personal information was not available publicly and at the conclusion of the trial, they would be shuttled to safety. Still, they shifted uneasily in their seats as the verdict was read.

Edwards more than earns his place on this list for his prominent role helping deliver one of the most diabolical disasters ever visited on the people of Brooklyn, preying on a low-income, inner-city communities ill-prepared to cope with the drug epidemic he unleashed. Prosecutors detailed to the jury how posses led by ruthless Jamaican drug lords, like Edwards, besieged Brooklyn and other U.S. cities, establishing networks of crack houses in the 1980s that flooded the streets with a cheap form of smoke-able cocaine. Edwards' crack empire spread as far as Washington, D.C., and Philadelphia.

On the streets, Edwards was known by the unimaginative nickname Uzi, simply because he often concealed a fully loaded automatic Uzi submachine gun on his person.

At its height, Edwards' narcotics operation generated tens of thousands of dollars a day, his gang's hierarchy of dozens of members and associates ran numerous drug spots in Brooklyn alone, mainly spread throughout Bedford-Stuyvesant, Crown Heights and Flatbush.

When someone got out of line, Edwards beckoned his henchman to beat, stab and/or shoot them to death. Jurors recoiled before the barrage of testimony of numerous violent assaults and torture sessions, the body count rising with each witness.

In one telling testimony about Edwards' ambivalence toward human life, the jury learned of how he ordered an underling to storm the corner of Sterling Place and Schenectady Avenue in Bedford-Stuyvesant and blast anyone who looked Jamaican.

Edwards was convicted on 42 counts, including conspiracy, narcotics trafficking, assault and murder. In sentencing Edwards, Federal Court Judge Raymond J. Dearie characterized him as a "pioneer" in the crack trade in Brooklyn, remarking on his intelligence that should have been channeled elsewhere, other than destroying thousands of lives in Brooklyn.

Dearie then slapped Delroy with seven consecutive life sentences, on top of a 15-year sentence and $1 million fine.

63
Mike Dowd – "The Cop Version of Goodfellas"

In the Brooklyn underworld, life *is* stranger than fiction.

Or at least wilder.

Mike Dowd was a corrupt New York City police officer, arrested in 1992 in possession of cocaine. Drug trafficking, though, was just one of this cop's many vices, who later estimated in court he committed hundreds of crimes while in uniform.

If it sounds like a made-for-the-movies thriller, that's because it was. In 2014 the documentary *"The Seven Five"* debuted, chronicling corruption in the 75th Precinct in East New York where Dowd led a band of crooked cops. Opening to positive reviews, the documentary was optioned by Sony for the full Hollywood treatment.

Corrupt NYPD Officer Michael Dowd

Unfortunately for the residents of Brooklyn's East New York, Dowd's story is all too true. At the time covered in the documentary's narrative, the mid-1980s through the early 1990s, Brooklyn was the epicenter of the crack epidemic. Amidst the mayhem, Dowd and his partner were each clocking $4,000 a week on the payroll of a violent drug gang.

Dowd was arrested, tried and convicted for his crimes, sent to federal prison for years, and then cashed in when he was enlisted by filmmaker Tiller Russell to provide play-by-play accounts of his corruption and thievery. The result is nothing short of breathtaking.

Armed with a badge, a gun and the public's trust, Dowd did more than tip off traffickers. Rolling up his blue sleeves he dove headlong into the drug trade. Some critics panned the documentary for its sensationalistic focus on Dowd's wild storytelling and lack of sensitivity to the ravages he wrought on the people of Brooklyn.

But man, what a wild ride it was while it lasted.

With the highest murder rate in the United States, the Seven Five was a notoriously dangerous beat, infested with drug gangs. With

Dowd a disillusioned police officer hard up for cash, it was a semi-automatic slide from bribe taking and information sharing, to extortion, drug dealing, gun running, armed robbery, assault and other crimes.

Dowd robbed street dealers at gun point. Short of murder, you don't get any more crooked than that as a police officer.

When Dowd's previous partner resigned from the force in the wake of a round of arrests in 1987, he was assigned a new partner, Ken Eurell. These brazen buddy cops connected with Dominican drug lord Adam Diaz and formed a ruthless partnership.

How diabolical was "The Diaz Organization?" Diaz and his drug gang, responsible for multiple homicides, operated super markets to sell his drugs. Not "open air drug markets" as a euphemism, but fully functioning grocery stores he commandeered to move his product.

Diaz needed Dowd and Eurell in his pocket to take his gang to the next level. The police officers even served as armed escorts to ferry drug profits along the dangerous Brooklyn streets of the crime-ridden 1980s era.

When the Suffolk County Police Department arrested Dowd and Eurell on drug charges, Dowd concocted a kidnapping plot with Colombians to pull off one last score and flee the country.

Little did he know that Eurell already dropped dime, leaping into the arms of the NYPD's Internal Affairs unit.

Dowd was arrested in 1991. Fallout from the corruption probe prompted then-NYC Mayor David Dinkins to create "The Mollen Commission" to explore police corruption, with the Seven Five considered the largest-ever scandal. Dozens of officers across the city were dragged in and interrogated. Dowd testified, though refused to name the names of fellow officers.

Eurell had no such qualms. For his snitching, Eurell never served prison time.

Dowd received 14 years, and served 13.

Following his eight-year-stint, Diaz was deported to his native Dominican Republic.

Those three and other key players in the drama participated in the documentary, which is highly recommended viewing.

Makes you wonder, who will play Dowd in the movie based on "The Seven Five?"

More recently, Diaz and Dowd teamed up again, in their post-prison lives, to hawk cigars from the Dominican Republic under the brand name "The Seven Five."

62
Jack Koslow – The Kill for Thrills Gang

he Brooklyn Thrill Killers 1954

The teenage brain is sometimes incapable of pumping the brakes. Yet there is a difference between reckless juvenile delinquency and psychopathic gang violence.

Such was the case in the early 1950s, when four sadistic teens from South Brooklyn self-styled themselves thrill killers. The notorious "Night of Horrors" case villainized comic books, sparking a national hysteria well earning this crew a spot on the

"Brooklyn's Most Wanted" rankings.

When authorities took down the Kill-for-Thrills gang, as they called themselves, Jack Koslow (18 years old), Melvin Mittman (17), Jerome Lieberman (17), and Robert Trachtenberg (15) quickly folded under questioning. Seems these cowards only found courage on the late-night streets of Brooklyn's waterfront when they could overpower their innocent victims.

This was not boys being boys behaving badly. This was a crew of vicious fiends.

Spilling the beans on the beating and torture of one black man, gang members blubbered on about a summer chock full of the old ultraviolence preying on street people in Brooklyn.

On the evening of August 16, 1954, these four jackals beat and kicked African-American factory worker Willard Menter in the shadow of the Williamsburg Bridge, burning him with their cigarette butts, before dragging his semi-conscious body down to the end South Fifth Street, where the torture continued. With Menter unconscious the beating only ended when the thrill-killers chucked his lifeless body into the East River to drown.

With the confessions, South Brooklyn police detectives were able to solve a string of open cases plaguing the area that summer. Ten days prior to the Menter murder, the gang set upon Reinhold Ulrickson, kicking him to death. In another attack they set a man on fire with gasoline, beat and whipped two young women in a municipal park, and perpetrated several other assaults.

The gang's gruesome handiwork caught fire in the media, holding them up as the 1950's poster-children for the dangers of juvenile delinquency.

Transcending the New York tabloids, many major U.S. outlets with national reach picked up the story, including *Time, Newsweek, Look* and *The New York Times*. Academic studies on juvenile delinquency also featured the case prominently.

Everyone had an opinion on what made these boys tick, with nationally renowned psychiatrists blaming the explosion of violence on the boys' sexual demons. "These boys appear to me to be bound together in a kinship of pathological dedications," Dr. Robert Hoffman declared. "They are probably homosexual ... [They] should be eliminated from society."

Despite the media frenzy and public outcry, two of the younger defendants avoided harsh penalties. Charges were dismissed against Lieberman due to lack of evidence, and a terrified Trachtenberg received leniency by turning on his chums, testifying against Koslow and Mittman.

Much of the coverage focused on crew-leader Jack Koslow, a self-affirmed racist Neo-Nazi, complete with Hitler mustache and anti-vagrant agenda. Did I mention that this merry band of Neo-Nazis were Jewish? *Inside Detective* magazine even dubbed Koslow the "Boy Hitler of Flatbush Avenue."

In a bit of epic courtroom theatrics, Koslow's attorney, the flamboyant theater buff Fred G. Moritt, recited a clever rhyme as part of his closing argument:

> Four little bad boys off on a spree,
> One turned State's evidence and then there were three.
> Three little bad boys, what did one do?
> The judge said, "No Proof," and then there were two.
> Two little bad boys, in court they must sit,
> And pray to the Jury, "please, please acquit."
> Neither judge nor jury were amused.

Koslow and Mittman were convicted on first-degree murder and sent away for life. When the verdicts were read, both boys wept in each other's arms.

Afterwards questions lingered related to motive. Why did they do it? Why didn't they testify in their own defense? Why were they prosecuted for some crimes, yet not others?

Comic books were demonized, when it came to light that the boys were avid readers of the "Nights of Horror" series. For years, academic studies and media reports continued to drag up the case, and it was referenced as proof there existed a link between comics and teen violence.

The New York State Joint Legislative Committee to Study the Publication of Comics, formed in 1949, took up an examination of *Nights of Horror* in a series of hearings in 1955.

Fortunately, the hearings never led to the ban of comics.

61
Ronald DeFeo – The Amityville Horror Killer

With a population of less than 10,000, Amityville is a sleepy hamlet in the town of Babylon on Long Island, NY. Prior to the 1970s, the small village's claim to fame revolved around former residents, including Annie Oakley, Will Rogers and Al Capone.

That all changed in November 1974, when Ronald "Butch" DeFeo Jr. murdered six members of his family, shooting them in cold blood at his parents' home in Amityville. The crime spawned a book, begetting a major motion picture, *"The Amityville Horror,"* that scared an entire generation silly back in the 1970s.

Yet long before the murders, movies and mania that followed, this was the story of a family from Brooklyn in turmoil.

Born in 1951, the oldest of five siblings, DeFeo was a troubled soul since early childhood. Ronald Sr. carved out a comfortable living for his family as a top sales associate at his father-in-law's Brooklyn Buick car dealership. This enabled the DeFeo clan to relocate to a more affluent area out on Long Island.

Despite the economic security, life in the DeFeo household was far from suburban bliss. The senior DeFeo was an overbearing presence in the home, exerting physical and verbal abuse on his namesake.

Overweight and bullied at school, the younger DeFeo chafed under his father's expectations. DeFeo's increasingly frequent outbursts as a teenager prompted his parents to pull in a psychiatrist. The sessions did little to improve the uncooperative Butch, and he stopped going. Heavy drug use led to more violent episodes and by the age of 17 DeFeo was expelled from high school, never to return.

With little in the way of career prospects, Butch joined the family business at the age of 18, where he again failed to live up to expectations. Unable to deal with their troubled child, DeFeo's parents showered him with expensive gifts and cash to keep the peace. Butch used the easy money to buy alcohol, drugs, and, disastrously, firearms.

With his home life fraying further, DeFeo became obsessed with guns. He threatened a friend in one incident on a hunting trip, and then later nearly killed his father during argument, a disaster that was only averted when the 12-gauge shotgun he brandished malfunctioned.

By 1974, DeFeo was an angry, drug-addicted, mentally unstable bomb just waiting to blow. That's when he concocted a clever scheme.

Charged with regularly depositing tens of thousands of dollars at the bank, proceeds from the car dealership's sales, DeFeo staged a robbery with an accomplice. He might have gotten away with the caper, yet as with most everything he did, Butch botched things and had a complete meltdown in front of police investigators.

Butch refused to cooperate with police, and when confronted by his father, he threatened to shoot him. As usual, the elder DeFeo backed off, his son storming away, humiliated and paranoid.

Not long after, on the morning of November 13, 1974, Butch shot both of his parents to death while they slept, with his hunting rifle. Butch then murdered his brothers, followed by his sisters, all in quick succession. The bloodbath took less than 15 minutes.

Butch showered, packaged up the bloody clothes and evidence, and then went to work at the dealership. He attempted to establish an alibi, feigning panic when he "discovered" the bodies.

DeFeo tried to divert suspicion to a Mafia soldier who had a previous dispute with the DeFeo family, but his ruse fell apart. Butch withered under questioning, quivering as he confessed to the heinous crimes.

At trial a year later, an insanity defense was rejected and on November 21, 1975, a jury found Butch guilty on six counts of second-degree murder. He was sentenced to six consecutive life sentences for the murders and is incarcerated at the Green Haven Correctional Facility in Beekman, New York.

A year later, the Lutz family moved into the "cursed" home. They lasted 28 days before fleeing the home and its blood-oozing walls. The first of several novels and movies chronicling their supposed haunting was produced in 1977: "The Amityville Horror: A True Story."

A movie based on that book was released two years later in 1979. Over the years several offshoots were produced, including a remake as recently as 2005.

60
Vyacheslav Ivankov – Little Japanese

Waves of Russian Jews immigrating to the United States in the 1970s reshaped the look and feel of Brighton Beach.

The demographic shift was so dramatic that the neighborhood adjacent to Coney Island abutting the Atlantic Ocean is now known as "Little Odessa." The area boasts more residents of Russian origin than anywhere else on the planet, outside Russia.

With the collapse of the Soviet Union in the 1980s, even more ethnic Russians and Ukrainians flocked to Brighton Beach and nearby Sheepshead Bay. They revitalized a flagging community plagued by high crime and commercial vacancy rates, adding a unique flavor to blend into that Brooklyn brand of the American experience.

Yet sprinkled amidst the thousands of hard-working, hard-accented immigrants jostling down bustling Brighton Beach Avenue now included some undesirable aspects of Russian culture. Men like Vyacheslav Kirillovich Ivankov, known on the streets as "Yaponchik," or Little Japanese, for his Mongolian facial similarities.

Born in Georgia behind the Iron Curtain of the Soviet Union and raised in the heart of Moscow, Ivankov rose to become the so-called "Red Godfather" dispatched to New York by underworld overlords to oversee criminal operations. Or so prosecutors later alleged.

As a young man, Ivankov made a name as a championship fighter, his skill with his hands attracting gangsters always eager to add muscle to their ranks. First incarcerated following a brawl, upon release Ivankov began his underworld rise dealing in black-market goods.

Arrested in 1982 and convicted on multiple criminal counts (robbery, weapons possession, drug trafficking, etc.), Ivankov was sentenced to 14 years in a Siberian gulag prison, where he embraced Russia's storied underground as a full-fledged "Thief in Law."

Much of Ivankov's early history is murky, but we do know he was released from prison early, rumored to be the bribing of a Russian court official.

However Ivankov managed it, he was out and headed to the United States by 1992, travelling under a valid visa portraying him as a film producer, and not a hardened criminal just released from a Siberian prison camp after serving 10 years hard labor.

Landing in America, Ivankov was soon spearheading criminal operations from a base in Brighton Beach, Brooklyn. Ivankov's Solntsevskaya crew numbered more than 100 gangsters, outfitting him with the largest Russian criminal group in operation at the time. With this crew of thick-necked thugs at his command, Ivankov hammered together the local loose-knit collection of Russian street gangs in Brooklyn into a single criminal enterprise.

In predawn raids in June 1995, FBI agents swept up Ivankov, charging him with a sophisticated extortion plot threatening an investment advisory firm operated by two Russian businessmen, to the tune of $2.7 million. As part of the plot, accomplices in Russia supposedly murdered a relative of one of the owners.

It was puzzling why Ivankov had exposed himself to prosecution by actively participating in the shakedown of the firm's principals. Wouldn't "The Red Godfather" delegate such a role?

At least that's what the defense argued.

International kingpin?

Mid-level Russian Mafia manager?

Misunderstood?

Whatever the case, Ivankov was sentenced to nine years and seven months at trial the following June.

U.S. federal investigators heralded the Ivankov takedown as a major dent in the rising Russian Red threat on the shores of Brooklyn. Ivankov protested from prison that they got the wrong guy, that there was no such international criminal conspiracy orchestrated by puppet masters in Moscow. Rather, Ivankov pointed to the rampant corruption and mismanagement plaguing Russian organized crime, both here and abroad, stating: "Russia is one uninterrupted criminal swamp," adding that the real criminals resided within the Kremlin.

With Americans morbidly fascinated with anything-Mafia, any and all trial tidbits of an assault on the hierarchy of a major Russian criminal organization operating out of Brighton Beach was big news.

Upon Ivankov's release from prison in July 2004, the U.S. government deported him to Russia to face murder charges regarding the demise of two Turkish nationals who were shot to death in a Moscow restaurant in 1992. Ivankov was acquitted at trial in 2005.

On July 28, 2009, while exiting a restaurant in Moscow, Ivankov was shot. It was suspected that Little Japanese was caught up in a gang war between mobster Aslan Usoyan, whom he was aligned with at the time, and rival Georgian crime boss Tariel Oniani.

Ivankov lingered in the hospital for 73 days before succumbing to his wounds. Little Japanese died on October 9, 2009, garnering widespread media coverage both in Russia and the United States.

59
Victor I. Barron - Corrupt Supreme Court judge

When disgraced Brooklyn State Supreme Court Justice Victor

Barron was convicted on bribery charges in 2002, presiding judge Nicolas Colabella summed it up perfectly.

"You've made almost a joke out of the Kings County judges," he said.

Neither Barron nor Colabella found the situation funny.

Arrested near his Marine Park home on East 36th Street, Barron was brought to justice in the same Brooklyn courtroom where he was once the ultimate authority. Facing a lengthy prison term and insurmountable evidence, Barron pled guilty. Sentenced to three-to-nine years in prison, Barron could have received five-to-fifteen years.

Transcripts of the court proceedings released after sentencing depicted Barron's whimpering defense, blaming his corrupt behavior on early onset Alzheimer's disease, or maybe it was Pick's disease. Yet earlier when wire-wearing attorney Gary Berenholtz recorded Barron cravenly calling for his kickback inside the Willoughby Street courthouse, the judge sure didn't sound like he was suffering from dementia.

Barron was snared seeking a payoff to fix an injury-settlement case. The Judas jurist agreed to trade the public's trust for his 30 pieces of silver – in this case a quarter-million dollars. The cash grab involved an injured-child automobile accident case, requiring a judge to sign off on a settlement. Barron knew this $4.9 million payout to the parents represented a $1.6 million payday for the plaintiff's attorney, Gary Berenholtz. So Barron hit up Berenholtz for $250,000.

When Berenholtz balked, Barron dropped the price of his soul to $116,000. Ultimately, Berenholtz secretly recorded Barron accepting $18,000, sealing the fate of the crooked judge.

In the aftermath of the case, Brooklyn D.A. Charles J. Hynes was left wondering why Barron had done it, as there was no evidence of a pattern of corruption, at least none they could find.

Hynes chalked it up to one of the oldest of human emotions: greed.

Barron was sentenced to more time than any other New York judge. He served 23 months of his sentence at the Clinton Correctional Facility in Upstate New York. Initially denied parole, in 2006 he was transferred, citing good behavior, to a Manhattan halfway house.

When last we heard from the disgraced former judge, he secured employment as part of the terms of his work-release program.

He was clerking.

No, not a *law* clerk.

Derisively dubbing him "Bag-Boy Barron," *The New York Post* reported how the Brooklyn University of Law grad landed a stock-clerk spot at Esti's, a clothing store on Coney Island Avenue catering to Orthodox Jewish women, earning $5.15 an hour.

Now that's a well-deserved piece of justice for this fallen former justice of the peace.

58
Levi Aron – The Butcher of Brooklyn

Located in the southwest corner of Brooklyn, Borough Park and its roughly 200 square blocks are home to the largest Orthodox Jewish community outside of Israel.

The neighborhood boasts scores of religious institutions and cultural centers serving this crowded sub-culture of New York City. It's a tight-knit village that looks after its own, wary eyes always alert, suspicious of outsiders not wearing the traditional black-and-white garb of the Hasidim.

On a late afternoon in the summer of 2011, the lurking threat was not easy to spot.

That's because the danger came from within.

That warm afternoon, eight-year-old Leiby Kletzky was excited. It was the first time his parents allowed him to walk home alone unaccompanied from a local community day camp.

When Leiby was late in arriving home, his family was mildly concerned. As minutes stretched to hours, nervousness became alarm. Family and friends fanned out, sounding the call that sent neighbors scurrying from the stone steps of Borough Park's densely packed multi-family homes. Word of the disappearance spread from home to home, block to block, mobilizing an entire community. Homes emptied as a massive manhunt ensued.

That evening, a family photo of little Leiby fronted a report of the disappearance airing on all local news stations. The New York tabloids ran with the story the following morning.

The terrifying mystery lingered nearly two days. It ended with the awful discovery of Leiby's little feet, severed and shoved inside the freezer of the home of a Jewish Borough Park resident. Police identified the suspect through surveillance-camera footage.

The rest of Leiby's decomposing remains were found in the garbage in a neighborhood adjacent to Borough Park.

Charged with the crime was Levi Aron, a nebbish hardware store clerk. Before his fingerprints were found on the body parts, Aron seemed harmless enough – at least he didn't look the type capable of murdering a child.

Sniveling Aron capitulated under questioning, confessing to the crime, but protesting adamantly that murder was not his intent. He described how young Leiby approached him to ask for directions. Aron then provided this suspicious account to investigators:

"He asked me for a ride to the Judaica Book store. While on the

way, he changed his mind and wasn't sure where he wanted to go. So I asked if he wanted to go for the ride -- wedding in Monsey -- since I didn't think I was going to stay for the whole thing since my back was hurting. He said OK.

"Due to traffic, I got back around 11:30 p.m. ... so I brought him to my house, thinking I'd bring him to his house the next day. He watched TV, then fell asleep in the front room. I went to the middle room to sleep. That next morning, he was still sleeping when I was ready to leave. So I woke him and told him 'I'll bring him to his house'... when I saw the flyers I panicked and was afraid.

"When I got home he was still there so I made him a tuna sandwich. I was still in a panic ... and afraid to bring him home. That is when I went for a towel to smother him in the side room. He fought back a little.

"Afterwards, I panicked because I didn't know what to do with the body... [I] carried parts to the back room, placing parts between the freezer and the refrigerator. I understand it may be wrong, and I'm sorry for the hurt that I have caused."

In a panic, Aron cut the small body into pieces, intending to dispose of it afterwards.

"The Butcher of Brooklyn," as Aron was dubbed by the media, was brought to trial in sensational fashion. The courtroom was mobbed by masses of mourning members of the Borough Park community.

Aron pled guilty to second-degree murder and kidnapping, and was handed a 40-years-to-life sentence.

Leiby's inconsolable parents accepted the decision to not seek the death penalty to avoid the pain of reliving the horrific crime in court and the papers.

His nickname may have been "Pittsburgh Phil," but Harry Strauss did most of his dirt on the streets of Brooklyn.

Throughout the 1930s as one of the more active members of Murder, Inc., that Brownsville-based crew of contract killers, Pittsburgh Phil rang up a staggering body count. By some low-end estimates, Strauss may have murdered 100 marks. However, that death toll may have been as high as 500 killings, not all of them under contract.

To put that tally into perspective, in 2015 the homicide rate for all of New York City was 339, according to statistics kept by the New York City Police Department.

Unlike many killers who prefer specific devices for delivering death, Pittsburgh Phil mastered multiple murder weapons. He'd beat you to death, burn you alive, bury you while you're breathing, string you up, shoot you, stomp you, smother you, slice you with a razor, stab you with an ice pick, or maybe just strangle you until you stopped squirming.

A psychopath with no regard for human life, Pittsburgh Phil stalked his victims, sometimes staking out future crime scenes for days to avoid detection and arrest. Intensely paranoid, Strauss never carried a weapon, unless he was pulling a job. As a known associate of Murder, Inc., Strauss knew he could be picked up by the police at any moment and brought in for questioning.

While he was arrested nearly 20 times, Pittsburgh Phil was untouchable. The few witnesses who came forward went wide-eyed once they learned they'd be testifying against a homicidal maniac.

Ultimately, like many of his brutal Brownsville brethren, Pittsburgh Phil was done in by gang-leader-turned-snitch Abe "Kid Twist" Reles, providing testimony that helped dismantle Murder, Inc.

In a 1940 trial, based on the song sang by Reles, Pittsburgh Phil and Martin "Buggsy" Goldstein were convicted of six murders, most prominently that of Irving "Puggy" Feinstein. Strauss strangled Feinstein to death, and then set the body on fire in a Brooklyn lot. A party to that crime, Reles revealed that Feinstein was targeted for murder by Albert Anastasia, so-called Lord High Executioner of Murder, Inc., when Feinstein ran afoul of Mafia boss Vincent Mangano.

In ghoulish testimony that must have shot a cold chill through the jury box, Reles's mother-in-law recounted how Pittsburgh Phil once asked her to borrow a clothesline …

… and an ice pick.

Facing execution in the electric chair, at a time when appeals did not drag out for decades, Pittsburgh Phil had his attorney mount a desperate ploy to convince the jury and judge that he was insane. He played the part full tilt, babbling and frothing on the witness stand, gnawing on items at the defense table in the courtroom.

Having murdered perhaps hundreds, there may have been something to his insanity act, but the judge and jury didn't buy it. On June 12, 1941, with all his appeals exhausted, Pittsburgh Phil went to the electric chair at Sing Sing in upstate New York, along with Goldstein.

56
Gerald Phillip "Gerry" Garson – Corrupt Supreme Court judge

Divorce proceedings and child custody battles can be some of the most emotionally wrenching experiences to endure.

The least you can hope for is a fair shake from the presiding judge, to rule by the book, even if it gets thrown at you.

So it was no wonder when "see-I-told-you-so" shouts of satisfaction went up when news hit in 2007 that former New York Supreme Court Justice Gerald Phillip Garson was convicted on three counts of bribery for rigging trials where he was the presiding judge.

Here's how it worked.

According to court testimony, Garson masterminded the scheme working through a "fixer" trolling the Brooklyn court system for desperate soon-to-be divorcées, tipping them off that a favorable outcome could be had, at the right price.

Once payment was made, the fixer steered them to the right lawyer, as in an attorney willing to be coached by Garson.

Garson navigated around the random assignment of judges by arranging bribes to court-employed techs to channel the right cases to his bench. During these trials, Garson was not a passive player, but a puppet master prepping the attorney beforehand, scripting the legal strategy to be acted out in court to minimize suspicion.

Garson was elected to the bench in 1997, placed on the ballot as the Kings County Democratic Party machine's nominee by Clarence Norman Jr., the long-running party chair later convicted on bribery charges. Ensconced in "Matrimonial Part 5B," in the Municipal Building on Joralemon Street in Brooklyn Heights, Garson presided over more than 1,100 cases. For years, he served as a judge apparently in good standing in Brooklyn.

Yet by the fall of 2002, the Brooklyn DA's office got wind that Garson was for sale, implicated in a complaint brought by Frieda Hanimov, who was in the midst of a hotly contest divorce and custody trial.

Hanimov was convinced her husband had bribed Garson through Nissim Elmann, the fixer, and Paul Siminovsky, an attorney tapped by Garson. Supposedly, an over-confident Elmann revealed the nefarious plot when he smugly informed Hanimov that she was too late. Her husband had already bought and paid for a favorable outcome.

Hanimov agreed to wear a wire and captured the damning testimony to topple Garson.

During the investigation, Siminovsky was picked up in Brooklyn, escorted to the Fort Hamilton army base in Bay Ridge, where he confessed during questioning, agreeing to wear a wire to capture Garson on recordings that could be used to take the jurist down.

Arrested and indicted in April 2003, suspended from the bench the following month, Garson chose to retire.

By 2006, rejecting a plea deal to admit to bribery charges in return for a 16-month sentence, the case proceeded to trial, even as Garson battled cancer that required surgery.

Siminovsky's testimony helped convict nine people associated with the scheme.

Following a 2003 indictment and several years of legal wrangling, Garson was brought before the bench in Brooklyn. While he evaded conviction on four counts of the indictment, Garson was slammed with one count of accepting a bribe, and two lesser counts of receiving rewards for official misconduct.

The judge became the jailed, hit with three-to-seven years in prison, of which he served 30 months before being released in 2009 to slither away.

Everyone took a hit in this case. The attorney, Siminovsky, cooperated, receiving a reduced sentence of one year in prison. The "fixer," Elmann, copped a plea and received 16-months-to-five years. The court employee who rigged the judge's assignments was handed one-to-four years. Even several previous "winners" who had fixed-cases fall in their favor received jail time, likely much to the jubilation of their former spouses.

In the aftermath of the convictions, no less than 50 motions have been filed to reopen divorce cases ruled upon by Garson.

The case has since been fodder for a *Law & Order* episode on television, covered extensively in the New York tabloids, and received dramatic re-telling on *CBS's 48 Hours* investigative news program on February 18, 2005, in a segment dramatically titled "Chamber of Secrets."

Stay tuned. Warner Brothers has optioned the rights to "The Frieda Hanimov Story," as *The New York Post* dubbed her the new Erin Brockovich, likening her to that famous whistle-blower.

55
Carl Kruger - Corrupt Brooklyn Politician

When it came to corruption, New York State Senator Carl Kruger was a full-service finagler.

In exchange for bribes and favors, the longtime lawmaker would lobby on behalf of your company or cause, push through legislation and basically do whatever needed to be done to keep the cash flowing into his greedy hands.

Until his avarice was exposed in dramatic fashion, Kruger was a popular state representative in one of the most diverse districts in Brooklyn. Kruger should have stuck to serving the best interests of New York State Senate District 27, covering the hardworking residents of Brighton Beach, Sheepshead Bay, Gravesend, Bergen Beach, Mill Basin, and Midwood.

Elected in a special election in February 1994, the former State Assemblyman had a noteworthy run in New York State's upper house, rising to Ranking Minority member on the Senate Committee on Aging, as well as assignments to the Crime Victims, Crime and Corrections, Energy and Telecommunications committees.

In fact, in 2007 when then-Senate Majority Leader Joseph Bruno (Republican) tapped Kruger (Democrat) as Chairman of the Senate Social Services Committee, it was the first time in New York history a minority-party senator was named to chair a committee.

Media-hound Kruger made headlines throughout the years. He was among the lawmakers suing then-Mayor Michael Bloomberg and the New York City Department of Education to block the dissolution of 32 community school districts (the suit failed) and legislation to prohibit use of electronic devices, like mp3 players and cell phones, in NYC crosswalks (also failed).

Kruger was a member of the infamous "Gang of Three" during the 2008 palace coup in Albany when Democrats threatened to cross the aisle and side with the Republicans (failed spectacularly, and all three were served prison time on offenses unrelated to that rebellion).

Kruger started to slide down the slippery slope of corruption in 2010, when the FBI and U.S. Attorney's Office in Brooklyn began investigating rumors of his shilling political favors for campaign donations.

Indicted on March 9, 2010, on bribery charges and corruption allegations related to a hospital merger, a story began to circulate that Kruger lived with his male partner, while that man's mother posed as Kruger's girlfriend. Considering his lack of support of same-sex marriage in the legislature, Kruger duplicitousness further fueled the media frenzy.

Kruger surrendered to authorities the following day.

Realizing a conviction automatically bounced him out of the State Senate, the Brooklyn senator resigned in disgrace prior to pleading guilty on corruption charges on March 20, 2011, openly weeping in court.

In sentencing Kruger, Judge Jed Rakoff of Federal District Court could have sent him away for 9 to 11 ¼ years, but showed leniency for Kruger's good deeds. Facing 50 years in prison on the initial indictment, Kruger's plea helped him secure a still-daunting seven-year stretch.

His companion, gynecologist Michael Turano, received a two-year prison sentence for his involvement in the corruption scandal.

54
Willie Sutton – "Because that's where the money is."

From trailblazing athletes to titans of business to award-winning performers, Brooklyn continues to produce pioneers across all walks of life.

The same goes for the criminal crafts.

When it comes to bank robbery, no name sticks out more than stick-up master Willie Sutton. One of the most prolific bank robbers of the 20th century, Sutton captivated the nation with coverage of his many bold prison escapes.

When asked by *New York Herald* reporter Mitch Ohnstad why he robbed banks, Sutton supposedly said, "Because that's where the money is."

This pithy phrase was later used as the logic behind "Sutton's Law," not an actual legal statute, mind you, but a maxim taught to medical students to encourage them to first focus on ruling out the obvious in medical diagnoses.

Thing is, Sutton denied ever making that statement. In his autobiography, Sutton accused Ohnstad of fabricating the quote, though he appropriated it when titling a later autobiography "Where the Money Was." In his own written words from that book, Sutton shared his obsession with robbing banks:

"Why did I rob banks? Because I enjoyed it. I loved it. I was more alive when I was inside a bank, robbing it, than at any other time in my life. I enjoyed everything about it so much that one or two weeks later I'd be out looking for the next job. But to me the money was the chips, that's all."

Though the bulk of his capers were conducted beyond the confines of the county of the Kings, Sutton cut his criminal teeth in Brooklyn, born in the borough on June 30, 1901, the fourth of five children.

Sutton's career seemed scripted for Hollywood, with all the stirring touches begging for a star treatment. Leaving school in the eighth grade, Sutton bounced around a series of jobs from clerk to gardener, with nothing lasting for more than a few months. Before long he set his sights on a career as a bank robber.

Sutton was not a thug, but a finesse thief, with an M.O. for pulling masterful heists in elaborate disguises. This persona of polished-gentleman-bank-robber captured the nation's imagination. Victims' testimonies of Sutton's gentle treatment and dashing demeanor heightened the public's fascination.

Yet Sutton captured national acclaim not only for his disguises and panache, but for his daring prison escapes.

In December 1932, serving 30 years for armed robbery and assault, Sutton scaled a prison wall by combining two separate nine-foot ladders, before slipping away into the night. He remained on the lam for more than a year.

Apprehended in February 1934, Sutton was sentenced to 25-to-50 years for the robbery of the Corn Bank Exchange. It took longer this time around, but Sutton once again pulled off a breath-taking prison escape in 1945, leading a 12-man exodus of cons burrowing out via a tunnel.

Unfortunately for Willie, this time around he was picked up the same day of the escape.

Severely punished for this fifth escape, Willie was walloped with a life sentence and packed off to the Philadelphia County Prison in Homesburg, Pennsylvania.

You'd think they'd be able to hold this Brooklyn boy, but not those prison bars.

On February 10, 1947, Sutton disguised himself as a prison guard, and that evening along with a fellow inmate lugged a ladder across the prison yard. Just as you'd imagine in a prison-break film, the massive spotlight found the two escapees, to which Willie waved them off, responding: "It's OK." Miraculously, he was not stopped, adding to the legend.

By 1950, still on the run, Willie earned a spot atop the FBI's Ten Most Wanted fugitives list.

Ultimately, Sutton's vanity was his undoing. Aware of Sutton's penchant for expensive clothes, clever investigators circulated his mug shot among high-end tailors. Sure enough, the son of a New York tailor spotted Willie on a subway. He followed Sutton and dropped a dime, and police soon took Willie into custody.

In addition to his life sentence + 105 years, a judge tacked on 30 more years to Willie's sentence.

This time, slick Willie was unable to slip out of prison.

For more than 17 years, Sutton languished in Attica State Prison in upstate New York before a federal judged freed Willie on Christmas Eve in 1969. By then, the 68-year-old bank robber was a broken man on parole, suffering from emphysema from a lifetime as a chain smoker, among other ailments.

In one last poke at popular culture's fascination with him, Sutton sat for a tongue-in-cheek commercial of the New Britain, Connecticut, Bank & Trust Company's launch of a photo credit card program in 1970.

Retiring to Florida, the infamous Willie Sutton passed away in Spring Hill in 1980 at the age of 79.

53
Ming Don Chen – The Sunset Park Massacre

Brooklynites are numb to most of the mayhem and violence in the big city.

Yet on October 27, 2013, even the most-hardened New Yorkers paused when news reports of an unspeakable crime started coming out of Sunset Park, Brooklyn.

At approximately 10:45 p.m. on 57th Street not far from the Brooklyn shoreline, police responded to a residence to investigate a possible stabbing.

What they found was much worse than just a knife attack.

NYPD officers from the nearby 66th Precinct in Borough Park discovered five people unconscious with multiple slash and gash wounds to their torsos.

Three of the young victims died at the scene, including Linda Zhuo (9 years old), Amy Zhuo (7), and William Zhuo (1). Shortly after, a fourth sibling, Kevin Zhuo (5), and mother Qiao Zhen Li (37), died at local hospitals.

Police ruled out a home invasion. The victims knew their attacker. Ming Don Chen, 25, a cousin of the children's father, was apprehended. In addition to the five murder counts, police charged Chen with resisting arrest, later upgraded to assault for attacking a police officer at the 68th Precinct.

Details of the crime emerged almost immediately, with the despondent Chen admitting to his actions.

Chen had arrived at the Sunset Park home of his cousin only eight days prior. The morning of the assaults, Qiao Zhen Li suspected something was wrong and attempted to contact her husband at work, though failed to reach him. Li did reach her mother-in-law in China, who in turn called her sister-in-law and shared her concerns with Chen's erratic behavior.

When the sister-in-law and her husband arrived at the apartment, Chen himself opened the door, splashed with blood, bare-footed. Chen had overpowered the woman and her small children, using a meat cleaver to hack the life from his victims. The sister-in-law called 911. Chen did not flee, and was arrested immediately.

Speaking to police through a Mandarin translator, Chen revealed his twisted motive. He arrived in America in 2004 illegally and had been homeless and unemployed for much of that time. Soon after appearing at the home of his cousin in Brooklyn, the transient laborer grew jealous, frustrated that they were successful while he languished in futility. He lashed out in a moment of resentful rage.

Two years later, Chen pled guilty to three counts of second-degree murder and two counts of first-degree manslaughter. He received 25 years in prison on each count, with the sentences to run consecutively.

Chen was 27 years old when he was sent away on October 2015.

Even in the underworld, there are things YOU ... JUST ... DON'T ... DO.

For the Italian Mafia, you don't kill a boss, unless the hit is approved by other bosses.

When a crew of rebellious upstarts gunned down Gambino Godfather Paul Castellano outside a Midtown Manhattan steak house, that rubout rubbed many Italian gangsters the wrong way.

Bartholomew "Bobby" Boriello would answer for that unsanctioned shooting, even though the architect was never called to task for that particular crime.

Standing a solid six-foot-three inches of mob muscle, Boriello was a gangster's gangster. Decades before he was best-bud-bodyguard for John Gotti, Boriello was a thick-necked thug from South Brooklyn coming up with future Gambino, Genovese, and Colombo crime figures.

Boriello's criminal career stretches back to the 1960s, when his older brother worked for Joseph "Crazy Joe" Gallo. Gallo ran a crew in the Profaci family and led an insurrection against tight-fisted family boss Joe Profaci. Long story short, Profaci died of liver cancer, Gallo was wacked in Little Italy and capo Joseph Colombo took over, re-naming the family after himself.

Life moved on.

In the wake of Gallo's murder in 1972, Stevie Boriello was neck-deep in the South Brooklyn rackets, his younger brother nipping at his heels, both aligning with the Gambino Crime Family.

The younger Boriello was a threatening presence in Carroll Gardens, Brooklyn, where he owned a social club operated by his brother. During his early days, Boriello was one of the usual suspects rounded up on suspicion in several gangland slayings.

Boriello eventually eclipsed his older brother and by the early 1980s was a made member and part of John Gotti's inner circle. Boriello was inducted into the Gambinos with John "Junior" Gotti, among other up-and-coming Mafioso. Assigned to Junior's crew, Boriello had his fingers in gambling, loan-sharking and extortion throughout Brooklyn, Manhattan and Staten Island.

Gotti trusted Boriello, evident in a series of sensitive assignments, including the murder of Louis DiBono, a major earner for the Gambinos. DiBono wrangled, among other things, a highly profitable contract to install fireproof materials at the World Trade Center in Lower Manhattan.

By 1991, Boriello was under investigation by multiple-law enforcement agencies. On April 13th that year, with his wife and daughters inside Boriello's Bensonhurst home on Bay 29th Street, he was gunned down on the street outside. The hit was a revenge murder for Boriello's participation in the Castellano hit. Lucchese Family Underboss Anthony "Gaspipe" Casso orchestrated Boriello's murder. John Gotti — who ordered the Castellano assassination so he could assume power — was untouchable, mainly because he was under such heavy surveillance by law enforcement.

In chilling detail later revealed by Boriello's wife, Susan, NYPD detectives Louis Eppolito and Stephen Caracappa visited the Boriello home days prior to the murder, inquiring when Bobby would be home. Eppolito and Caracappa are better known as the infamous "Mafia Cops" who were on the Lucchese payroll. They were casing the home for Casso, providing advanced recon to carry out a plot to assassinate the assassin.

Boriello was one of three Gambinos targeted for death for the

Castellano murder by Genovese boss Vincent Gigante and Lucchese boss Vittorio Amuso. Gambino family underboss Frank DeCicco was blown apart by a car bomb in 1986, and soldier Edward Lino was murdered by none other than Caracappa and Eppolito in 1990.

51
Abe "Kid Twist" Reles – The Canary Who Couldn't Fly

Today the shores of Coney Island are enjoying somewhat of a renaissance.

Millions of investment dollars are washing in, with plans for hotels and modern amusements and attractions envisioned. A new 5,000-seat semi-outdoor amphitheater opened in the summer of 2016, complementing the 7,500 MCU stadium unveiled in 2001, home to the New York Mets farm team the Brooklyn Cyclones. And the famed New York Aquarium is undergoing a massive renovation.

Nearly gone is the gritty, rough-and-tumble destitution of the 1970s, the vacant storefronts of the 1980s, and the homeless encampments under the boardwalk of the 1990s.

Yet this latest makeover is hardly Coney Island's first reclamation. The Depression years of the 1930s sullied the former seaside mecca, transforming it for a time into the "Sodom by the Sea." Sure the droves still drove down to its shores in the summertime. But Coney Island's concessions suffered as Luna Park slid into bankruptcy.

Lording over the beach was Coney Island's Half Moon Hotel, a once-magnificent Spanish Colonial-style monolith perched seaside just off the well-trodden boardwalk. It was there that occurred such a notorious gangland episode, it seemed to sum up the full scope of neglect and corruption plaguing not just Coney Island and Brooklyn, but that entire era in criminal lore.

In fact, nowhere in gangland is there an unsolved mystery as ingrained into the cartoonish noir mythos of the mobster as the events that occurred at the Half Mo

on Hotel. It revolved around Abe "Kid Twist" Reles, a gangster despised as much by the public — for his prolific career as a hitman for Murder, Inc. — as by the underworld — he flipped for the feds and became an informant after being indicted on a murder count in 1940.

Keep in mind that this was decades before turning informant was accepted as a viable career option for Brooklyn gangsters. Rarely did the cops and robbers cooperate, even though the death penalty was not only legal in New York State, it was used more frequently. Apparently appeals did not drag out indefinitely as they do today.

You might say the fate of Kid Twist was a cautionary tale for his peers.

Born into poverty in 1906 in Brownsville, Brooklyn, to Austrian-immigrant parents, Reles and his family barely survived on what his father made, first in the garment industry, then later selling knishes on the streets of Brooklyn. Leaving school at a young age, the young Reles bullied his way through the back alleys and gambling dens of Brownsville, linking up with future Murder, Inc. all-stars Martin "Buggsy" Goldstein and Harry "Pittsburgh Phil" Strauss.

The diminutive Reles made up for his small size with outrageous violence and was most certainly a psychopath, with a predilection for ice picks. Reles favored this weapon, as death could be misconstrued by medical examiners as a naturally caused brain hemorrhage. Prone to random acts of violence for the most minor offenses (he once murdered a parking-lot attendant for not retrieving his car quickly enough), Reles stepped up in the Brooklyn rackets working for the Shapiro brothers.

When Reles was busted and sent away for two years to a juvenile-detention facility and the Shapiro brothers abandoned him, the die was cast for an epic gangland rivalry.

Reles cut a back-alley deal with Meyer Lansky propelling Reles higher up the criminal food chain in Brooklyn. He expanded into labor racketeering, loan sharking, extortion and a wider array of criminal activities — not to mention taking a leadership role in Murder, Inc.

By the 1940s, though, the law caught up with Reles. Facing insurmountable evidence on multiple murder counts likely to land him in the electric chair at Sing Sing, Kid Twist turned informant.

Reles' testimony was critical in the indictment and prosecution of numerous key crime figures of that period, including Louis "Lepke" Buchalter, Harry Strauss, Louis Capone, Mendy Weiss, Harry Maione, Frank Abbandando, Irving "Knadles" Nitzberg, and his longtime partner "Buggsy" Goldstein.

With the help of damning testimony provided by Reles, all of these members of Murder, Inc. were convicted and executed by electric chair.

Next up in the crosshairs: Albert Anastasia.

Anastasia was not only a co-leader of Murder, Inc., he was (more importantly) a high-ranking Made member of the Mafia. Among the many hats worn by "The Mad Hatter," Anastasia coordinated contract killings for the mob.

With Anastasia under indictment and an epic trial set for November 12, 1941, Reles was the most-wanted criminal in the underworld. With a massive murder contract hanging over his head, authorities stashed Reles out of sight, under constant watch by no less than six officers.

The Half Moon Hotel seemed like an ideal spot for safekeeping until the trial.

Then the *expected* happened.

On the morning of November 12th, Reles *fell* to his death from Room 623 on the sixth floor.

As the cover story went, Reles was trying to escape, and had tied bedsheets together, before *accidentally* plunging to his death.

Sure he did.

The next day the five New York City policemen guarding Reles were busted down in rank, but not removed from the force. Years later, in 1951, a grand jury found Reles' death to be accidental, as a result of his escape attempt.

The case against Anastasia fell apart.

Years later, infamous mob turncoat Joseph Valachi stated: "I never met anybody who thought Abe went out that window because he wanted to."

In a fitting epitaph, the newspapers named Reles "The Canary Who Could Sing, But Couldn't Fly."

50
William Cutolo – Wild Bill

They called him "Wild Bill" for a reason.

Actually, many reasons.

William Cutolo rose through the ranks of the Colombo Crime Family on the hard streets of Brooklyn and played a key role in the bloody Colombo Family War of the early 1990s.

Cutolo specialized in labor racketeering and related crimes, wresting control over District Council 37, which oversees dozens of labor unions throughout New York City. For years he siphoned off union dues from the hard-working rank and file, kicking a percentage upstairs to his Colombo chieftains.

Manning this lucrative spigot, Cutolo spewed a steady stream of no-show jobs, where Colombo family members were paid as union employees, but never performed actual work. Having a legitimate job on the books helps fend off parole officers and IRS investigators.

Over the years, Cutolo cultivated a reputation as a gentleman gangster, hosting fundraisers for Leukemia-related charities, even dressing up as Santa Claus for the annual National Children's Leukemia Association gala.

Behind the scenes, though, Cutolo was a cut-throat gangster.

Born in the Basilicata region of Italy, Guglielmo "William" Cutolo came to America as a young boy and grew up in Brooklyn. Drawn into the Colombo Family working his way up as a solider in Pasquale Amato's crew, Cutolo later reported directly to acting-family-boss Victor Orena. Cutolo surrounded himself with a notorious crew, based out of Bill's Friendly Bocce Italian social club in the Bath Beach section of Brooklyn.

Cutolo's ability to earn fueled his meteoric mob rise. Named president of Teamsters Union Local 861, he later resigned under a cloud of suspicion. That was fine with him, as he would muscle in on District Council (DC) 37, a local of the American Federation of State, County, and Municipal Employees, as well as Local 400 of the Industrial & Production Workers Union.

Cutolo earned the nickname "Wild Bill" after viciously beating a man with a wooden baseball bat. It helped that Wild Bill favored cowboy boots and hats, which were in fashion in the 1980s, even in Brooklyn.

Yet it was Wild Bill's involvement in the Colombo's civil war that cemented Cutolo's place in Brooklyn mob lore.

On the street, acting boss Vic Orena positioned himself to seize control of the family from Carmine Persico when "the Snake" was sentenced to life in the Commission Case and named his son Alphonse Persico as acting boss.

Cutolo was a member of the Orena faction.

The first shots fired in the war came June 21, 1991, with the attempted hit on Orena commissioned by Persico. Orena responded by siccing Cutolo on Persico stalwart Gregory "The Grim Reaper" Scarpa. Scarpa survived. Less than a week later, Cutolo murdered Persico henchman Henry Smurra in Brooklyn.

Not long after, Cutolo got into a gun battle with Joel Cacace, wounding the Persico loyalist.

Following more murders and gun battles, the final body in the war dropped when Orena Captain Joseph Scopo was murdered by John Pappa, a young psychopathic drug dealer trying to make a name for himself on the streets.

Meanwhile, Orena was sentenced to prison, essentially ending the war in Persico's favor. This left Cutolo in a precarious position, as he was on the losing side and directly responsible for at least three murders during the war.

Cutolo survived, but was busted down from captain to solider.

By 1994, Cutolo was on trial for racketeering along with a group of Colombo members and family associates, though all were acquitted. Upon his release from prison in 1999, Alphonse Persico extended an olive branch to smooth things over by bumping up Cutolo to the post of underboss.

Yet the winds changed violently when Alphonse Persico was

convicted on a gun charge and sent away to prison. Fearing Cutolo would lead another insurrection, Carmine Persico decided to remove Wild Bill as a threat once and for all.

On May 26, 1999, Persico called Cutolo in for a meeting. Wild Bill was dropped off by an associate in a park in Bayside, Queens.

He was never seen alive again.

Later, investigators learned that Colombo gangsters Thomas Gioeli, Dino Saracino, and Dino Calabro met Cutolo, escorting him to Saracino's basement where Wild Bill was murdered. For years Cutolo lay buried in a Mafia graveyard in an industrial park in Farmingdale, Long Island.

In 2007, after an earlier mistrial, both Alphonse Persico and underboss Jack DeRoss were convicted of Cutolo's murder, due to testimony and recorded conversations provided by Cutolo's family, including his son, William Jr. Both gangsters were given life sentences.

When they dug up Cutolo, there was one distinguishing feature that helped investigators identify the body.

Like many of the cowboys of old, Wild Bill died with his boots on.

49
John Wojtowicz – Dog Day Afternoon

What makes one crime more notorious than all the others?

Is it the *hey-I-know-that-bank* setting? The *you-couldn't-make-this-stuff-up* motive? The *are-you-kidding-me* cast of characters? The *that-could-be-me* innocents with guns held to their heads?

All of the above?

Little did John Wojtowicz know that on the morning of Tuesday, August 22, 1972, when he and two armed accomplices stormed the Chase Manhattan Bank at 450 Avenue P and East Third Street out on the edge of Gravesend, Brooklyn, that they would be the center of a hostage crisis unfolding on live television.

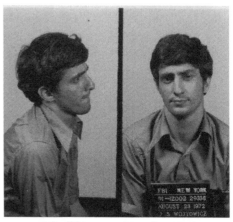

John Wojtowicz Mugshot 1972

He was just trying to pay for his boyfriend's sex-change operation.

The botched Brooklyn holdup led to a dramatic 14-hour hostage siege captured in a compelling *Life* magazine article, "The Boys in the Bank," by P.F. Kluge and Thomas Moore.

That led to the provacative 1975 film "Dog Day Afternoon" directed by Sidney Lumet and starring Al Pacion, John Cazale, and Charles Durning. And that led to six Academy Award nominations in 1975, winning the Oscar for Best Screenplay.

Those of us from Brooklyn know that nowhere is the summertime slaughter on the senses as insufferable as when we descend into the depths of the dog days of summer, the hottest days on the calendar. I imagine that when Wojtowicz walked down Avenue P that morning he saw those familiar waves of shimmering heat drawing up from the Brooklyn blacktop.

In the Northern hemisphere during the summer months at sunrise, Orion's hound, the Dog Star of Sirius in the constellation Canis Major, is visible just above the Eastern horizon. The ancient Greeks lamented such glimpses of the Dog Star, for they knew of the infernal heat sure to follow.

Anyone from Brooklyn knows how strange things can happen during the dog days of summer.

While based on the events of that dog day afternoon, the film departed from reality in key aspects, as itemized in a rant written by Wojtowicz and submitted to *The New York Times* upon the film's release.

The more recent 2014 documentary, "The Dog," hewed closer to the fantastic facts provided by Wojtowicz, who died before its release.

Flash back to August 1972. Wojtowicz, 27 years old, was a married man and Vietnam veteran living a double life of lies. A gay man exploring his sexually in New York's underground at a time when the gay rights movement was in full swing, Wojtowicz decided to rob a bank to pay for his boyfriend's sex-change operation.

Now *that's* a backstop for a movie, and the plot only thickened from there.

Brooklynites love a good under-Dog story, even when the protagonist is more anti- than hero. As outrageous as it seemed at the time, especially for its provacative sexuality and anti-establishment themes, the film depicted a watered-down version of Wojtowicz.

As detailed in the subsequent documentary, several salacious details of self-proclaimed pervert Wojtowicz were never covered in the film, such as how he insisted on sex the night before the heist from one of his accomplices. Bobby Westenberg acquiesed. In that article to *The New York Times* in 1975, Wojtowicz estimated 30 percent of the movie was true, though he was a big fan of Al Pacino's portrayal.

Who wouldn't want a young Al Pacino to play them in a movie about their life?

Wojtowicz left his wife, and by 1971 was involved with Ernie Aron, a.k.a. Liz Eden, a pre-op transgender ushered to the scene during the standoff. They were married in December, though the ceremony was symbolic as gay marriage was decades from becoming legal. When Eden became obsessed with a sex-change operation, Wojtowicz disapproved initially, but changed his mind following her failed suicide attempt.

As depicted in the film, that was the intent of the robbery, before it devolved into a 14-hour, media-televised hostage crisis. Hundreds of Brooklynites crowed the streets in front of the bank to gawk at the unfolding drama.

There was no happy ending here. One accomplice, Westenberg, fled the scene as the caper began, while another was shot dead by the FBI. Wojtowicz, who surrendered, was sentenced to 20 years in prison for armed robbery. He served less than six years before being parolled.

Wojtowicz sold the rights for the story for the film, receiving $7,500 and one percent of the film's net profits. The money was used to fund Eden's operation.

Unfortunately for Wojtowicz, following the surgery, Eden flat-left him, saying she never wanted to see him again. Distraught, Wojtowicz attempted suicide by slicing his wrists. Yet like many things he did in his life, Wojtowicz failed. Eden died in 1987 due to AIDS-related complications.

Despite the sad ending, for that one steamy dog day afternoon in Brooklyn in 1972, Wojtowicz sure made a ruckus on that Gravesend, Brooklyn street corner.

In a cheeky postscript to this story, Wojtowicz applied for a security job at Chase Manhattan Bank after his release from prison. Needless to say, he was rejected.

Wojtowicz died of cancer in 2006.

When Frankie Yale was gunned down on 44th Street while driving through Borough Park during the height of Prohibition-Era Brooklyn, it was the first time a Thompson submachine gun was used in New York for a mob-related assassination.

It would not be the last.

Despite his Ivy-League nickname, Yale was born Francesco Ioele in Longobucco, Italy, immigrating to the United States at the turn of the 20th century.

As a young thug, Yale ran with John Torrio and the infamous Five Points Gang in Lower Manhattan, before moving into Brooklyn when Torrio decamped for Chicago in 1909.

Yale wasn't a particularly imposing physical presence, but he was every bit the thug from a young age, involved in several homicides. As early as his late teens, Yale was a combatant in a showdown in a Coney Island pool hall, leaving more than one body in his wake.

Seven years later, Yale hung out his own shingle for a Coney Island joint he called The Harvard Inn. In keeping with the Ivy League-theme, he started going by the surname Yale, a take-off on his given name Ioele, while also using Uale.

One night while working at The Harvard Inn, a young Al Capone offended the sister of street-soldier Frank Galluccio. Galluccio over-retaliated in vicious fashion, slashing a scar on the face of the most infamous gangster of the Prohibition Era.

Unlike the close-knit Sicilian gang bosses of Brooklyn of that time, Yale schemed with Italians of different regions of Italy. Yale murdered or outmaneuvered rivals in his rise to lead "The Black Hand," the collective term for the extortionist Italian gang factions operating along the Brooklyn waterfront. That brought him into direct competition with the opposing "White Hand" Irish gangs.

From prostitution and extortion to gambling, hi-jacking and, once Prohibition was passed, bootlegging, Yale had his Black Hand in all major Brooklyn waterfront rackets by the 1920s. He even owned a Bensonhurst funeral parlor on 66th Street and 14h Avenue, which was quite a convenience, considering his other lines of businesses. When questioned by authorities about his occupation, Yale said, "Undertaker."

In addition to Capone, Yale mentored other underlings who went on to prolific criminal careers, including Albert Anastasia and Joe Adonis.

Yale was also responsible for one of the pivotal contract killings of the early American mob, when he parachuted into Chicago to gun down entrenched boss James "Big Jim" Colosimo. Big Jim had brought Torrio out to Chicago earlier. However, when Big Jim hesitated to jump into bootlegging, Torrio marked him for death. Yale's hit on Big Jim paved the way for Torrio and Capone to seize the bootlegging rackets and reshape the underworld of the Windy City.

Back in Brooklyn, Yale was fighting a running battle with the Irish gangs and other Italian upstarts, trading bullets and body blows in the bars and back alleys along the thriving docks.

Yale barely escaped a 1921 assassination attempt, but took a bullet to the lung that severely debilitated the boss. Months later, Yale's brother Angelo was gunned down on Cropsey Avenue in Bath Beach, a retaliation hit for an earlier murder at the Harvard Inn, of Ernesto Melchiorre. An enraged Yale targeted Silvio Melchiorre, the contract killer who masterminded the hit on Angelo.

Yale escaped yet another assassination attempt in 1923, when a carload of gangsters mistook his driver for Yale. Frank Forte had been driving Yale's wife and two daughters home when they were fired upon. Yale's wife and the children escaped physically unharmed. Forte was shot to death.

By 1928, Yale was a top bootlegger and racketeer in New York, having defeated Irish factions by murdering key gang bosses, yet found himself at odds with none other than former protégé, and now Chicago kingpin, Al "Scarface" Capone.

From his territory in New York, Yale was supposed to assure safe passage of Capone's Chicago-bound illegal Canadian liquor shipments.

Big Al's trucks began to disappear.

Big Al sent a goon to investigate quietly and report back his findings.

Big Al was not happy with the report.

On July 1, 1928, while at one of his clubs on 14th Avenue in Bensonhurst, Brooklyn, Yale picked up the phone to field a distress call that something was wrong with his wife. He burst out of his club and jumped into his Lincoln coupe, running right into the crosshairs of a Buick full of tommy-gun-toting Chicago hitmen.

Yale's Lincoln was armor-plated, but the windows had yet to be bullet-proofed.

Frankie Yale's funeral was the most extravagant send-off in New York mob history, befitting a giant that ran the rackets in Prohibition-age Brooklyn.

It took nearly 40 cars to transport the massive arrays of flowers from Yale's wake to the cemetery.

47
Joe Waverly Cacace – The Colombo Family War

How tough was Joel "Joe Waverly" Cacace, Sr.?

On a cold December day in 1976, three bandits ambushed Cacace in a brazen hold-up at his Sheepshead Bay florist shop.

They picked the wrong gangster to stick up.

Bleeding from a gunshot wound, lead later left in his chest by doctors, Cacace wrestled a gun away from one crook, shot him, and then blasted after the other two fleeing bandits. Cacace then dumped the

Joel Cacace Mugshot

dead body in the back of his Buick, and while bleeding profusely drove himself to the 61st Precinct on Coney Island Avenue. An ambulance later rushed Cacace to Coney Island Hospital for treatment of his non-life-threatening gunshot wounds.

The incident inflated Cacace's already formidable street credibility in Brooklyn.

Rising through the ranks of the Colombo crime family, Cacace was involved in some of the most notorious episodes in Brooklyn crime lore.

Carmine "The Snake" Persico trusted Cacace as one of his top enforcers, even after the Colombo Family boss languished in prison. Persico was swept up on RICO charges as part of the epic Commission trial of the late 1980s that locked up the upper ranks of the five New York crime families.

While incarcerated, an infuriated Persico issued the death warrant for William Aronwald, a former supervisor of the federal Organized Crime Strike Force in the Manhattan U.S. Attorney's office, who also served as chief of the criminal division in the Brooklyn office.

Handed the contract, Cacace assembled a hit squad of Colombo soldiers with plenty of notches on their guns – Vincent and Enrico "Eddie" Carini, and Frank Smith. Cacace provided the hit team with a slip of paper with Aronwald's name. Staking out Aronwald's Brooklyn law office, they tailed him and later shot him at a laundromat near his Queens home.

Unfortunately for everyone involved, they shot the wrong Aronwald – not William, but George, his 78-year-old father, an administrative law judge no less. Father and son Aronwald shared a law office.

It was bad enough they killed the wrong man, but to murder a judge was bad business all around for the five families, and other Mafia gang bosses demanded punishment.

The Carini brothers fell first, discovered dead by lead in separate cars in Sheepshead Bay. Frank Smith was spared by the Colombos, who later regretted their mercy when he became a cooperating witness for the federal government.

To close the loop and cover himself, Cacace even hit the hit team that murdered the Carini brothers, gunning them down at the Carini funeral.

Wait, it gets better.

After the Carini assassinations, Cacace married Eddie Carini's widow, Kim Kennaugh, but the marriage resulted in a divorce. Kennaugh moved on with her life, finding love again and marrying NYPD officer Ralph Dols.

Cacace could not move on.

Feeling humiliated by the marriage to Dols and in a position to do something about it now as acting street boss for the Colombo family, Cacace ordered underboss Thomas "Tommy Shots" Gioelli to take out Dols. Gioelli recruited underlings Dino Calabro, a capo, and soldiers Dino Saracino and Joseph "Joey Caves"

Competiello, to murder Dols. They carried out the assassination in August 1997, surprising Dols outside his home and gunning him down.

The murder ripped through Brooklyn, bringing down a world of heat on organized crime.

Cacace was acquitted at trial for ordering the Dols assassination, despite cooperation from hitman Calabro that fingered his former boss. Testifying in court for the federal government, Calabro swore he never knew Dols was a police officer until the day following the murder, when the story made front-page news.

The jury didn't buy the testimony of either Calabro or Comptiello, acquitting Cacace and Gioelli of the crime. However, Cacace pled guilty to multiple counts of murder and racketeering in return for a 20-year sentence in 2004.

Cacace is incarcerated in Tucson, Arizona, with a 2020 release date, though is still under indictment for other crimes. It is unlikely he will haunt the streets of Brooklyn ever again.

46
The Shapiro Brothers – Meyer, Irving & William

The Shapiro Brothers (Meyer, Irving and William) formed an undeniable force in the New York labor rackets in the 1920s and 1930s.

These sinister siblings were cut-throat murderous bastards.

From their powerbase in the Williamsburg section of Brooklyn, the Shapiro brothers operated a diverse portfolio of criminal activity, including bookmaking, prostitution, loansharking, extortion, robbery and, during Prohibition, bootlegging.

Above all other crimes, though, their primary racket involved infiltrating New York's booming garment industry in Brooklyn. The torrent of poor Russian Jews to the United States, coupled with a sharp uptick in demand for manufactured clothes and innovations in production technology, fueled the industry in Manhattan and Brooklyn. As the industry was driven largely by immigrant labor, racketeers like the Shapiro Brothers were able to exploit workers and extort manufacturers.

The Shapiro gang was also notable for recruiting upstart criminal teenagers Abe Reles and Martin "Buggsy" Goldstein, nasty thugs who later served as core members of Murder, Incorporated. They were not aligned for long. Goldstein and Reles ran afoul of the Shapiros once they started collaborating with Jacob "Gurrah" Shapiro (no relation to Meyer, Irving and William) and Louis "Lepke" Buchalter toward the end of the roaring 20s. In a running rivalry, the Shapiros ambushed Goldstein and Reles, who managed to escape unscathed.

Reles' sweetheart would not be so lucky.

Set upon by the despicable Meyer Shapiro one night, the young lady was kidnapped, beaten and brutally raped. This sickening revenge crime spun Reles off into a rage, magnifying the intensity of the war.

By 1931, Reles' Murder, Inc. allies Joseph and Louis Amberg had murdered Irving Shapiro, shooting him down in a Brooklyn street near his home. Then, they caught up with Meyer. His bullet-riddled corpse was found slumped against a wall in a tenement basement on Manhattan.

Goldstein and Reles completed their terrifying trifecta in the summer of 1932, conveniently accepting the contract hit Buchalter took out on Willie Shapiro. They buried his beaten and bloody broken body, while still alive and moaning, out in the marshes of Canarsie. Willie's body was never found, but Reles spilled the beans to investigators years later when he flipped for the feds and became a cooperating witness against the mob.

45
John Hatcher –
The Bloody Hatchet

Law enforcement stares down the many faces of evil every day, seeing so much of what the rest of us would want to unsee.

So when members of law enforcement speak in absolute terms, it carries weight.

"He _was_ the crack epidemic," characterized John Gilbride, Special Agent in Charge of the Drug Enforcement Administration's (DEA) New York Office, reported by Murray Weiss in the March 5, 2007, edition of *The New York Post*. Gilbride even lumped Hatcher in with drug kingpins Nicky Barnes, Kenneth "Supreme" McGriff and Lorenzo "Fat Cat" Nichols, all street legends in New York's illicit narcotics trade.

Hatcher led the vicious East New York drug gang known as the Rugby Boys, pursued by the DEA in a six-year investigation. During the reign of the Rugby Boys, Hatcher helped drive the rise of the crack-cocaine epidemic in 1980s Brooklyn. The poison they peddled destroyed thousands of lives, laying waste to entire blocks they invaded. Law enforcement was caught off-guard at the time by the drug's rapid spread and resultant violence.

"[The Rugby Boys were] one of the most brutal drug distribution gangs that I've ever heard about and I've been in law enforcement for 26 years," remarked Dan Anderson, a Special-Agent-in-Charge of the DEA's New York office, captured in a March 6, 2007, *Washington Times* article by journalist Tim Reid.

When federal prosecutors brought down Hatcher, the drug lord sidestepped a death-sentence by agreeing to cooperate, copping to his role in no less than 80 shootings, racking up 30 slayings. The Rugby Boys were so prolific in their murder and mayhem, Hatcher's confession took four months to process and corroborate before investigators mounted prosecutions.

With Hatcher's cooperation, law enforcement took out the upper echelon of the Rugby Boys, a gang that clocked more than $1 million per week at its height.

"There were times when we actually had to stop him and say, 'That's enough for today,' " DEA Special Agent John Profetti said, recalling one grim session when Hatcher described an assault when one disobedient henchmen was stabbed, shot, choked, set on fire and then doused with a pail of urine.

John Hatcher did not have to turn to crime. Unlike most major drug traffickers of that era, Hatcher was not brought up in a criminal culture. His father owned a popular record shop in Canarsie, Brooklyn. One brother was an officer at the United States Naval Academy, another was a Christian minister.

Yet by his early teens, Hatcher was flexing on the streets of Brooklyn, first as a pick-pocket before graduating to burglary and armed robbery.

After running with violent Jamaican drug gangs that infested Brooklyn, Hatcher hatched the Rugby Boys recruiting other like-minded local lost boys. Violent and streetwise, but with a cunning mind for business, Hatcher flourished in the drug trade. His organization swelled as he recruited the lost boys from Brooklyn corners, right as crack hit the street. As a smoke-able, more-addictive, less-expensive alternative to cocaine, crack exploded in use in the inner city, creating armies of zombified addicts.

From his Park Slope lair, Hatcher lived large the life of the gangster in everything he did, from how he dressed and talked, to how quick he'd drop a body to send a warning.

In 1991, a member of Hatcher's crew grazed an NYPD officer,

mistaking him for a rival gangster. Hatcher took the collar, serving eight years in prison. With Hatcher locked up, a lieutenant bought his drug spots for $70,000 and made payments totaling some $200,000 to Hatcher's wife and father. Upon release, Hatcher stepped back into the game, now with the added street cred prison time lends.

In 2000, Hatcher was involved in a drug deal gone bad, shooting and killing a New York City bus driver caught up as a courier. The debacle attracted the attention of law enforcement, and one of Hatcher's lieutenants, Charles Thomas, was soon under surveillance. Thomas was later linked to a credit card scam, providing the leverage investigators would use to flip him.

By 2001, a joint taskforce including the DEA, the NYPD and the U.S. Postal Inspector was gathering evidence on multiple Rugby Boys, culminating in a massive sweep the morning of May 13, 2002.

Hatcher had a hunch his time on the street was over.

On the stand, Hatcher testified against his former partners to save himself, sending shock waves throughout the drug trade in Bedford-Stuyvesant and East New York. Many of his former partners were sent away for life sentences, individuals he collaborated with over decades.

Eligible for the death penalty, Hatcher saved his life by cooperating.

John "Bloody Hatchet" Hatcher is incarcerated in an undisclosed federal prison in a protected unit where he will live out the rest of his natural life.

44
Lemrick Nelson - The Crown Heights Riots

Talk about making a bad situation worse.

In 1991, the relationship between the African-American and Orthodox-Jewish communities of Brooklyn was strained, a rivalry simmering for years.

Though the city elected its first African American mayor in David Dinkins in 1989, it was not long removed from the violent racially motivated murders in Gravesend (1982), Howard Beach (1986) and Bensonhurst (1989).

On the Monday evening of August 19, 1991, at 8:21 p.m., in the Crown Heights section of Brooklyn, a Mercury Grand Marquis station wagon driven by Yosef Lifsh, part of a three-car motorcade escorting Lubavitcher Hasidic spiritual leader Rabbi Menachem Schneerson, careened out of control.

Tragically, seven-year-old African-American boy Gavin Cato was struck and killed, and his cousin Angela Cato was severely injured.

The situation spun out of control quickly, sparking three days of civil unrest and rioting in Brooklyn, where 43 residents and 152 police officers were injured.

Immediately following the accident, as multiple ambulances arrived, an anxious crowd formed, jostling the station wagon driver and the vehicle's other occupants. They fled in the Hatzolah ambulance, ordered by the police to escape the crowd as the situation deteriorated. That's when rumors spread that the Hatzolah ambulance prioritized the Jewish men over the injured and dying black victims.

Then the notorious Crown Heights Riots of 1991 exploded.

Cameras rolled as the enraged crowd overturned police vehicles, damaged property, and chucked bottles and rocks at police.

It would get worse.

Several blocks away, Yankel Rosenbaum, a 29-year-old Australian University of Melbourne graduate student in America performing his doctoral research, wandered into the path of the raging mob. He was set upon by a group of up to 20 seething protestors. They chanted, "Kill the Jew."

Beaten and stabbed numerous times, Rosenbaum was rushed by ambulance to the hospital. Initially expected to survive, he died when one of his four stab wounds was not addressed for more than an hour. Charges were upgraded. Police collared 16-year-old Lemrick Nelson, the Crown Heights resident who stabbed Rosenbaum in the back. Rosenbaum fingered Nelson before he was rushed from the scene.

The son of poor immigrants from Trinidad, a product of a broken home, Nelson lived with his mother in a shelter for battered women before she abandoned him near his second birthday. By the time he reached that fateful night in 1991, Nelson was already a troubled youth.

Three days of rioting ensued, broadcast live around the world. This wasn't just Brooklyn news, but the latest racial flashpoint to flare up for a media more than willing to fan the flames night after night, front page after front page.

Following three trials (the first ended in acquittal, the second a hung jury), Nelson was convicted of violating the civil rights of Rosenbaum and sentenced to 10 years in prison.

Initially, Nelson proclaimed his innocence, but by 2003, in the face of strong evidence, he admitted to stabbing Rosenbaum. At trial, while the defense did not refute that Nelson attacked Rosenbaum, the attorneys maintained that his violent actions were not racially motivated. So-called hate crime criminal convictions come with harsher penalties.

The legal proceedings dragged out for a decade with much of the coverage focused on the racial divide in America, dragging Nelson along for the ride, shining a harsh spotlight on the murderer.

Though the incident occurred in 1992, Nelson was not convicted until 2003, then released from prison in 2004, given credit for time spent in prison prior to formal conviction.

Years later in the fall of 2010, Nelson himself was stabbed in the head with an icepick following a road rage incident. Nelson survived that attack.

Later in December that same year, Nelson was picked up for drunk driving when police found him unconscious in a car near Newark Airport, an open bottle of Scotch in the vehicle.

43
James Parker - Brooklyn's Own Fatal Attraction

In the autumn of 1996, as the children of Bay Ridge were returning to school shrugging off the last lingering vestiges of summer, mourners shuffled into Our Lady of Angels Church on 73rd Street and 4th Avenue to pay their last respects to Danielle DiMedici.

In the national media, DiMedici came to epitomize a textbook-example of how impotent authorities can be in protecting a woman stalked by an obsessed, determined, violent ex-boyfriend.

Exactly one week prior, following nightmarish months of harassment, DiMedici was slain by her ex-boyfriend, James Parker. DiMedici was seven months pregnant with Parker's daughter. She planned to call the baby Athena, after the Greek goddess of wisdom and courage.

At 24 years of age, Parker was trouble from the start for the much younger 17-year-old DiMedici.

After assaulting a previous girlfriend in the 1980s, Parker served a year and a half in prison. His rap sheet included arrests for drug-related offenses, burglary and grand larceny, and at the time of DiMedici's murder he was violating parole stemming from a 1993 drug conviction.

After being kidnapped, beaten and abused, DiMedici was given a necklace alarm by NYPD detectives, an order of protection and a 24/7 armed NYPD guard on her home. The frightened DiMedici never activated the alarm, said police.

Tragically, the NYPD removed the 24-hour police-guard protection from DiMedici just days before Parker invaded her home on September 14, 1996. The police coverage was reduced to periodic drive-by check-ups after police reviewed a tape recording of a call in which Parker pleaded with DiMedici to marry him. She refused.

Afterwards, the NYPD was criticized by the family in the media. The Brooklyn prosecutor's office, who earlier disagreed with the possibility of lifting the 24-hour police protection, was never notified. After the murder, a statement from the prosecutor's office claimed emergency measures would have been taken to remove DiMedici from the home, had their office been made aware of the development.

The NYPD said at the time that lifting the 24-hour protection was warranted, as Parker had not been seen in the area in weeks. Parker was on the lam, with a warrant out for his arrest stemming from an earlier beating he delivered to the pregnant DiMedici.

The prosecutor had asked the department to stay the order to remove the protection, intending to initiate relocation of DiMedici and family members as early as that coming Monday.

Unfortunately, Parker never answered for his crime, taking the coward's way out. At approximately 10 a.m. on the morning of

September 14, 1996, a rage-filled Parker held DiMedici and 11 members of her family at gunpoint in their Borough Park home at 4305 10th Avenue, near 43rd Street.

The stand-off lasted more than two hours.

With police surrounding the building and sharpshooters perched on rooftops, a chilling scream shot through the air: ''You must get in here because he's going to kill everybody!''

As police stormed the building, Parker turned the gun on DiMedici, also shooting her grandmother Barbara Hussey, her uncle Edward Hussey and the uncle's girlfriend Larissa Solovsky. DiMedici died of her wounds at the scene. The other three survived.

Parker turned the gun on himself.

DiMedici's unborn daughter also perished.

Since the tragedy, the case has been profiled in numerous books and campaigns by advocates fighting for tougher measures to address domestic violence against women.

42
Evsei Agron - The Russian Godfather

From the ashes of the Russian Revolution of 1917 rose ruthless criminal gangs known as Vorovskoy Mir or "Thieves World."

After the formation of the Soviet Union, the new regime attacked these criminal groups, bent on eradication. Dictator Joseph Stalin rounded them up in the 1930s, exiling them to deplorable prison camps in the wilderness, forging a hardened species of criminal, more vicious and irredeemable than any the underworld has ever seen.

They were known as the Vory v Zakone, or "Thieves in Law."

Some would find their way to Brooklyn.

This secret society had a strict code that demanded total submission to the thieves' life. Membership required that the thief-in-law served hard time and had no legitimate ties to society (no formal address, nor legitimate business dealings nor real jobs). A Vory v Zakone could only earn money through criminal means. Period. End of discussion.

Thieves-in-Law were discouraged from having families, though not outright prohibited. And absolutely, under no circumstances, were they to cooperate, or even associate with the government or authorities.

Evsei Agron was a Thief-in-Law.

Born in Leningrad, Agron served seven hard years in a Gulag prison for murdering a man, earning his entry into the underground organization. After his release, for a time he ran a successful prostitution and gambling operation in Hamburg, Germany, before he made his way to America.

On October 8, 1975, Agron washed up on shores of Brooklyn, awash in a wave of thousands of Russian Jewish immigrants granted entry during the 1970s. As a Thief-in-Law, Agron commanded instant street credibility when he arrived in Brighton Beach. That Brooklyn seaside community was a much bleaker place in the early 1970s, with high store vacancy and crime rates. Out of that urban blight, Soviet émigrés molded a thriving community, with the largest concentration of Russian people outside of the homeland.

In whispered tones among the Soviet Jews of Brighton Beach, Agron was known as "The Godfather," raking in thousands of dollars every week preying on his own people. Conditioned to fear government officials and not look to the authorities for protection, they were easy targets for Agron's lucrative extortion racket that he ran from the El Caribe Country Club on Strickland Avenue.

Agron was known to carry a cattle prod, a particularly painful device he used to torture-shock stubborn victims until they agreed to pay or do his bidding.

Ambushed in Coney Island in 1980, Agron survived being shot in the stomach. When no one stepped forward, retaliation was not so easy. As Agron was so hated in Brooklyn's underworld it was difficult to identify the shooter.

Agron continued his climb. While establishing operations in Russian communities in six other U.S. cities, Agron nurtured a mutually beneficial partnership with the Genovese Crime Family in Brooklyn. With the Italians, Agron gained access to political connections and muscle. For the Italians, Agron brought them into new lucrative schemes and enabled them to expand their Brooklyn sphere of influence.

Another ambush followed in early 1984. This time Agron was shot in the face and the neck. Once more he survived, though he would bear the facial scarring the rest of his life.

That attack led to an all-out war with Russian gangster Boris Goldberg and his heavily armed crew. A dramatic sit-down ensued in May of 1984 at Agron's offices at the El Caribe, with Agron making a massive display of force, calling in dozens of his men who surrounded the building.

On the morning of May 4, 1985, Agron was leaving to go to the Turkish baths on the Lower East Side of Manhattan, as he did every week. He was ambushed in the hallway of his apartment, shot twice in the head.

This time Agron did not survive.

The brief and bloody reign of Evsei Agron was over, and Marat Balagula, one of his ruthless lieutenants, stepped into the breach as leader of the Russian mob in the United States.

Phil Foglietta - Poly Prep Football coach Who Molested Players

Nestled in a picturesque campus not far off the Verrazano Narrows Bridge in Dyker Heights lies the Upper School of Poly Prep Country Day School, one the first private boys' schools founded in Brooklyn.

Established in 1854 in Downtown Brooklyn, Poly Prep offered the affluent families of Brooklyn an elite boarding-school-style of education. The institution still operates a Park Slope campus for its lower grades. The lush Dyker Heights facility was created in 1915 on 25 sprawling acres carved out from adjacent Dyker Beach Golf Course.

Since its founding, Poly Prep enjoyed a stellar reputation as a bastion of excellence in Brooklyn, known for both academic and athletic achievement.

Yet today when you plug "Poly Prep" into a search engine, the results returned are far more notorious.

Former football coach Philip Foglietta was an institution within the institution, from 1966 through 1991 building the Poly Prep program into a Brooklyn powerhouse.

Then he abruptly sailed off into the sunset.

When successful coaches retire, it's usually a planned affair, thought out well in advance. Yet rather than taking his victory lap around the private school prep league, Foglietta's sudden departure seemed strange. And even as the former coach was lauded for his contributions in a retirement dinner at the Manhattan Athletic Club, ugly rumors were in the air.

It was four years before the full truth emerged publicly. For decades Foglietta preyed upon the innocent boys at Poly Prep, a serial rapist and child molester, repeatedly accused of awful indiscretions dating as far back as 1966, the very first year he joined Poly Prep.

By 2002, Poly Prep's administration was in full-on crisis mode, fending off accusations of covering up Foglietta crimes for years, allowing him to remain on staff with access to more potential victims. There were even rumors that members of the school's administration threatened his accusers to silence them.

Did the administration of Brooklyn's beloved Poly Prep protect child-rapist Foglietta to win football games and raise money? That was the question in the minds of many Brooklynites when the story broke and the parade of victims started stepping forward.

In 2002, the administration issued a letter to alumni that Poly Prep had "recently received credible allegations that sexual abuse had occurred at Poly Prep more than 20 years ago by a faculty member/coach ..."

Foglietta was the prime suspect, though the notice didn't identify him by name.

In 2004 the first victim stepped forward publicly. Former student-athlete John Paggioli filed a suit against the school, later dismissed due to the expiration of the statute of limitations. In New York State, a minor who is a victim of sexual assault must file a civil suit within five years of turning 18 years of age.

In 2009, a dozen former students banded together to mount a $20 million Racketeer Influenced and Corrupt Organizations Act (RICO) case against Poly Prep, an unusual use of the statute. The court documents allege the potential for hundreds of possible victims, facilitated by a pattern of corruption and cover-ups perpetrated by the institution spanning decades.

The damning accusations alleged Poly Prep's administration

turned a blind eye to Foglietta's criminal activity, because he delivered a winning football program. A successful sports program is quite a recruitment asset for any private institution.

The breadth and depth of the crimes, the lurid nature of the sexual assaults, the sheer volume of victims, and the unusual application of RICO – normally used to attack organized crime – set the stage for a high-profile legal showdown. This had major implications beyond Brooklyn. Should the plaintiffs prevail, it would set a legal precedent other accusers could use, in lieu of statute-of-limitations obstacles.

In a stunning decision, in August 2012, Judge Frederic Block of the Brooklyn District Federal Court announced two of the 12 victims' RICO claims could move forward. The decision drew national attention.

Poly Prep diffused the situation, settling out of court with the plaintiffs, while issuing a public apology to the victims. The institution continues to wrestle with legal actions that will never bring peace to the hundreds of victims, and its reputation is irreparably tarnished.

Unfortunately, Foglietta was never held accountable for his crimes.

He died in 1998, years before the allegations saw the light of day.

At the time of his death, the school established a scholarship fund in his memory.

That scholarship has since been removed.

40
George Parker – The Man Who Sold the Brooklyn Bridge

Since opening to international fanfare in 1883, the Brooklyn Bridge has been so much more than a modern marvel of engineering.

From Court Street out to Coney Island, as children whenever we did something we weren't supposed to, our mothers would set the same snare before the scold.

"Well if he jumped off the Brooklyn Bridge, would you?"

Then there's the age-old litmus test of gullibility used to dismiss our childhood tall tales.

"If you believe that, I have a bridge to sell you."

This wasn't just a Brooklyn thing, but adages appropriated coast-to-coast, even showing up in a 1949 Bugs Bunny cartoon. Even back then the nation was enamored with everything Brooklyn.

Remarkably, though, there were people gullible enough to buy the Brooklyn Bridge.

In fact, it was sold many, many times.

Just not legally.

A "Confidence Man" usually specializes in a specific scam, perfecting the con over time. You've got your Spanish Prisoner (today's reader may recognize this updated as the Nigerian Letter Scam), your Fortune-telling Frauds, your Gold Bricks, and your False Injury Insurance Swindles.

George Parker's swindle was selling property he did not own during the early 20th century, often to unsuspecting immigrants or tourists. Parker sold Broadway theater shows, the Statue of Liberty, Madison Square Garden, even the Metropolitan Museum of Art. When selling Grant's Tomb, he drew sympathy posing as the heartbroken grandson of the famed Civil War hero and former U.S. President.

Yet Parker is best known for selling the Brooklyn Bridge, several times.

Image this man's powers of persuasion, to convince someone he not only owned a New York City landmark, but was willing to part with it at a discount.

Then imagine the shock on the faces of his victims, the mornings they showed up on the bridge with their work crews attempting to set up toll booths, only to be unceremoniously booted off the span by smirking local police.

Like most successful Confidence Men, Parker tinkered with his sting over time. He rented offices to establish a legitimate setting for negotiations. He produced high-quality forgeries of all the necessary legal documents. And he targeted recently arrived immigrants coming through Ellis Island who appeared to be men of means.

Some of his sales were for up to $5,000, a massive sum at the time. However, he accepted far less in most instances, given that he kept selling it, reportedly twice per week for up to two years.

Alas, like all shysters' shills, there is no perfect crime. As persuasive as Parker was, even he was still fallible.

Arrested on fraud charges multiple times, at least one judge had had enough of Parker and on December 17, 1928, right before Christmas, he was sentenced to life in prison in Kings County Court in Downtown Brooklyn.

Packed off to Sing Sing, Parker spent nearly nine years in prison until his death, enjoying minor celebrity status, impressing prisoners and guards alike with tales of his outlandish capers. It seems cons and corrections officers are especially taken with creative criminality.

Parker was not the first, nor the last, to sell the Brooklyn Bridge. There were other imitators, such as William McCloundy, a.k.a. I.O.U. O'Brien, sent to Sing Sing for a two-and-a-half-year stretch for his version of the scam.

Yet no one before or since ever approached the sales volume achieved by Parker and his wonderful con.

39
Christopher Furnari – The 19th Hole Crew

Ever see a fit gangster over 50?

Me neither.

Most mobsters don't get to live life into old age. If *the life* doesn't get them life behind bars or land them in the cemetery, then years of excess, stress and just bad living usually lead to premature death.

Christopher Furnari Mugshot

Not Christopher Furnari. When Furnari, known on the streets as "Christie Tick," was sentenced in his early 60s, he never thought he'd see the light of day beyond prison walls, and rightfully so. During the epic Mafia Commission Trial of the 1980s, this legendary Lucchese mobster was handed a 100-years-might-as-well-be-death sentence. At the time, he was already 62 years of age.

However, after serving 28 years behind bars, in 2014 Furnari made headlines when a parole board granted him a miraculous reprieve and released him from prison.

He was 92.

Has there ever been a gangster that lived into his 90s?

Ever?

Furnari was not just *any* gangster. Christie Tick was a capo (and later Lucchese consigliere) that ran one of the most powerful crews from a Mafia stronghold deep in the heart of Bensonhurst. The so-called "19th Hole Crew" was named for one of Brooklyn's most infamous mob nests, a cocktail lounge perched on 86th Street and 14th Avenue right off the Dyker Beach Golf Course, a public city-run facility on the shores of southwest Brooklyn.

Among his claims to criminal fame, Furnari mentored young wiseguys Anthony "Gaspipe" Casso and Vittorio "Vic" Amuso. Before rising through the ranks to lead the family, Casso and Amuso ran the Bypass Gang, a highly successful burglary ring that reported up to Furnari. Furnari sponsored the two for formal mob induction, or to be "made," in 1970.

It was Casso who later stepped in to control the Luccheses after the Commission case locked up the family's upper echelon. (Casso actually declined boss Philip "Rusty" Rastelli's request to become the acting street boss, and wisely proposed Vic Amuso to the top post, fully aware that the position would draw intense attention from media and law enforcement.)

Born in 1924 in the Dyker Heights section of Brooklyn to immigrant parents from the Furnari section of Sicily, Christie Tick kicked off his criminal career at a young age. By the 1940s, Furnari had already served time on two separate armed-robbery convictions, and was sent up for a third stint, convicted on rape charges, that would keep him in prison through 1956.

Upon release, Furnari found a home within the Brooklyn arm of the Lucchese Family. Formally inducted into the mob in 1962, he was elevated to crew captain two years later.

While the Lucchese Family has its roots in the Bronx, Furnari helped develop the smaller Brooklyn faction in Bensonhurst. Furnari and his underlings had their hands in a wide range of rackets, from labor racketeering and gambling, to drug dealing, extortion and loansharking.

When Furnari was elevated to consigliere of the Luccheses, he was a much-sought-after advisor and mediator, both within the clan and outside the family.

By 1985, Furnari was swept up into the Mafia Commission case and indicted on RICO charges (Racketeer Influenced and Corrupt Organizations Act). While out on multi-million-dollar bail, Furnari continued his criminal conniving, including working with Casso and Russian gangsters from Brighton Beach on a massive gas-tax scheme that threw off millions of dollars for multiple New York criminal organizations.

Furnari's time on the streets ended on November 19, 1986, along with virtually the entire leadership of the Luccheses and the other Mafia families. Furnari was convicted on all charges, including labor racketeering, extortion and murder, that of former Bonanno family boss Carmine "Lilo" Galante. He was sentenced to 100 years without the possibility of parole.

While in prison, Furnari's attorneys argued the no-parole stipulation should be removed, due to the tainted testimony of witnesses, including Casso, who had since flipped for the feds.

Despite the intent that Furnari never see the light of day, he secured an early release in the autumn of 2014, after serving 28 years of his sentence.

38
Darryl Littlejohn - The Murder of Imette St. Guillen

In the Old Dutch tongue of the founders of New York, they called it "Bruklein," or "The Broken Land."

That is a fitting name for Fountain Avenue in East New York, a forgotten place broken off from the rest of the city.

In 2006, down Fountain Avenue way could be found a dangerous stretch of car lots and looming brick buildings, scrawled with graffiti, strewn with garbage, old tires, abandoned vehicles, orphaned shopping carts.

The perfect place to ditch a body.

In this filthy place during the bitter winter of that year, in a gully where Fountain Avenue empties under the Belt Parkway, NYPD officers discovered the lifeless body of Imette Carmella St. Guillen. They found the 24-year-old John Jay College of Criminal Justice graduate student, cut down in the prime of her life, naked and bound in a blanket, her eyes and mouth taped shut.

The murder mystery surrounding St. Guillen exploded in the New York tabloids, before quickly going national. It developed into the heartbreaking big-city story of an innocent, beautiful young woman set upon by a hulking fiend.

At the time of her death, St. Guillen had been studying criminal justice, ranked in the top five percent of her class. She was scheduled to graduate just a few months later that May.

On the evening of February 24, 2006, St. Guillen met up with friend Claire Higgins at a Chelsea bar called The Falls. They spent the evening celebrating St. Guillen's birthday, drinking and laughing late into the night. Higgins left the bar around 3:30 a.m., and then called St. Guillen shortly thereafter, receiving assurances from St. Guillen that she would soon call it a night.

That was the last time anyone who cared for St. Guillen saw her alive.

The next evening the NYPD fielded an anonymous call that led them to the body dumped in that gully on Fountain Avenue along the shores of the broken land.

St. Guillen's cracked fingernails let investigators know she'd fought desperately for her life. An autopsy revealed she'd been sexually violated and beaten. The cause of death was asphyxiation, from having a sock shoved down her throat, and her mouth and nose sealed with tape.

Stretch of Fountain Avenue Where Body of Imette St. Guillen Was Found

The NYPD's Special Victims Unit fielded the case, leading them back to The Falls. Eye-witnesses said St. Guillen had been served alcohol well beyond the point of inebriation. She was last seen with a bouncer from The Falls, Darryl Littlejohn, an ex-con who served 12 years on drug and robbery convictions. Working as a bouncer was in direct violation with his parole-mandated curfew guidelines.

Littlejohn was taken into custody, and charged with kidnapping, unlawful imprisonment and first-degree murder. Further investigation yielded DNA evidence linking Littlejohn to St. Guillen. A search of his apartment and vehicle produced more damning evidence. Cell phone tower records placed Littlejohn in the Fountain Avenue location in Brooklyn at the right time when the broken body of St. Guillen was discarded.

When Littlejohn's van was featured on a news broadcast, another victim stepped forward from an earlier attack. She narrowly escaped his clutches.

With Littlejohn in custody on the St. Guillen murder, prosecutors opted to first try him for that earlier abduction. At trial, Littlejohn was found guilty and received a 25-years-to-life sentence.

Later, in 2009, Littlejohn was tried for the St. Guillen murder in a high-profile trial. He was found guilty of first-degree murder and related charges and received another life sentence, to be served consecutively with his previous sentence.

As for The Falls, and its role in serving an already-intoxicated woman, the ownership settled out of court with St. Guillen's family, and eventually went out of business.

Due to the publicity of the case and the negative light cast on New York nightlife, St. Guillen's tragedy inspired changes in laws and regulations. In 2007, New York City enacted legislation requiring security cameras at the entrances to nightclubs possessing cabaret licenses.

37
Christopher Thomas - The Palm Sunday Massacre

In the Christian faith, Palm Sunday is the final Sunday of Lent, the beginning of Holy Week, and commemorates the triumphant arrival of Christ in Jerusalem, days before he was crucified.

Culminating on Easter Sunday, signifying the reincarnation of Jesus Christ, Holy Week has a solemn undertone that starts with Palm Sunday. It incorporates concepts of rebirth and celebration of the Christ.

In Brooklyn in 1984, Palm Sunday took on a more somber tone. The headline in *The New York Post* the next morning said it all.

"Showed No Mercy."

That day in Brooklyn, Christopher Thomas shot to death 10 people in an apartment at 1080 Liberty Ave. in East New York, Brooklyn

– a brutal mass murder that made headlines across the country.

It was christened "The Palm Sunday Massacre."

The innocent victims included three adult women, one teenage girl, and six children. Only a single survivor was found amidst all those bodies that day, an infant girl.

To this day, Thomas adamantly professes his innocence, despite overwhelming evidence to the contrary, according to court records. Thomas accused Enrique Bermudez, a convicted cocaine dealer and husband of one of victims, Virginia Lopez. Thomas maintains that the crime was drug-related and had nothing to do with him. Bermudez found the bodies and called police. Lopez was pregnant with Bermudez' child.

Detectives suspected the crime was related to the drug trade. However, that theory was disproven when investigators learned of Thomas' obsession with Bermudez, whom he accused of having an affair with his wife.

Investigators uncovered enough evidence to prove Thomas' guilt beyond a reasonable doubt.

Later at trial, citing Thomas' "extreme emotional disturbance," due to his drug-addled state while committing the crime, Thomas was handed 10 manslaughter convictions.

He was sentenced to 83 to 250 years in prison.

This story had a redeeming postscript that allowed it to resurface in the media years later.

Joanna Jaffe, a police officer on the scene who picked up the blood-spattered 13-month-old child, Christina Rivera, from the carnage that day, just couldn't let her go.

Jaffe stayed in contact with Christina throughout her childhood. Eventually, at the age of 14, Rivera moved in with Jaffe, who adopted her once Rivera's grandmother passed.

Chief Joanna Jaffe is now the highest-ranking officer in the NYPD.

It's one of those few Brooklyn hard knock stories that had a happy ending.

In the underworld, there is always someone waiting in the wings to rise.

Boris Nayfeld, known as Biba on the streets of both Belarus and Brighton Beach, landed in Brooklyn in the late 1970s as a Soviet Jewish refugee under the Jackson-Vanik Amendment. (Signed into law by U.S. President Gerald Ford in 1975, the Jackson-Vanik Amendment to the Trade Act of 1974 was instrumental in eliminating barriers to the emigration of Soviet Jewry.)

Nayfeld notched his first arrest in 1980, a bust in Nassau County on grand-larceny charges. He pled down to petty larceny and was released.

Nayfeld had an extensive criminal repertoire, as an experienced thief, drug dealer, and strong-arm thug. He soon hitched his wagon to Evsei Agron, a rising Russian Mafia star who would rule the Brooklyn rackets in the 1970s and 1980s.

Following years of loyal service as Agron's bodyguard and chauffeur, Nayfeld was standing outside his boss's apartment on Ocean Parkway when Agron was gunned down inside in the lobby of the building in 1985.

When gangster Marat Balagula took Agron's place atop to Brighton Beach mob, Nayfeld became an enforcer for the new regime. Later when Balagula was undone by a massive gasoline bootlegging scheme, Nayfeld stepped up to take over the Brighton Beach rackets.

It's no wonder Nayfeld rose through the ranks, as he was a particularly violent man and ominous presence in Brighton Beach. He was often accompanied by his equally menacing brother Benjamin, a former member of the Soviet Union's weightlifting team. The duo formed a frightening criminal combination in Brooklyn.

In addition to his homegrown Brooklyn rackets, Nayfeld orchestrated an international heroin-smuggling ring that funneled shipments from Thailand to Europe and then on to New York for broader distribution stateside. This included partnerships with both Italian Mafia groups and Latino street gangs.

It was during the 1990s that Nayfeld engaged in a war with Monya Elson, who came to Brighton Beach right about the same time as Nayfeld, later specializing in theft and scams.

In 1991, Nayfeld became enraged when a car bomb was discovered in the vehicle he had been driving. His daughters were in the backseat. The bomb was spotted as he dropped the girls off at their school. Investigators determined that the amount of explosives not only would have destroyed the vehicle and killed it occupants, but was powerful enough to level an entire Brooklyn block.

Nayfeld struck back when on May 14th that year, one of his henchman opened fire on Elson on busy Brighton Beach Avenue in broad daylight. Despite catching five bullets in his stomach, Elson survived the attack.

More attacks and counter-attacks ensued, including one instance where an assassination attempt using an Olympic marksman was aborted at the last second when Nayfeld got spooked, his vehicle fleeing the scene. That year, in Los Angeles, a Nayfeld assassin had Elson in his sights at close range, but failed to kill the rival boss when his gun jammed. He did manage to wound him.

With the violence escalating and bodies dropping on both sides from bombings, kidnappings and shootouts, by 1993 Nayfeld was on the lam, ducking a federal warrant for his arrest on drug charges.

That was when perhaps the most dramatic exchange of the war occurred. A crew of Nayfeld assassins ambushed Elson and family members in front of their Sheepshead Bay apartment on July 26, 1993. Elson was shot multiple times, his wife Marina hit with a partial shotgun blast to the face, and his nephew taking grazing fire. All three survived.

Nayfeld would eventually be arrested in January 1994 on the outstanding drug trafficking charges.

Nayfeld was released by authorities in 1998 and now lives in Staten Island, according to the U.S. Attorney's Office.

As of late, Nayfeld was picked up on an extortion charge in January 2016.

Preet Bharara, the United States Attorney for the Southern District of New York, announced that Boris Kotlyarsky and Nayfeld were arrested for extorting $125,000 from a victim who they claimed Nayfeld had been hired to murder.

In the complaint, an unnamed Russian businessman had allegedly offered Nayfeld $100,000 for the hit. Nayfeld was willing to accept cash but did not follow through on the contract.

35
Louis Buchalter - Lepke

Louis "Lepke" Buchalter bumped off enough victims to bump him up relatively high on this list, as a member of that sinister wave of pre-war mobsters that infiltrated New York's labor unions.

During the 1930s, the Brooklyn Jewish gangster was a high-ranking member of Murder, Inc., the execution squad credited with perhaps 1,000 murders. Buchalter also holds the dubious distinction of being the only major mob kingpin to be executed after being convicted of murder.

Born on the Lower East Side of Manhattan in 1897, Buchalter never had a legitimate shot at a straight life. His mother, Rose Buchalter, called him "Lepkeleh," or "Little Louis" in Yiddish, and the moniker stuck, belying his larger-than-life rage. You don't rise through the ranks of the underworld with the nickname "Lepke" unless you're a complete bad ass.

Buchalter's brothers turned out relatively fine, (a Rabbi, a Pharmacist, and a Dentist walk into a bar...). Yet "Little Louis" lacked adequate supervision from an early age. Buchalter's father passed when he was 12 and his mother relocated to Arizona for health reasons, leaving behind the unruly Lepke to be minded by his sister, Sarah.

Lepke leapt into a life of crime, first arrested as a teen for assault and burglary. Packed off to an uncle in Bridgeport, Connecticut, Lepke later slid in for a stint

Wanted Poster for Jacob Shapiro and Louis Buchalter 1937

in the Cheshire Reformatory before returning to New York. An

18-month-stay in Sing Sing on grand larceny followed in 1917, then another 30-month conviction for attempted burglary.

Released from Sing Sing in 1922, the hardened Buchalter hooked up with childhood-chum-cum-career-criminal Jacob "Gurrah" Shapiro, forming a frightening partnership. The two set about sucking the life out of Brooklyn's thriving garment industry. At the time, Jewish sweatshop owners were more than willing to share a few shekels to save their kneecaps and avoid job actions.

Around this time, Buchalter and his gangster cronies aligned with the Italians, linking with Tommy Lucchese, future boss of the Mafia family named for him, forming a cross-ethnic-criminal-cabal well equipped for corrupting the garment industry.

In the late 1920s, Buchalter avoided prison on multiple murder counts, including rubbing the life out of underworld players like Jack Diamond and Jacob Orgen. But for the most part, Buchalter kept his head down and shunned attention, understanding the police pressure notoriety drew.

In the 1930s, Buchalter played a prominent role in the gang of contract killers that became Murder, Inc., evolving into a murderous arm of the Mafia. Albert "Lord High Executioner" Anastasia would field the murder requests from the Mafia families, and turn them over to Buchalter who would farm out the contracts to a cadre of cold-blooded killers. The arrangement was preferable to the Mafia, as Murder, Inc. members were not directly associated with the Mafia families. Within a short time, the bloody business was booming, with Buchalter even accepting an increasing number of out-of-town contracts.

By the height of the Great Depression in the mid-1930s, Buchalter was raking in hundreds of thousands of dollars each year from his involvement in many rackets. Yet, the heat was on and the notoriety he worked so hard to shun finally found him and his fellow murderers.

With investigators closing in, Buchalter and Shapiro went on the lam. In his absence, authorities indicted Buchalter on a drug charge in 1937. A manhunt ensued for the next two years before Buchalter finally surrendered in 1939, to none other than J. Edgar Hoover, head of the Federal Bureau of Investigation. Shapiro had already turned himself in by then.

In separate trials, Buchalter was convicted on narcotics trafficking, then extortion, and sentenced to decades in prison he would never serve.

In 1941, Buchalter was indicted on multiple murder counts and on November 30 was convicted of first-degree murder for the killing of Joseph Rosen, a Brooklyn candy-store owner and former union truck-driver Buchalter suspected of cooperating with District Attorney Thomas Dewey.

Buchalter received more notoriety when his appeal made it all the way to the U.S. Supreme Court, before the conviction was affirmed, seven justices to zero, with two abstaining.

In 1944, his appeals exhausted, "Little Louis" was led from his cell in Leavenworth Federal Prison, where he'd been serving his time on the racketeering convictions. On March 4th, along with two of his underlings, Buchalter went to the electric chair at Sing Sing.

34
Troy Hendrix Kayson Pearson – The Murder of Romona Moore

In the early summer of 2003, the body of Romona Moore was found nearly eight weeks after the 21-year-old disappeared from the Canarsie-area apartment she shared with her parents.

The Hunter College student, a native of Guyana, was brutally raped, tortured, and then murdered. The ghastly crime drew headlines for its brutality, while sparking a court battle between Moore's parents and the New York City Police Department.

Investigators learned that on the evening of April 24th, Moore was last seen leaving a friend's Brooklyn apartment. According to that witness, Moore was heading to the Burger King fast food restaurant on Remsen and Church avenues.

Moore was never seen alive again.

Police officers responding to the 911 call to her Remsen Avenue apartment filed a missing person's report. Weeks passed with few promising leads. Police informed Moore's family that as she was a grown woman, her disappearance may not have been an indication of foul play. The family took offense.

Moore's aunt later received an anonymous phone call, directing her to an address on King's Highway. When police from the nearby 67th precinct arrived to investigate the burned-out building, they soon discovered Moore's decomposing body, wrapped in a blanket. She'd been dead for more than a week.

Anonymous tips led police to Troy Hendrix and Kayson Pearson, the two local hoods who abducted Moore, dragged her to the basement of Hendrix's home, drugged and chained her to a pole before subjecting her to days of torture, rape, and eventually murder.

Not more than four days after murdering Moore, the same two suspects raped a 15-year-old girl in that basement. She survived by freeing herself from her bonds while the two fiends slept. She testified at their trials.

A third despicable character emerged during testimony, a pal of Hendrix who witnessed Moore chained in the basement. While he did not participate in the violence, he did nothing to aid Moore, even after he returned home to Maryland.

Both suspects turned on each other during questioning, blaming one another for the crime and offering to testify. Fortunately, investigators collected enough DNA samples and evidence to reject their offers.

During the trial, Pearson smuggled in a makeshift weapon made from sharpened plastic and assaulted a court bailiff and his attorney. That attack produced a mistrial, though the defendants would not escape justice.

In sickening court testimony, the psychopathic Person claimed, "We did it for fun ... That day, Jan. 19, 2006, was the most fun I have had in my entire life."

Both were convicted of first-degree murder and related offenses and sentenced to life without the possibility of parole.

In a statement, then Brooklyn District Attorney Charles Hynes shared: "I am hard-pressed to find a more evil case. I am satisfied that these defendants will never see the outside of a prison cell."

The legacy of Moore's murder lingered, as her mother brought a federal suit against the NYPD for its handling of the case, arguing that detectives did not pursue this case of a missing black woman with the same level of intensity as disappearances involving white women.

The suit referenced the case of Svetlana Aronov, a rare-books dealer who disappeared around the same time as Moore, kicking off a massive manhunt. Aronov, a white woman from the affluent Upper East Side of Manhattan, was found several weeks later, drowned in the East River. Her funeral services were being held at the time Moore's body was discovered.

In 2008, the suit was cleared to move forward by a Federal Judge in Brooklyn, however another judge threw the case out in 2014.

Famed Hollywood director Martin Scorsese's 1990 blockbuster film "Goodfellas" gave us a romanticized look inside the violent orbit of Paul Vario, the East New York Mafia gang boss associated with some of the most high-profile crimes of the 1970s.

Paul Vario Mugshot 1970s

On screen, Vario's character, "Paul Cicero," played by actor Paul Sorvino, is an ominous elder statesman. You sense the menace seething beneath the surface. The real-life "Paulie" was even more intimidating, with bulging animosity that propelled him to the leadership of one of the most powerful Mafia crews in the golden age of gangsterism.

Physically imposing standing six foot three inches tall, weighing in at a beefy 250 pounds, Vario leveraged every inch of his massive presence to terrorize. Vario was known to abruptly beat down men and women. He once thrashed a woman with whom he'd been romantically involved. In a fit of jealousy, she made the miscalculation of informing Vario's wife Phyllis of their dalliances.

The bully Vario was more than a Brooklyn brawler. He used his ruthless cunning to climb the ranks of the Lucchese Crime Family from associate to leading one of the family's core crews as a caporegime.

Scorsese got it right. Obsessively suspicious and paranoid, Vario never used telephones, communicating to underlings surreptitiously through his inner circle. From his home base in

East New York, Brooklyn, Vario's crew was violent and varied in its criminal activities, from extortion and armed robbery, to hijacking, gambling and, against family orders, drug trafficking. As a soldier and later captain, Vario was the target of numerous investigations, jailed on counts of bookmaking, loan-sharking, burglary, tax evasion, bribery, assault and more.

Vario's name was linked in the headlines to infamous crimes and criminals under his watch. Jimmy Burke, played in the movie by Robert De Niro and renamed Jimmy Conway, was the mastermind behind the high-profile Lufthansa haul, the largest airport heist in history, from the cargo terminal at Idlewild Airport (since renamed John F. Kennedy International). Vario's crew generated millions of dollars hi-jacking shipments and trucks out of that airport for years.

Then there was Henry Hill, a low-level associate of the family, who went on to write the book that was the basis for the Scorsese classic.

By the early 1970s, Vario was the underboss of the family, drawing intense scrutiny from law enforcement. He faced off against the federal government in a series of trials, from witness tampering and bribery to an insurance scam. In 1973, the government successfully prosecuted Vario on tax evasion charges and sent the gang boss away for six years. Doing his time on the notorious "Mafia's Row" in the federal lockup in Lewisburg, Pennsylvania, Vario received far better treatment than was the case in the prison's general population.

Released early in 1975, Vario was demoted from underboss by new boss Anthony "Tony Ducks" Corallo. In 1978 the infamous Lufthansa Airlines robbery netted the gang $5 million in cash and nearly a million dollars in jewelry. As Mafia crew chief, Vario received his honorary kickback, a sizable cut of the proceeds of the heist.

In 1984, Vario was convicted again, this time of fraud, based partly on testimony from Henry Hill, who by then was cooperating with the government to get out from under sentencing on a drug conviction. A judge handed Vario four years in prison for, of all things, providing Hill with a no-show job when he was released from prison years prior.

While in federal prison, the following year Vario was indicted on racketeering and extortion charges, among other counts, related to criminal activity at JFK.

On May 3, 1988, Vario died in prison while serving 10-to-12 years following investigations fueled by the cooperation of Henry Hill, who would outlive his old boss by nearly 25 years.

32
Carlo Gambino

How cold and calculating was Carlo Gambino?

There's a story involving Gambino and Dominick "Mimi" Scialo, a ruthless enforcer for the Colombo Mafia Family who controlled rackets in Coney Island. Scialo was obnoxious and vulgar, especially when he drank. In 1974, spotting Gambino in an Italian restaurant, he loudly insulted the Don. Scialo had to be restrained by other Colombo soldiers.

Carlo Gambino Mugshot 1930

Gambino did not lose his temper, not even to utter a single word in response. He just looked at Scialo with a cold stare.

Scialo's body was later discovered sheathed in concrete flooring of Otto's Social Club in South Brooklyn.

You don't get much bigger in Brooklyn than the Boss of Bosses, but Carlo Gambino was in it for the power, not the fame.

"The Godfather" author Mario Puzo supposedly based his literary creation, Vito Corleone, the central character in his gangster mythology, on a composite of gang bosses Gambino and Frank Costello.

However, while Costello was born the same year as Don Corleone, and both were bootleggers with pockets full of politicians, unlike Gambino, Costello was imprisoned on numerous stints and ousted by the ruling Mafia Commission. In his entire criminal career, Gambino served less than 22 months, and that was way back in 1937 through 1938.

Gambino had more in common with the fictional Godfather. Like Puzo's Corleone, Gambino shunned the spotlight, leading a low-key lifestyle that enabled him to avoid incarceration, even as he was under constant surveillance.

Both real and fictional mobsters had three sons and a single daughter, were heavily involved in extortion, illicit gambling, loan sharking and numerous other rackets, both issued staunch edicts against narcotics trafficking. Realizing drug-dealing draws intense attention from law enforcement, Gambino's top-down message to every member of his crime family was simple: "Deal and Die."

Like Corleone, Gambino accomplished what few gangster did, dying of natural causes, passing away at home in 1976. That was quite a feat, considering his long violent history to rise to the penultimate peak of organized crime.

Born in Palermo, Sicily, Carlo's family was aligned with the Honored Society, a criminal organization in Sicily, when he stowed away on a merchant ship in 1921 heading for America.

Gambino found employment as a butcher, with a sideline in bootlegging, aligning with the D'Aquila Mafia faction dominated by his relatives the Castellanos, from Brooklyn. By the end of 1921, Gambino was formally inducted as a "Made Man" in La Cosa Nostra, the Italian American Mafia.

In 1926, Gambino married Catherine Castellano, his cousin, in a ceremony in Brooklyn. The young couple made their home in Kings County, first at 1692 83rd Street, then later 8302 17th Avenue.

Chafing under the rule of Joe "the Boss" Masseria, then later Salvatore Maranzano and Philip and Vincent Mangano, Gambino threw in with a group of "Young Turks" that included Charles "Lucky" Luciano, Meyer Lansky, Benjamin "Bugsy" Siegel, Frank "Prime Minister" Costello, Gaetano "Tommy Three-Finger Brown" Lucchese and Albert "Mad Hatter" Anastasia. Led by Luciano, this faction overthrew the Sicilian old-guard and established the Mafia Five Family structure that would dominate the underworld for decades.

When Anastasia was assassinated in 1957, Gambino was a suspected triggerman on the hit, conspiring with Vito Genovese. Gambino took the wheel, assuming control of a crime family now named for him, and vastly expanded its reach into many lucrative rackets nationwide into multiple cities, including gambling, loansharking, hijacking, labor racketeering, deeply penetrating waterfront unions.

In addition to Anastasia, Gambino participated in plots against fellow mob bosses of the Profaci and Bonanno Mafia clans, and is rumored to have orchestrated the murder of Joe Colombo and Crazy Joe Gallo. Yet he himself was never the target of a hit.

At the height of his reign, Gambino's organization had 30 crews on the street with upwards of 700 members by some counts from law enforcement, grossing hundreds of millions of dollars per year.

Then, following more than five decades of crime, the FBI finally indicted Gambino in 1970, for hijacking, while the U.S. Supreme Court ordered his deportation, the wily boss foiled federal authorities with a series of heart attacks, delaying prosecution.

Gambino died of a heart attack on October 15, 1976. His funeral mass, held three days later at the Church of Our Lady of Grace in Brooklyn, drew thousands of attendees and onlookers, including police officers and politicians.

The family that bears his name still exists in Brooklyn to this day.

31
Joey Fama - The Murder of Yusuf Hawkins

Some crimes transcend the criminal act, trampling the fabric of how we see ourselves.

The reprehensible murder of Yusuf Hawkins — an innocent 16-year-old African-American boy chased down, then gunned down by an angry white mob on the streets of Bensonhurst in 1989 — was such a crime, setting back racial relations in New York City for years to come.

Before the violent shooting, before the months of protest marches, before the media storm, and before the drawn-out trials, there was a teenager looking to buy a used 1982 Pontiac priced at a reasonable $900.

The evening of August 23rd was hot when Hawkins and three of his friends travelled from East New York, less than 10 miles to the northeast, but light years away from the Italian-American enclave of Bensonhurst, circa 1989.

Hawkins and his friends had no idea that when they stepped off the train that night that they'd landed in the wrong place at the worst possible time for a group of young black men. By tragic coincidence, at the same time Hawkins and his pals were exiting the 20th Avenue train station on the N line, a mob of bat-wielding Italian American teens were working themselves into a frenzy.

Earlier, a local girl, Gina Feliciano, threatened the local boys that she had invited black youths to her birthday party. This followed an earlier racially charged confrontation between locals and visiting African-American boys. Feliciano had been warned to not invite them into the neighborhood.

Feliciano stirred the pot with her ex-boyfriend, Keith Mondello, who took the bait, rallying the local troops for an ambush. In the ensuing confrontation, the bewildered Hawkins was shot by Joseph Fama, who also grazed one of Hawkins' friends. The other boys barely managed to escape with their lives.

Hawkins was rushed to nearby Maimonides Hospital in Borough Park, but never made it out of the ambulance alive, immediately igniting a firestorm.

This wasn't just groups of youths fighting in the streets, but a modern-day lynching. In fact, the attack came during the mayoral election of David Dinkins, who would become New York City's first black mayor. Dinkins used the lynching term in making the murder a central issue during his campaign. Dinkins also stated incumbent Mayor Ed Koch shared some of the blame for New York's racial issues at the time. Weeks later, Koch's bid for a fourth term was defeated by Dinkins.

Wandering into a twisted feud, Hawkins was guilty of nothing more than the color of his skin.

Bensonhurst, at the time, was still heavily Italian-American, mostly blue-collar hard-working middle-class people. But in the nearly weekly marches that followed, the neighborhood was stained with the stigma of a bastion of racism, the media capturing despicable images of Bensonhurst youths hurling racial insults at the marchers, some holding aloft watermelon. The first march was led three days after the attack, followed by regular protests in the area, all broadcasted nationwide on nightly news programs.

Ultimately, eight Bensonhurst youths were brought to trial, though only four were convicted, including Feliciano's former boyfriend, Mondello, 19 years old at the time. He received a prison sentence of five-to-16 years as ring-leader. He was acquitted of the murder charges, but incarcerated on a slew of other counts, including rioting, weapon's possession, menacing and more.

Fama, then 18, was convicted of second-degree murder, for acting with "callous disregard for human life," and sentenced to 23-and-$2/3^{rd}$ years to life.

While Mondello was freed from Attica prison after eight years, Fama remains incarcerated, steadfastly professing his innocence.

30
Marat Balagula - The Russian Tony Soprano

Marat Yakovlevich Balagula navigated the underworlds of Italian and Russian organized crime in Brooklyn, and was responsible for a substantial upgrade in sophistication among the "Organizatsiya."

Born in 1943 in Orenburg, Russia, at the height of World War II, Balagula's family fled in a mad dash ahead of the fearsome German Wehrmacht fighter squadrons. During the war, his father, Jakov, served as a lieutenant in the Red Army, and afterwards settled into a relatively comfortable life as a factory worker.

The Soviet regime drafted young Balagula into military service at 19, where he served in an administrative capacity. Leveraging these skills when he transitioned into Russian civilian life, Balagula managed a food cooperative, while pursuing his education at night, earning a business degree with concentrations in mathematics and economics. This administrative and business-school experience served Balagula well later when he dove into the murky world of Russia's black market.

In his early 30s in the late 1970s, Balagula took advantage of the Jackson-Vanik Amendment to uproot his family for American shores. He landed briefly in Washington Heights, where the family struggled, before settling in Brighton Beach.

Balagula's criminal career hit an upswing when he aligned himself with brutal Brooklyn Russian mob boss Evsei Agron, and before long he rose to become the top lieutenant for the godfather of Brighton Beach. When Agron was assassinated on the streets of Brooklyn in 1985, Balagula stepped into the breach.

Both before and after Agron's demise, Balagula drew upon his economic background to bring a higher level of criminal sophistication to the Russian rackets, establishing and expanding an impressive array of fraudulent white-collar schemes.

Now ensconced as the new power on the southern shores of Brooklyn, Balagula more tightly structured the loose-knit Russian crime groups and gangs. Both within and beyond Brooklyn, Balagula bolstered his criminal trade lines, setting up cross-border smuggling operations spanning the globe.

Meanwhile back in Brighton Beach, Balagula nurtured a promising relationship with the entrenched Italian mafia. It was through this Italian connection that Balagula truly made his mark on the Brooklyn criminal underworld, concocting a brilliant gasoline bootlegging scheme by illegally siphoning off pennies-per-gallon of tax revenue that yielded hundreds of millions of dollars for the Italians and Russians.

Balagula wisely grasped that there was more than enough money pumping out of the scheme, enough so that he could hand over two cents per gallon to the Italians as protection, and still make his millions. Balagula implemented the scam and it hummed along nicely, until the Colombo Crime Family learned of it and leaned on the Russian crime lord. He ran to his contacts in the Lucchese family for cover. Balagula had grown close to the infamous Lucchese gangster Anthony "Gaspipe" Casso, partnering on various schemes, including most unusually, a diamond mine in Sierra Leone, involving the smuggling of so-called blood diamonds out of Africa.

Though Balagula had a fearsome reputation, paying protection to the Italians did not exactly enhance his street credibility in Brighton Beach. Russian gangster Vladimir Reznikov not only shot up Balagula's Midwood office, killing and wounding several of his employees, he shoved a gun in his face at the Russian Mafia hotspot Odessa, a nightclub Balagula owned on Brighton Beach Avenue.

Balagula promised to pay.

When Casso got wind of Reznikov's muscling in on his Russian partner, he sent word to have him come back to Odessa to pick up the money. Mafia soldiers Joseph Testa and Anthony Senter, the so-called Gemini Twins, were waiting in the parking lot and shot him to death.

Meanwhile, the pressure was getting to Balagula and he suffered a heart attack, motivating him to convalesce at home where he could be better protected from assassination.

In the mid1980s, Balagula became embroiled in a massive credit card scheme, convicted in federal court when he went on the lam, fleeing to Europe, where he was picked up three years later in Germany. Extradited back to the United States, he was locked away to serve eight years for the credit card case. In a subsequent trial on the gasoline scam, ten more years were tacked onto his prison sentence.

Balagula was released from prison in 2004 and has yet to resurface in Brooklyn's underworld.

29
Carmine Persico – The Snake

Since rising to top of the Colombo crime family in 1973, Carmine John Persico, Jr., has known a total of four years of freedom.

Currently serving 139 years for racketeering and related criminal offenses, Persico is a legend for his daring criminal exploits. Like the time he was shot in the face during an epic gun battle, spit out the lead and drove himself and a wounded underling to the hospital.

Survivor of multiple gun battles and gang wars – Check.

Overseer of a sprawling criminal enterprise for decades – Double Check.

Carmine Persico
Sentencing 1986

Owner of perhaps the coolest nickname in the Mafia – Triple Check.

"The Snake's" storied criminal career started on the mean streets of Brooklyn, from his days leading the Garfield Boys downtown, the forerunner to the notorious South Brooklyn Boys.

Born in Brooklyn in 1933, Carmine and two other brothers would join the mob. Theodore and Alphonse later became captains in the Colombo Family, though "Allie Boy" died of cancer in 1989.

Growing up in rough and tumble Carroll Gardens and Red Hook, Carmine Jr. dropped out of high school at 16 and scored his first serious collar at 17, for beating a rival to death in Prospect Park.

He evaded prosecution due to lack of evidence.

In his early 20s, Persico graduated from street gangs to go work for the Profaci Family, the predecessor of the Colombo Family. By then he was involved in everything from armed robbery to loansharking. Aligned with the notorious Gallo Brothers, Persico participated in the hit on mob boss Albert Anastasia, colluding with Vito Genovese and Carlo Gambino. Genovese hated Anastasia. Gambino, Anastasia's underboss, wanted him out of the way so he could take control of the family.

Persico, like the Gallo Brothers and most street-level members of the Profaci Family, fostered deep resentment toward the tight-fisted boss for his reluctance to share the family spoils. The wily Persico double-crossed the Gallos, then attempted to murder Larry Gallo, earning his nickname as "The Snake."

In 1962, Profaci died, yet the internal war with the Gallo brothers raged on under new boss Joseph Magliocco. Joe Gallo sought to pay back Persico's treachery with an attempted bombing and subsequent ambush. Persico escaped the bombing, though during the attack was shot multiple times. That was when Persico drove himself to the emergency room.

Persico soon went away on an extortion wrap. While the Snake was in prison, Magliocco failed in a bid to take over the Commission, prompting Joe Colombo to orchestrate a coup that brought him to the seat of power, renaming the group the Colombo Family. Persico was named a captain under the new regime and flourished upon his release from prison.

Persico gained more notoriety when mobster-turned-infamous-government-witness Joe Valachi singled him out in testimony for his involvement in multiple rackets, including labor-union infiltration, loansharking, gambling, extortion and more. It was Persico's ability to earn for the Colombo Family that rocketed him to the upper echelons of organized crime in New York.

Yet legal troubled dogged Persico. Following a succession of trials in the 1960s, he was sent back to prison for eight years on a hi-jacking conviction. In that trial, Valachi loomed once again as a key witness for the government.

On the streets, with Persico imprisoned, "Crazy Joe" Gallo on the loose, and family boss Joe Colombo paralyzed from a bullet fired at an Italian-American Civil Rights League rally in Manhattan, the Colombo family was in turmoil. Meanwhile, Persico was hit with an additional 37 counts stemming from a loansharking operation. A jury acquitted him on all charges. That tends to happen when terrified witnesses claim they can't identify the defendant.

With Colombo sidelined, and acting boss Joseph Yacovelli not the true power in the family, Persico's crew seized control. Cleaning up unfinished business, a Persico hit squad wiped out the Gallos in an infamous hit at Umberto's Clam House in Little Italy on April 7, 1972.

The following year, after 17 years in prison, the Snake's son, Alphonse "Allie Boy" Persico was released from prison and tapped as acting boss until his father was released six years later. Yet freedom was fleeting, as in 1981 Allie Boy pled guilty on conspiracy charges in a bribery case. He was sentenced to five more years in a federal lock-up.

Persico was released from prison, undisputed head of the family. Yet another indictment followed in 1984, on multiple racketeering counts aimed at the upper echelon of the Colombo family. A national manhunt kicked off when Persico went on the lam, and he was added to the FBI's "10 Most Wanted List." Persico was turned in by his cousin. He had been hiding at his suburban home in Wantaugh, NY. The following year he was indicted, along with the heads of the other New York families, and successfully prosecuted as part of the epic "Mafia Commission Trial."

In 1986, he received a 39-year sentence from one trial, and a 100-year sentence on the Commission case. The sentences were to run consecutively, pretty much eliminating Carmine Persico's chances to ever see the light of day as a free man.

Still, Persico continued to pull the strings on the streets for years to come, including the epic "Colombo Family War" of the 1990s.

Persico is currently housed in the federal prison in Butner, North Carolina, with a release date of March 20, 2050.

He would be 117 years old.

28
Dominick Napolitano – Sonny Black

Dominick "Sonny Black" Napolitano's nearly *made* Federal Bureau of Investigation (FBI) agent Joseph D. Pistone, a.k.a. Donnie Brasco.

Allowing Pistone to infiltrate his wing of the Bonannos in the late 1970s through early 1980s cost Napolitano his life. The embarrassing debacle was retold in the hit film "Donnie Brasco," starring Johnny Depp as Pistone and Michael Madsen in a sinister star turn as the Bonanno captain Napolitano.

While Madsen delivered a classic performance, it must have been difficult to truly recreate Napolitano's horror when FBI agents revealed that one of his most-trusted soldiers, privy to scores of scores, was not just a snitch, but an undercover FBI agent.

Pistone got very close to Sonny Black. They partied together, played tennis, socialized. Pistone was even invited up to Napolitano's inner sanctum atop the Brooklyn black tar roofs where he raced his prized pigeons, a passion of several aging Brooklyn gangsters.

For Napolitano, it was more than the realization that Pistone's testimony would cripple the Bonanno family for years to come, and destroy his crew. More ominously, he knew someone had to be held accountable for inviting this disaster.

And he knew that someone had to be him.

Until that point, Napolitano enjoyed a successful run in organized crime. Born and raised in Williamsburg, Brooklyn, "Sonny Black" didn't get his nickname for dark, dastardly deeds. Born blonde, his hair turned grey prematurely, hence Sonny's need to dye it black. Yet make no mistake, while Napolitano may have been vain, he was still a vicious criminal. You don't rise to the rank of capo in a crime family without being a hardcore gangster.

A rival of future family boss Joseph Massino (the first seated five-family boss to turn government witness), Sonny Black ran his end of the Bonannos from a powerbase in Brooklyn, with a satellite spinoff in Florida that he negotiated with legendary sunshine-state boss Santo Trafficante, Jr.

Napolitano ran his crew from the Motion Lounge and the Italian-American War Veteran's Club, both on Graham Avenue in Williamsburg, Brooklyn, as well as The King's court, a nightclub in Holiday, Florida. By the time the Pistone bombshell exploded in his face, Sonny Black also had a sizable gambling business in Orlando.

Napolitano was a soldier loyal to the faction of the family run by future boss Phillip "Rusty" Rastelli. After the assassination of Carmine "The Cigar" Galante, Rastelli's rose to lead the *family*, and the loyal Napolitano was raised up to captain. However, despite Rastelli's status as seated boss, there was dissention in the ranks from a rival faction in the family, led by captains Alphonse "Sonny Red" Indelicato, Dominick "Big Trin" Trinchera and Philip Giaccone. Napolitano and Massino, both capos under Rastelli, conspired on a triple homicide that wiped out the three rival captains in an epic ambush.

Napolitano's fatal error was in allowing Pistone to get so close to him. He planned to have Pistone inducted into the Bonanno Family. Pistone was only taken out of action when he received a direct order from Napolitano to murder a fellow wiseguy.

There is a classic FBI surveillance picture taken of Napolitano just after the FBI visited The Motion Lounge and wiped the smirk off his smug face by slapping down multiple pictures of Joseph Pistone, the agent, not Donnie Brasco, the gangster. In a surveillance photo taken right after the encounter, Napolitano's troubled face is one of betrayal and bewildering disbelief.

In the wake of the Pistone revelation, Bonanno capo, and Napolitano rival, Joe Massino engineered Napolitano's death. In the end, Sonny Black knew it was coming. Summoned to a sit-down, Napolitano slid his watch and jewelry to the bartender of The Motion Lounge, as well as the keys to his apartment.

Someone would have to feed his pigeons.

They drove Napolitano to a home in the Flatlands section of Brooklyn. As he entered, he was shoved down the stairs. Bonanno captain Frank Lino and family associate Ron Filocomo opened fire.

When the first volley failed to kill him, Napolitano didn't cower in fear.

"Hit me one more time and make it good." And that's exactly what they did. His body was later discovered out on South Avenue in Staten Island.

His hands had been cut off, an old Mafia warning about introducing the wrong people into the *family.*

27
Yasser Ashburn – The Folk Nation

For nearly a decade, Yasser Ashburn – a.k.a. Supa Swerve 6 – lay siege to the Ebbets Field Houses in Crown Heights, Brooklyn, until the dismantling of his violent drug gang in 2011.

As "Big Homie," or lead shot-caller for the vicious Six Tre Folk Nation gang, Ashburn led a running battle against a rival Crips set that littered the streets with dozens of dead and wounded on both sides.

Years before Ashburn led the Six Tre to war, he made headlines in 1999. Fifteen years old at the time, Ashburn was charged in the stabbing death of another Brooklyn youth, resulting from a fight during a pick-up basketball game. Ashburn walked on that count, acquitted by a second jury after the first failed to return a verdict.

In the years that followed, Ashburn and his crew terrified residents at the Ebbets Field Houses, notorious New York City public housing looming on the site where once sat the famous baseball field of the Brooklyn Dodgers. Prosecutors charged gang members with racketeering, drug trafficking and related crimes, including robberies, assaults and murders, within Brooklyn and beyond.

Following a dramatic three-week trial in Brooklyn federal court, Ashburn, along with lieutenants Jamal Laurent and Trevelle Merritt, were all found guilty on numerous counts.

This included the murders of Courtney Robinson, Brent Duncan, and Dasta James.

Following the verdict, Loretta E. Lynch, United States Attorney for the Eastern District of New York, stated:

"Today's verdict is a victory for the residents of the Ebbets Field Houses and the Brooklyn community. For far too long, the defendants and their fellow gang members terrorized this community, murdering innocent young men and committing other violent crimes in their attempt to control what they mistakenly believed was their turf. These defendants will now be held to account for their crimes."

Included at trial, the prosecutors focused on an incident on April 20, 2008, when Courtney Robinson jumped in to protect his nephew in a fight against Folk Nation during a birthday party in an apartment at the Ebbets Field Houses.

Ashburn left the party, returning shortly after with a gun.

He shot Robinson in the back, killing him.

The trial also covered the murder of 18-year-old Brent Duncan by gang member Jamal Laurent. Duncan, a member of a rival Crips set in Brooklyn, was killed during a robbery in 2011.

At the age of 33, convicted on murder and racketeering counts, Ashburn received two life sentences, with an additional 10 years added for good measure.

For his crimes, Jamal Laurent was handed five consecutive life sentences.

As for the Ebbets Field Houses, in a January 12, 2016 article in *The New York Post* entitled "Ebbets Field Apartments are getting a makeover," journalist Selim Algar wrote:

"The owners of the once-notorious Flatbush housing complex are renovating and rebranding the property in an effort to secure massive rent hikes in a rapidly gentrifying section of Brooklyn near Prospect Park. A marketing campaign, complete with slick videos touting proximity to the Brooklyn Museum and Botanical Garden, offers units ranging from $1,300 a month for studios to $2,500 for three bedrooms. The sprawling complex was once rife with gang and drug activity."

26

William Boyland Jr. - Corrupt Scion of Brooklyn Political Dynasty

William Boyland Jr. had it all.

Yet it seems the trust and adoration of his constituents was not enough.

The son of Brooklyn Democratic royalty rose to prominence in his own right. By 2003, Boyland secured the same seat in the New York State Assembly his father and uncle held before him, representing the people of some of the poorest neighborhoods in America.

It is a remarkable success story, if you exclude the latter chapters in Boyland's career.

Boyland's uncle first arrived in the Assembly in 1976, though died in office of a heart attack in 1982. His younger brother, Boyland's father, William Boyland Sr., went on to serve successfully for 20 years. Meanwhile, Boyland's sister, Tracy L. Boyland, served in the New York City Council, where she was appointed Chairwoman of the Women's Issues Committee.

Conversely, Boyland will go down in history as a corrupt politician who received one of the harshest prison sentences ever imposed on a lawmaker in New York State history. His descent in to the abyss was completed in 2014 when a federal judge slammed him with a 14-year prison sentence on bribery, extortion and fraud charges.

This was more than a politician behaving badly. To appreciate the level of betrayal, you need to know the district Boyland represented, the 55th Assembly District, one of the most disadvantaged areas of the country. These are the oft-notorious neighborhoods of Brownsville and Ocean Hill, and sections of neighboring Bushwick, East New York and Crown Heights. These are not affluent communities, but neighborhoods with desperately poor enclaves plagued with by crime, narcotics trafficking, and neglect.

They needed a champion to fight for them in Albany.

They got William Boyland Jr.

Boyland's stunning sentence followed years of suspicion, investigation and legal wrangling. In November 10, 2011, a bribery trial ended in acquittal. Boyland should have quit while he was behind. Yet only weeks later, on November 27, he was arrested on new charges, based on recordings capturing Boyland soliciting bribes, while still under indictment.

Boyland was for sale.

The assemblyman accepted thousands of dollars in cash bribes, filed phony expense reports to bilk the New York State Assembly, steered state contracts illegally to businesses and non-profits, and shook down local businessmen, trading favors for cash. He was not a passive participant, but aggressively pursued bribes, even advising bribers how to game the state-grant system, all for a price.

Boyland was even caught filing expense reports for inflated costs associated with the secret sessions with undercover agents, where he was soliciting more bribes.

While Boyland argued in court for a lighter sentence based on his service to the community, the government produced evidence of the opposite, including how he stole tens of thousands of dollars in funds that had been earmarked for the elderly, the most vulnerable segment of the people he was supposed to be championing.

Within days of his initial acquittal, Boyland was secretly recorded by undercover agents soliciting yet another bribe.

On March 18, prosecutors slapped Boyland with additional mail-fraud charges stemming from false expense reports. Boyland was acquitted of some charges, then successfully prosecuted on other bribery counts.

During the sentencing, in handing down the whopping 14-year-term, Judge Sandra L. Townes of Federal District Court in Brooklyn slammed Boyland at his sentencing, remarking on his lack of respect for the law. She added she was "not seeing any redeeming characteristics of the defendant."

Yet Townes actually cut Boyland a break, as prosecutors sought the 20-year maximum.

As per New York State Assembly rules, based on his conviction, Boyland was automatically stripped of his seat. Following a hotly contested special election in 2014, the vacant seat was won by Latrice Walker, a local Brooklyn attorney, longtime advocate for the people of Brownsville and former Counsel to U.S. Representative Yvette D. Clarke.

Boyland was not the only corrupt politician Brooklyn produced, but was certainly among the most brazen, and historically significant considering the length of his sentence.

25
Heriberto Seda - The Brooklyn Sniper

As far as anyone knew, Heriberto Seda was a 30-year-old high school dropout loser from Brooklyn. Seda, though, had grand aspirations.

Apprehended in 1996, Seda was tagged "The Copycat Zodiac Killer,"

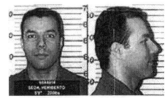

Heriberto Seda
Mugshot 1996

convicted of murdering three, wounding four.

The original Zodiac Killer, who terrorized Northern California throughout the late 1960s into the early 1970s, claimed up to 40 victims. That villain has yet to be apprehended.

Initially known as the "The Brooklyn Sniper," for his preferred form of serial homicide, Seda killed in spurts, first in the 1990s with a series of shootings. Seda then went dormant, remerging in 1992 for a longer spree that ended with his unexpected arrest in 1996.

Like the Zodiac Killer, Seda sent taunting letters to the media, starting with the less-than-subtle pronouncement "This is the zodiac ..." sent in 1990 to *The New York Post* newspaper and television news program *60 Minutes*. Seda added his own twist, signing his letters as Faust, the fictional character who sold his soul to the devil.

Police suspected initially that the letters were a hoax, yet after piecing together enough similarities from numerous crime scenes, they warned the public. The case grabbed headlines nationwide, placing the residents of Brooklyn on edge waiting for the next body to fall.

Following the flare up in 1990, the Zodiac Killer seemed to go underground, until *The New York Post* received a letter in 1994, claiming five more attacks, four of them fatal, reigniting the police investigation.

Seda's violent, unhinged nature was his undoing. During an argument with his half-sister Gladys Reyes, critical with her for her choice of unsavory friends, Seda shot Gladys in the rear. She escaped to a neighbor's apartment and called police.

After a stand-off in Brooklyn, with Seda exchanging gunfire with officers, he surrendered into custody. When Seda wrote down his account of the incident, eagle-eyed Detective Joseph Herbert noticed similarities between the designs Seda doodled and the letters from the Zodiac Copycat.

Gotcha!

Let's just say Seda wasn't exactly a master criminal.

From the zip-guns used in the attacks, seized from Seda's East New York apartment in Brooklyn, to fingerprint and DNA evidence on the letters sent to police, to the testimony of dozens of witnesses, the evidence against Seda was overwhelming. He was convicted of 17 counts, including murder, attempted murder, assault, weapons possession, and other crimes. A federal judge slammed Seda with 83 years and four months in prison.

Incarcerated in 1998 at the age of 30, Seda has yet to stand trial for several Zodiac Copycat-linked murders, though he will languish behind bars until he is eligible for parole, at the age of 113.

24
Louis "Pretty" Amberg – Inventor of the Sack Murder

They called him "Pretty," though Prohibition-era gangster Louis Amberg was anything but attractive.

As "Pretty" himself liked to tell it, one day on a Brooklyn street corner, a representative from the Ringling Brothers travelling circus offered him a job, as "The Missing Link."

Amberg loved to share that story.

No one knows exactly what happened to the Ringling Brothers' barker.

How dangerous was Pretty Amberg? When a psychopathic serial killer like Abe "Kid Twist" Reles says, "The word was that he was kinda nuts," you know you've descended pretty far into the abyss.

Amberg is notorious on numerous counts. He was suspected in no less than 20 murders, though crime historians speculate that body count may be as high as 100.

Amberg also had a reputation for eluding justice. Arrested dozens of times on suspicion, he was never convicted. Victims and witnesses who managed to survive the time between Amberg's arrest and trial never had the nerve to finger him in open court. That is, once they realized who he was and what he would do to them.

Amberg was much more than a murderer. Among some gangland historians, Amberg is considered the absolute worst Jewish criminal America ever produced, and was identified as such by author Maximillian Zellnerin in his book "The Book of American-Jewish Gangsters: A Pictorial History." (Published by CreateSpace; January, 2013.)

Among his claims to fame, Amberg is credited with inventing the so-called "Sack Murder," a particularly diabolical form of torture-homicide technique. Amberg restrained his victims by binding them with a long single strand of wire connected around their legs, arms and neck. He then placed them in a sack, hence the name. Struggling to break free from the painful binding, the victims strangled themselves, in a most bloody and painful manner.

Discovering these bloody sacks was quite gruesome work for investigators.

The brutal tale of the life of Pretty Amberg is reflective of his era. Born in 1897 in Russia, Amberg arrived on American shores as a young boy. His poor family settled in the predominately Jewish section of Brownsville, Brooklyn. His father was a fruit peddler, a trade Amberg appropriated, but with a twist. He went door to door, banging until the residents opened, then threatened them with violence and arson until they bought. By his teens, Amberg was the scourge of Brownsville.

Pretty Amberg later received mythic notoriety, when famed newspaperman and author Damon Runyon wrote of him, recounting how the gangster purchased a laundry business, because he needed sacks to dispose of his corpses.

As he grew in age and rage, Amberg and his brothers – Oscar, Joseph and Hyman "The Rat" – vied with other major criminal groups of Prohibition-era Brooklyn, including Jacob "Gurrah" Shapiro, "Little" Franke Teitelbaum, Louis "Lepke" Buchalter and the Shapiro Brothers (no relation to Gurrah).

As the 1920s wore on, Amberg's despicable reputation grew, based in no small part to his awful behavior in public. At restaurants, he was known to spit in strangers' food for kicks. If they complained, he stabbed them in the face with a fork. In fact, he stabbed famed-comedian Milton Berle in the face, after Berle insulted Amberg during his act at the Vanity Fair Club.

In addition to labor racketeering, the Amberg brothers ran a lucrative loan-sharking ring, preying on the Jewish immigrants who could not secure loans from financial institutions. They charged an unconscionable 20 percent interest rate, per week. Amberg personally dealt with delinquent debtors, sending just the right message on Brooklyn's streets.

When Prohibition became the law of the land, Pretty Amberg graduated to bootlegging and was very protective of his turf. One day, famed gangster Jack "Legs" Diamond approached Amberg about a partnership. Diamond broached the subject of visiting Brownsville, to which Amberg responded, "We'll be pals, Jack, but if you ever set foot in Brownsville, I'll kill you and your girlfriend and your missus and your whole damn family."

Dutch Schultz offered to come in as a partner, which basically meant Schultz was positioning for a takeover. Amberg warned, "Why don't you put a gun in your mouth and see how many times you can pull the trigger?" When Schultz sent some of his goons to set up shop a block away from an Amberg operation, they were assassinated within 24 hours, sparking the short-lived Schultz-Amberg War.

Pretty's brother Joey Amberg was the first victim of that gangland conflict, ambushed on September 30, 1935, along with his driver, in a garage on Blake Avenue in Brooklyn.

Schultz was the next to go, though not at the hands of the Ambergs. He was bumped off by the Luciano-Lansky combination in October 23, 1935.

Later that same evening, at 1:35 AM, Pretty Amberg's naked, mutilated corpse was discovered in a burning car near the Brooklyn Navy Yard. It took days to identify the badly burned corpse.

As for who killed Pretty Amberg, pick a suspect. Schultz may have ordered the hit, though it may have been Murder, Inc. filling a contract put out by Luciano. A third theory is that he was bumped off by previous partners he chiseled out of the proceeds of an armed robbery.

Fittingly, when police found Amberg's body, his hands and feet were bound with wire.

23
Carmine Galante - The Cigar

In the underworld, sometimes a picture is worth a thousand headlines.

Crime-scene photographs are shockingly brutal, yet nothing so elegantly articulates the savagery of a life of crime and its mortal consequences. One such frozen fatality found in Brooklyn's criminal archives was captured when a quaint eatery in Bushwick, Brooklyn, on July 12, 1979, exploded into one of the most infamous crime scenes in mob history.

It was an ordinary summer afternoon on a Thursday, a bit before 3PM. Bonanno crime boss Carmine "Lilo" Galante was finishing his lunch at Joe and Mary's Italian-American Restaurant, located at 205 Knickerbocker Avenue, just a couple blocks off Flushing Avenue. Galante's nickname "Lilo," or "The Cigar," reflected how he was so often seen with a cigar clenched in his jaws.

Joining Galante that afternoon were Bonanno capo Leonard Coppola, and solider and restaurant-owner Giuseppe Turano, who also happened to be Galante's cousin. Seated at another table were two bodyguards, Baldassare Amato and Cesare Bonventre.

Carmine Galante Mugshot 1943

Little good they would be for Galante that day.

It's a bit surprising, even reckless, that Galante was dining in the open air-patio of the restaurant, even if he was surrounded by armed underlings. Galante was not exactly popular that summer, muscling in on drug operations, engaging in profit-sharing disputes with ganglords from other families and feuding with a host of dangerous characters.

Yet that's just the type of brash Mafioso Galante was since his youth.

Born in 1910 in East Harlem, Galante was an intense, troubled young man, sent to reform school at the age of 10 following early brushes with the law. As he grew, young Carmine only got worse. Dropping out of school to run with the Italian street gangs on the Lower East Side of Manhattan, by the time Galante was in his early 20s, he was in prison, where he was diagnosed as psychopathic.

In the ensuing years, Galante spent several years in and out of prison on assault raps. At one point, Galante nearly went away for a longer bit for the murder of a police officer during a botched armed robbery, though he avoided a lengthy sentence due to lack of evidence.

During a subsequent hold-up, though, where another police offer was wounded, as well as a young boy, Galante was forced to plead guilty to attempted robbery. He received a 12-year sentence that kept him off the streets until 1939. By the time he was released, Galante was a hardened criminal and diagnosed psychopath, with a violent temper and well-earned reputation for violence. He served as a hitman and muscle for Vito Genovese, underboss of the Luciano Crime Family, though he later aligned with another Mafia family, the Bonannos.

A one-time driver for mob boss Joseph Bonanno, Galante was dispatched to Montreal, Canada, to run a heroin-distribution ring. Deported from Canada back to the United States, Galante's involvement in the drug trade continued, leveraging his Sicilian Mafia connections.

By 1958, Galante was on the run, evading arrest on drug-tracking charges. He was picked up on the Garden State Parkway the following year.

Following a mistrial, during a subsequent trial Galante was handed a 20-year sentence in 1962. Within days of his release 12 years later he ordered a bomb planted at the doors of the mausoleum of his hated rival, Frank Costello. Then after Bonanno boss Philip "Rusty" Rastelli went to prison, Galante made a power grab, considering himself the rightful heir to the Bonanno throne.

In the ensuing years, Galante engaged in a running rivalry with the Gambinos, knocking off at least eight of their members, while he continued his drug trafficking before being sent back to jail on a parole violation in the late 1970s.

Waging a high-profile campaign to grab as much of the lucrative drug trade as he could, Galante drew much unwanted law enforcement attention to organized crime.

Moreover, Galante never cooperated easily with his peers in the other New York Mafia families and the plot found widespread Commission support. Genovese boss Frank Tieri initiated the plot to take down Galante. The conspirators soon found willing collaborators among dissenters from within Galante's own organization, disgruntled with the Don's tight-fisted treachery. Not only did Rastelli want Galante out so he could resume his position at the top the Bonanno Family tree, even the exiled former boss Joe Bonanno gave the nod.

Galante's long and winding road was about to come to its end at Joe and Mary's Italian-American Restaurant in Bushwick on that summer afternoon in 1979. Smoking his trademark cigar, Galante was startled when three assassins wearing ski masks stormed in and opened fire.

Afterwards, a photographer captured one of the most iconic images ever taken of a mob assassination, depicting Galante's disheveled corpse, sprawled amidst strewn furniture and piles of broken plates, a cigar still clenched in his jaw. The scene ranks up there with other important mob rubouts, like Crazy Joe Gallo at Umberto's Clam House in Little Italy and Paul Castellano outside Sparks Steak House in Midtown Manhattan.

Turano and Coppola were also gunned down by the assassins. Mysteriously, Galante's Sicilian bodyguards did nothing, sitting stoically as the hitmen opened fire, according to witnesses.

They were not even wounded in the attack.

Interesting.

Supposedly, Alphonse "Sonny Red" Indelicato, a caporegime in the Bonanno family, ordered the hit, carried out by a squad including Anthony Indelicato, Dominick Napolitano, Dominick

Trinchera, and Louis Giongetti.

Later, chucking another conspiracy theory onto the pile, as chronicled in Philip Carlo's excellent 2006 gangland book "The Ice Man: Confessions of a Mafia Contract Killer," notorious contract killer Richard Kuklinski also took credit for the murder.

Regardless who gunned down Galante, he hastened his demise through avarice as much as arrogance, and his truly self-destructive tendencies.

22
Israel Narvaez - The Mau Maus

If a gang leader sees the light, converts to Christianity and dedicates his life to inspiring younger people to avoid the mistakes he made, does that redeem him?

Ask his victims.

Or, ask the survivors, the family members, the friends, the children.

Israel Narvaez is one such story of redemption from that sullied era in the 1950s when gangs overran Brooklyn's streets – a period when prison, drugs and violence claimed the lives of a generation of our young men and women.

Gang-leader Narvaez not only got a second chance at life, he wrote a classic book on escaping the streets titled, "Second Chance: The Israel Narvaez Story."

Long before the best-seller hit bookstores, Narvaez was a ruthless gang leader terrorizing the streets of Brooklyn, one of the founders of the Mau Maus, a violent Puerto Rican gang that gained notoriety in the 1950s.

Narvaez cut his criminal teeth in a gang called the Apaches. When that outfit splintered under the weight of heroin addiction and infighting, Narvaez defected, aligning with an African-American gang in the Fort Green public housing projects called the Chaplains. They granted his franchise request to spin off the Mau Maus, initially dubbed the Mau Mau Chaplains.

This was mid-1950s Brooklyn and gangs were everywhere, carving out their patches of black tar and broken concrete with blades, bats, and bullets. Narvaez was in the thick of the violence, best friends with Nicky Cruz, another infamous gang lord from that period. The potent partnership of Narvaez and Cruz powered the rise of the Mau Maus and they waged bloody turf battles with rival factions from 1956 through 1958.

Then one day Narvaez and Cruz crossed paths with street preacher David Wilkerson soapbox-speaking from a Brooklyn corner in the summer of 1958, pleading with them to embrace Jesus and abandon gang life. The message resonated with Narvaez, for a time. Afterwards, Cruz remained with Christ. But for Narvaez, the call of the streets was too strong. Before long he was back in Brooklyn pounding the pavement harder than ever as undisputed sole leader of the Mau Maus.

That winter, Narvaez and several Mau Maus became embroiled in a high-profile incident held up by the media as a bellwether warning of just how bad the racial gang fighting had gotten on the streets of New York. Gang murders were nothing new. But something about the audacity of this attack struck a chord in the city.

Anthony Lavonchino was a member of the Sand Street Angels, an Italian gang from nearby Farragut frequently at odds with the Mau Maus. Not long before that day, February 23, 1959, Lavonchino set upon Tico, a loyal Mau Mau, for the crime of strolling with Lavonchino's sister.

In retaliation for that beating, Narvaez and other gang members, including Carl Cintron, Carlos Reyes, and Melvin Torres, struck back in a big way, ambushing Lavonchino in front of the Brooklyn Paramount Theater, just as a movie was letting out. Shot in the head, Lavonchino died at the scene from his wound.

Cintron was collared as the shooter and the other Mau Maus were soon in custody.

For his role in the killing, Narvaez was sentenced to four-and-a-half years in prison, providing plenty of time to reflect on gang life. Upon release, Narvaez found his way back to the Christian faith, while publishing his best-seller about his life on the unforgiving streets of Brooklyn.

Today, Narvaez is a pastor and motivational speaker for a ministry he founded in Everett, Washington, geographically located about as far west of Brooklyn in the continental United States as you can get before stepping into the Pacific ocean.

21
Anthony Spero – The Old Man

No one did more to perpetuate the myth that the mob kept the peace in Brooklyn than Anthony Spero.

Spero loved Brooklyn.

Spero sponsored an annual July 4th public display of affection in Bath Beach, featuring a buffet and fireworks display choking the boulevard of Bath Avenue with the smoke of tens of thousands of dollars' worth of explosives. (Among his many rackets, Spero had a big summer sideline peddling illegal fireworks.)

Spero loved birds.

He was an ardent practitioner of the urban sport of pigeon racing across the uneven black-tarred rooftops of Bath Beach and neighboring Bensonhurst.

Yet there was so much more to Anthony Spero than being a big Brooklyn booster.

When not racing pigeons or passing out fireworks, "The Old Man," as the long-time Bonanno crime boss was known on the streets, was a vicious gang lord, with a small army of foot soldiers filling out his Bath Avenue crew. Spero was a thief, a drug dealer, a labor racketeer and a murderer.

How ruthless was Anthony Spero?

During Spero's federal racketeering trial in 1999, Alphonse D'Arco, former underboss of the Lucchese crime family, testified of a conversation he had with the Old Man in the early 1990s discussing Mafia informants. According to D'Arco, Spero said that not only should they whack the rat, but his entire family, including children, should be murdered to send a message.

The myth that the mob kept the streets of Brooklyn safe is a falsehood. Spero and his brutal brethren were not protecting the people of Kings County, but fleecing them and flooding their streets and schools with drugs.

Coming out of the 1970s, organized crime still had a stranglehold in Brooklyn. Young men from blue-collar backgrounds dropped out to replenish the ranks of the various crews competing for the corners of Brooklyn. Crime was up across the board, from car theft to burglaries to murders. When drugs hit the streets in a big way in the 1980s and 1990s, it was a disaster for Brooklyn.

Men like Spero profited on the pain of thousands of families broken by the drug epidemic.

Spero was formerly inducted into the Bonanno crime family under the regime of Carmine "Lilo" Galante on June 14, 1977. Future boss Joseph Massino attended Spero's induction ceremony in Brooklyn. Spero was a Galante disciple and thrived as a soldier, and later consigliere, as well as two-time acting boss of the *family*.

In 1984, in one of the most highly publicized mob murders in history, Galante and a bodyguard were murdered at Joe and Mary's Italian-American Restaurant in Bushwick, Brooklyn. In the aftermath of that hit, Phillip "Rusty" Rastelli was raised to boss, Spero to consigliere. By 1987, with both Rastelli and underboss Massino incarcerated, Spero was named acting boss of the *family*.

Throughout the 1990s, the murderous Spero engineered a series of killings that came back to haunt him in court. In 1990, he ordered a hit on Louis Tuzzio, a Gambino associate who had fumbled a murder contract for the Bonanno family. The next year, he again ordered a slaying, this time the target was Vincent Bickelman, a street thug who had the dimwitted idea to burglarize the home of Spero's daughter, Jill. In his defense, Bickelman didn't actually know he was knocking over the home of the beloved daughter of a mafia boss.

Later, Spero ordered the murder of the man he had bump off Bickelman, Paul Gulino, a low-level associate in the Gambino's Bath Beach crew, who overstepped when he assaulted a family capo.

Spero ordered many more murders, despite being locked away on a two-year prison stint for gambling in the mid-1990s. With his rise in the rackets came increase notoriety. A federal investigation led to 2001 convictions for Spero in the Tuzzio, Bickelman and Gulino murders, as well as assorted racketeering charges.

At 73 years old, The Old Man was sentenced to life in prison, where he died six years later at the Butner Federal Correctional Complex in North Carolina.

Today, due to the hard work of law enforcement, most of the wiseguys have retreated, died, or disappeared from Bath Beach. For the most part, the once-thriving social clubs and street corners where these criminals congregated, on 13th Avenue, 18th Avenue,

Bath Avenue, 11th Avenue, and parts of Staten Island, they're all gone now.

The taxpayers should know that protecting them on the streets of Brooklyn are the men and women of the New York City Police Department, the Drug Enforcement Agency, the Federal Bureau of Investigations, and other law enforcement units. They are the best of the best.

That's who keeps your Brooklyn streets safe.

20
Devernon LeGrand – The Reverend

This was a different kind of crime family.

Though they called him "The Reverend," there was nothing holy about Devernon "Doc" LeGrand and the house of horrors he kept in Crown Heights, a four-story home at 222 Brooklyn Ave.

From the outside looking in, during the early 1960s LeGrand was the pastor of St. John's Pentecostal Church of Our Lord. But behind those heavy doors LeGrand led a depraved cult.

LeGrand lured young women into the church, who investigators characterized as concubines. LeGrand dispatched them daily across the city to panhandle. These habit-adorned young women became a regular recognizable 1960s NYC fixture in many neighborhoods.

When they returned each night to LeGrand's "House of Horrors," as it was dubbed by *The New York Post*, the women were forced to take dangerous narcotics, including Angel Dust, the hallucinogenic drug phencyclidine (PCP). Having since fallen out of favor due to harsh side effects, PCP produces intoxication, hallucinations, and euphoria in low to moderate doses, as well as suicidal impulses, aggressive behavior, convulsions and seizures.

The drugged women were sexually abused and raped on a regular basis.

On the first floor of the multi-story building on the corner of Brooklyn Avenue, LeGrand preached, calling himself "the Bishop," while upstairs the women and children were imprisoned in a warren of small makeshift rooms. Many of the children were kept in cages, starved, beaten.

LeGrand fathered 46 children with his victims, and the panhandling brought in more than a quarter of a million dollars a year. With those ill-gotten gains, LeGrand purchased the Crown Heights property and funded construction of a compound on 58 lush acres in Sullivan County in upstate New York.

LeGrand paid cash, much of it in rolls of panhandled coins.

According to eye-witness testimony from victims and neighbors, there was always a wild party raging within the walls of 222 Brooklyn Avenue. But by the mid-1970s, the party seemed over, as the cult began to unravel during a series of trials.

In 1975, LeGrand and his son, Noconda, were convicted of first-degree rape for the vicious assault of a woman who barely escaped with her life. That was followed by a 1977 conviction in the beating death of two teenage sisters LeGrand lured into his nightmare. LeGrand and his stepson killed the two innocent girls, before dismembering the bodies, fearing that they would testify against him in an upcoming case on the earlier rape charges.

Later that year LeGrand was also convicted of murdering and cutting up the body of his daughter-in-law. Gladys Stewart, married to another LeGrand stepson, was cooperating secretly with prosecutors when she tried to leave her husband. LeGrand and his stepson attacked her, along with her 16-year-old sister.

During the next two hours, LeGrand sent his members down to a room on the first floor while he and his stepson tortured and stomped the two sisters to death, as the others listened in horror.

They sang hymns to drown out the screams.

LeGrand was slapped with a 25-years-to-life sentence for the rape and three murders. After serving the initial 25-year sentence, LeGrand came up for parole first in 2001, denying his guilt and insisting he was the victim of lying witnesses.

Locked away in the remote Shawangunk Correctional Facility in Wallkill, NY, the unrepentant reverend was denied parole on multiple occasions.

Though LeGrand was convicted of three murders, more members of his flock are still missing. Investigators ripped up the floor in the basement of the building on Brooklyn Avenue on two separate occasions, though the search failed to yield additional bodies.

In 2006, Devernon LeGrand died in prison at the age of 82.

19
Justin A. Volpe – Abner Louima

"It's Giuliani Time!"

This incendiary slander set the city afire in 1997, *supposedly* uttered by racist police officers in the bowels of a Brooklyn precinct as they sodomized Abner Louima, a Haitian immigrant, with a broken-off broom handle.

This was exactly the opportunity left-leaning opponents of then NYC-mayor Rudolph Giuliani's aggressive quality-of-life policing policies needed. Those three words rocketed the case into the stratosphere, drawing civil rights activists like moths to a Molotov cocktail.

Yet those words were never said, at least not by NYC Police Officer Justin Volpe. They were offered by Louima, to the media. Louima later retracted the statement, but the fuse was lit.

Volpe, an NYPD officer charged to "Protect and Serve," as the NYPD's official motto prescribes, instead chose to Persecute and Sodomize. Torturing Louima in that vile manner in the 70th Precinct in Central Brooklyn, Volpe sickened not just the residents of the Midwood, Ditmas Park, and Prospect Park neighborhoods he was sworn to shield, but the rest of the nation as the headlines started pumping out.

In 1997, Abner Louima was a Haitian immigrant who had arrived in America six years prior, working as a security guard at a plant in the Flatlands section of Brooklyn. Out with friends on the night of August 9th, Louima stepped in the middle of a fight between two women at Club Rendez-Vous, a popular East New York nightclub. The situation escalated and the police from the nearby 70th Precinct were called in, leading to a confrontation. Volpe was one of the responding officers.

After a struggle in the club, Volpe claimed Louima struck him. He later retracted that accusation. Based on the trumped-up accusation, Louima was dragged down to the stationhouse, charged with disorderly conduct, obstructing government administration, and resisting arrest.

On the way to the 70th precinct house, Volpe and other officers beat Louima with nightsticks and radios. At the precinct house, Louima was strip-searched and tossed in a cell, where the beating continued. Then, in a bathroom of that station house, Volpe sexually assaulted the imprisoned, helpless Louima.

At trial, jurors heard of how Volpe strode through the station holding aloft the bloody, excrement-soiled weapon, as he snarked, "Took a man down tonight."

At Coney Island Hospital the following day, emergency-room

nurse Magalie Laurent suspected Louima's injuries were the result of police brutality and notified his family. The NYPD's Internal Affairs unit, charged with investigating such charges, launched a probe.

The assault required no less than three painful surgeries to repair injuries to Louima's colon, rectum and bladder. He was hospitalized for almost three months.

Within weeks of the attack, the word was out and thousands of protesters took to the streets, heralding the so-called "Day of Outrage Against Police Brutality and Harassment" march on the 70th Precinct on August 29.

Famed *New York Daily News* journalist Mike McAlary won a Pulitzer Prize in 1998 for his extensive reporting on the Louima case.

At trial, though Volpe initially pled not guilty to violating Louima's civil rights, he changed his plea to guilty midway through, in the face of insurmountable evidence. For his crimes, Volpe was sentenced to 30 years in prison, without parole, on December 13, 1999.

Later, NYPC Officer Charles Schwarz was convicted for participating in the assault in the bathroom and sentenced to 15 years in prison, though Volpe identified another officer, Thomas Wiese. Schwarz' conviction was overturned on appeal, though he was later convicted of perjury and handed five years.

Louima won an $8.75 million settlement from New York City in 2001, the largest such claim at the time.

18
Greg Scarpa –
The Grim Reaper

Organized crime figures thrive on inspiring fear – and on the streets in Brooklyn, the more gruesome, ghastly and ghoulish the reputation, the better.

Greg Scarpa Mugshot

Such is the case with career criminal Greg "The Grim Reaper" Scarpa, whose Mafia moniker conjures up scythe-wielding specters of evil personified – exactly the type of street cred needed to rise up the ranks of a crime family.

Scarpa was also known as "The Mad Hatter," a nickname not nearly as fearsome as "Grim Reaper," but enough to make other wiseguys look sideways. Yet Scarpa's unsuspecting criminal co-conspirators should called him "The Big Snitch," as for three decades he was an informant for the Federal Bureau of Investigation.

Born in 1928 in Brooklyn, this son of Italian immigrants got a rough start, forced to deliver coal at the tender age of seven. The rough experience hardened the young Scarpa.

Seeing his older brother Sal embrace the more lucrative and less-laboring path of crime, Scarpa idolized *the life*. By his teens, Scarpa was doing enough dirt to get noticed by Profaci-family solider Charlie LoCicero, who took the future gangster under his wing.

From running numbers to loansharking to shakedowns, Scarpa's knack of excessive brutality earned him a reputation, especially among delinquent debtors.

"Making his bones" for the Profacis by committing murder, Scarpa was "Made," or formally inducted into the family in 1950, then set about specializing in truck hi-jacking, leading to an early arrest in his career. Facing a lengthy prison term, Scarpa caved and agreed to become a government informant. Scarpa not only peddled the family secrets for his freedom, but received cash payments for his tips, nurturing a long and mutually beneficial relationship between Scarpa and his FBI handlers.

The tale of the Mad Hatter has a romantic twist, albeit a bit bizarre, when he swept 17-year-old Linda Diana off her feet. The only problem was, Scarpa, 35 years old at the time, already had a wife, Connie. Like many mobsters, Scarpa simply carried on the affair, setting up house with Linda in Brooklyn, even fathering two children, Linda and Joseph. (Watch the *Investigation Discovery* television series "I Married a Mobster," featuring both "Big Linda" and "Little Linda.")

By 1963, the Scarpa story took a wild turn, when the FBI earmarked him for an outrageous mission. Remember, the early 1960s was the height of the Civil Rights struggle in America, where huge swaths of the nation were still bitterly divided and paramilitary racist organizations such as the Klu Klux Klan held sway in the shadows. Scarpa was recruited by the FBI to go down to Mississippi and locate the bodies of three slain Civil Rights workers, by any means necessary. Their disappearance was the focus of the hit film "Mississippi Burning."

Supposedly, after Scarpa returned, the bodies were located.

In the ensuing years, Scarpa led a charmed life eluding prosecution. His reputation as the most ruthless mob executioner in New York grew with his murder count. And little did everyone know, he remained on the streets because of his cooperation with the FBI. That bloody bliss would not last forever.

In 1986, Scarpa was hospitalized, requiring surgery for a hiatal hernia, and required an emergency blood transfusion. He rejected pre-screened blood from the hospital, not wanting the blood of an African American coursing through his veins. Instead, Scarpa received a transfusion from one of his underlings with a matching blood type.

It was a fateful decision that cost Scarpa his life, as that contributing gangster was a bodybuilder who shared dirty needles, contracting HIV that he passed along to Scarpa in the transfusion during the operation.

Back on the streets, Scarpa was soon thrust into the spotlight. With Carmine "The Snake" Persico jailed for life following his conviction in the Commission Case, acting boss Vic Orena attempted to take over the family, initiating the Colombo Family War of the 1980s that would claim a dozen lives. Scarpa flourished as a daring gunman racking up plenty of bodies for the victorious Persico side.

In 1993, Scarpa's body ravaged by his disease, suffering from full-blown AIDS, he pled guilty and was convicted on multiple counts of murder and racketeering.

Wasting away, Greg Scarpa died from the disease less than a year later in a federal prison in Minnesota.

17
Frank Abbandando – The Dasher

Nicknames are funny things.

When he was young, fleet-footed Frank Abbandando from Brooklyn was so quick playing baseball they called him "The Dasher."

That wasn't on some peewee sandlot team, but on the 1928 team at the Elmira reformatory in upstate New York. The 18-year-old Abbandando was serving a stint for nearly kicking to death New

York City police officer Hampton Ferguson.

Ferguson had attempted to arrest Abbandando.

The *nerve*.

The speedy sobriquet took on a new meaning following Abbandando's release, who reinvented himself as a serial rapist who sprang out from the shadows to snatch up unsuspecting women down dark Brooklyn streets and alleyways.

Oh, there's more when it comes to the dastardly Dasher of Downtown Brooklyn.

Frank Abbundando Mugshot 1940

Apparently, rape was more of a diversion for Abbandando, whose primary predilection was as one of the more prolific contract killers for the infamous Murder, Incorporated, that group of psychopathic for-hire hitmen who did the bidding of the Mafia from their powerbase in Bushwick.

Born in Avellino, Italy, to Lorenzo Abbondandolo and Rosaria Famighetti, "The Dasher" dashed to America as a boy, part of a large family of 12. His life of crime started early on the poverty-stricken streets of Brooklyn, first as a petty thief and extortion artist, preying on the hard-working immigrant shopkeepers of the Ocean Hill neighborhood of Brooklyn.

After joining "The Ocean Hill Hooligans," a particularly violent street gang, Abbandando quickly rose until he was second only to the misnamed Harry "Happy" Maione. By his late teens, Abbandando had his hand in everything from gambling and loan sharking to extortion, armed robbery and, ultimately, murder.

The Dasher fashioned himself quite dashing, a clothes horse who spent lavishly on designer duds and luxury automobiles he drove around Ocean Hill and Brownsville looking for female victims to whet his rape fantasies and perverse sexual appetites. When he was done with them, he stabbed the poor women in the chest with an ice pick to eliminate any witnesses.

Throughout the 1930s, as the Italian Mafia rose to prominence with the organization of the Five Families in New York and the ruling Commission, Abbandando found a home with the Jewish gangsters of Murder, Inc. He alone is suspected in more than 30 murders for "The Combination," another nickname for that murderous crew of killers.

How much was a life worth to Abbandando? Apparently about $500, his going rate for homicide-for-hire, a sizable sum in Depression-era Brooklyn, though he often accepted less. Abbandando was also involved in a number of high-profile murders of the time, including the systematic dismantling of rival gang the Shapiro Brothers.

As the 1930s drew to a close, Murder, Inc. had outlived its usefulness, unable to outrun a massive body count that drew federal agents like flies on corpses down dark Brooklyn alleys.

Looking at a looming death sentence, gang leader Abe "Kid Twist" Reles rolled on his crew and agreed to cooperate with the government. Since the 1920s, Abbandando and Reles had collaborated on scores of scores, gleefully dropping many bodies together, including the killing of Brooklyn loan shark George Rudnick.

Suspected of sharing information with police, Rudnick was brutally stabbed 63 times with an ice pick by Abbandando. Reles testified that he personally assigned the Rudnick murder to Abbandando.

At trial, in a brash moment straight from a gangster classic, Abbandando took his position on the witness stand, leaned over and quietly threatened the judge.

Who does that?

For a psychopath who eluded prosecution for so long, Abbandando was flabbergasted when found guilty of murder, though his conviction was set aside on appeal. The following year at retrial, on April 3, 1941, Abbandando was once again found guilty of first-degree murder. He was sentenced to die in the electric chair.

While six more members of Murder, Inc. would be executed as a result of Reles' cooperation, Kid Twist mysteriously flew out a window of a hotel in Coney Island, dying upon impact. (Yes, that notorious snitch too made this list of "Brooklyn's Most Wanted.")

For Abbandando, it was too late. Already on death row at Sing Sing, the upstate New York prison in Ossining, the deadly Dasher was finally dealt his due on February 19, 1942.

16
Monya Elson –
The Russian Brigade

The streets of Brooklyn have been home to all kinds of criminal groups, from sets, squads and syndicates, to posses, packs, crews, cliques, crime families and "The Combination."

But in the 1990s Russian gangsters from Brighton Beach belched out a new type of criminal organization – a "Brigade." Or, more specifically, Monya's Brigada, named for international Russian crime lord Monya Elson.

In 1995, while on the run from investigators, Elson was nabbed in Italy, then later extradited back to New York to answer for his crimes. Charges included multiple mob murders, international narcotics trafficking, racketeering and much more.

For years, Monya's Brigade was the terror of "Little Odessa," the nickname given to Brighton Beach, as the seaside Brooklyn community boasts the largest Russian-born population in the world outside of the mother country.

Elson landed in New York at the tail end of the 1970s, riding a wave of immigration washing up on the shores of Brighton Beach. From credit card scams to counterfeiting to drug trafficking, armed robbery, and extortion, Elson and his Brigade built up a broad portfolio of criminal activity by the early 1980s.

In one scheme, Elson and an underling disguised themselves as Hasidic Jews and visited jewelry merchants. Posing as interested buyers, while Elson's partner distracted the diamond dealer, Elson swapped out the real deal for fake zircons. This was just one of many clever crimes Elson masterminded.

In more serious crimes, Elson was charged with murdering three Russian mob associates as well as the attempted murder of a fourth target. This included the father-son homicides of Vyacheslav and Alexander Lyubarsky, and Alexander Slepinin. All three murders were committed in 1992. The fourth charge, for attempted murder, was for the January 1991 car bombing of rival Russian mob boss Boris Nayfeld, who survived.

Elson's war with Nayfeld's organization brought Monya's Brigade increased notoriety. During tit-for-rat-a-tat-tat retaliatory strikes, Elson survived an ambush in front of his Sheepshead Bay home, catching several bullets, while his wife was shot in the face with dozens of shotgun pellets. She lived. His nephew also survived that attack, only to be gunned down later in the war in a shooting, also allegedly orchestrated by Elson's nemesis Nayfeld.

Surviving subsequent attempts on his life, and ducking indictments on murder charges and other counts, Elson fled Brooklyn for Europe, where he was tripped up in a money-laundering case in

Italy.

Elson was extradited to the United States, tried and convicted on the murder counts and other crimes, and sentenced to a lengthy prison term.

15
Romano Ferraro - The Predator Priest

They should have known the Reverend Romano Ferraro had a callous disregard for the feelings of children when he delivered a stunning sermon in 1986 that caused a national uproar.

During his sermon for religious-instruction students in the first-through-sixth grades at St. John Vianney Roman Catholic Church in Colonia in Middlesex County, Ferraro said Santa Claus did not exist and there never was a Rudolph the Red-Nosed Reindeer nor a North Pole.

Now was that *really* necessary?

The story made headlines and newscasts coast to coast. In a statement the church, the pastor of St. John Vianney, Rev. Francis J. Sergel, wrote, "'It is unfortunate that Father Ferraro in his zeal to emphasize the spiritual dimensions of our celebrations may have appeared to diminish the importance which many, especially children, attach to some of the cultural and secular aspects of this season."

What kind of monster would say such things to children? Two weeks after the Dec. 6th sermon, Ferraro took a leave of absence from the church for "personal and parochial" reasons. Unfortunately for the fiendish Ferraro's many victims, submarining St. Nick was the least of his transgressions.

Ferraro's lengthy, lurid career as one of the most prolific pedophile priests in American history began when he was ordained by the Diocese of Brooklyn in 1960.

It is not unusual for priests to be shuttled around from parish to parish. In fact, it is a fairly common practice. Like the military, the Catholic Church will reallocate its resources to balance staffing levels. When one priest retires or requests a transfer, another is relocated. Reassignments also help ensure the Gospel message doesn't grow stale.

However, then there is "Priest Shuffling," a shameful practice where Roman Catholic Church administrators reassign priests suspected or accused of child abuse, shuttling them off to another parish, hoping the problem goes away.

Lacking good conscience, church officials would not disclose the pedophile's past crimes to the new parish. They should have reported these predators and not unleashed them on new flocks of victims.

And certainly not 32 times.

That could mean Ferraro was the most shuffled priest in American history, but as the Catholic Church never kept records of the evil practice, we'll never know.

We do know that Ferraro's sick trail cut across six states (Florida, Missouri, New Jersey, New York, Rhode Island, and Vermont). In addition to the six dioceses – Brooklyn, New York, Rockville Centre, Metuchen (NJ) and St. Louis (MO) – Ferraro's prolific pedophilic criminal career including five stints as hospital chaplain. He was even a criminal abroad for time, let loose for a time on a parish in the Philippines.

If you were a young Catholic school boy or played in a Catholic Youth League in Brooklyn in the 1960s and 1970s, as I did, it's frightening to think this predator likely crossed your path. In that period, Ferraro was assigned to multiple locations in Brooklyn, including Holy Family (Flatlands Ave & Rockaway Parkway), Madonna Residence for the Elderly, Regis Pacis Votive Shrine (65th & 12th Ave.), St. Francis Xavier (Carroll St. & 6th Ave.), St. Joseph's (185 Suydam), St. Lucy's (Kent & Park Ave.), St. Rosalia's (63rd & 14th Ave.), as well as stops at St. Rose of Lima (in Far Rockaway), Parson's Manor (in Jamaica), St. Rita's (on Staten Island), St. Aloysius (in Queens), St. Francis Xavier (in the Bronx), and Wyckoff Heights Hospital in Queens).

They just couldn't get rid of this guy.

During his 42-year-career, he spent approximately 13 years on leave, including a 10-year mandatory sideline starting in 1973. Who knows what he was doing during those periods, but he did come back, and by 1983 he again had full access to parishioners of all ages.

A few years later Ferraro made his notorious "Santa is Dead" sermon, and not long after that, the accusations started to fly.

By 1988, the Catholic Church was fielding multiple charges regarding Ferraro and running for cover.

The Catholic Church made a six-figure settlement to make one case go away, even as others cropped up. All in all, Ferraro admitted in open court to sexually abusing "perhaps dozens" of young boys. The Catholic Church's shuffling of Ferraro 32 times helps corroborate that assertion, at the high end of the estimate.

Arrested in 2002 and convicted in 2004 in Massachusetts for raping a boy there, Ferraro is serving life.

There's a special circle of hell reserved for priests who prey on young children.

God willing, someday Ferraro will be shuffled there one day.

How the Mafia hath fallen.

Joe Massino Mugshot 2003

Doesn't Omerta, the Mafia's code of silence, mean *anything* anymore?

For Brooklyn Bonanno gang boss Joseph Massino, apparently not.

Some say Massino was the Last Don of the Italian Mafia in America, but he's better known for one of its firsts. Massino was the first *seated* boss of one of the Five Families to cooperate with the federal government.

Born in New York City on January 10, 1943, the murderous Massino first killed for the mob in his early 20s, fulfilling a contract put out on Bonanno family associate Tommy Zummo. By then, Massino was already a rising star in the *family*, developing a reputation as a solid earner and a prolific hi-jacker, often with his future brother-in-law Sal Vitale at his side.

In 1975, Carmine "The Cigar" Galante, then head of the family, rewarded Massino's loyalty, formally inducting him into the mob. Massino was sponsored for membership by mob-mentor and future-family boss Phillip "Rusty" Rastelli.

Later, Massino secretly delivered a request to the Mafia Commission on behalf of Rastelli, imprisoned at the time, requesting for permission to whack an out-of-control psychopathic Galante. With the Bonanno's renegade boss drawing intense heat for his reckless drug trafficking, and seeding resentment for his refusal to share the proceeds, the hit was sanctioned. Assassins gunned down Galante in broad daylight in an Italian restaurant in East York. Afterwards, Massino was elevated to captain in charge of his own crew. Rastelli spent nearly his entire tenure as boss of the family behind bars, save for two years of freedom.

In 1981, with a trio of Bonanno captains plotting Rastelli's fall, Massino orchestrate the now-infamous triple-homicide of Alphonse "Sonny Red" Indelicato, Dominick "Big Trin" Trincera and Philip Giaccone.

Not long after, Massino seized an opportunity to remove another *family* rival, fellow Bonanno captain Dominick "Sonny Black" Napolitano, after Napolitano proposed for membership a thief and Bonanno associate named Donnie Brasco. Brasco was actually active undercover FBI Agent Joseph Pistone. His infiltration of the Bonannos, facilitated by a friendship with Napolitano, rocked the family. Someone had to answer for the Donnie Brasco debacle.

Napolitano, Benjamin "Lefty" Ruggiero, who initially sponsored Pistone, and Anthony Mirra, also close to Pistone, were all murdered on Massino's house-cleaning orders.

When six Bonannos were rounded up in 1981 on evidence gathered by Pistone, Massino went on the lam when he got word he was next. Massino was charged *in absentia* with conspiracy to murder in the triple homicide of the captains, hijacking and other counts. Massino surrendered to authorities in July 1984. His racketeering trial began April 1986, with Massino implicated by the testimony of others, including Pistone.

In January 1987, Massino was sentenced to 10 years in prison. Rastelli received 12.

With consigliere Anthony "The Old Man" Spero the acting street boss and the incarcerated Rastelli in failing health, everyone knew underboss Massino was the real power in the family. He ran his criminal empire from behind bars, including ordering multiple murders, usually through his brother-in-law Sal Vitale.

Within days of the death of Rastelli, a sit-down of the family's captains officially elevated Massino to boss, at only 48 years of age. Vitale was promoted to underboss.

In the aftermath of the infamous Mafia Commission Case of the 1980s that swept away the leadership of New York's Five Families in waves of RICO indictments and life sentences, by 1991, Massino was being hailed as "The Last Don."

Massino instituted strict edicts on secrecy and ordered family members to keep low profiles, insisting his captains no longer meet. However, elevation to the pinnacle of the New York Mafia only made Massino more of a target for law enforcement. It did not take long for federal investigators to recruit a parade of underworld underlings to testify against Massino.

In a stunning betrayal, that included Sal Vitale, Massino's brother-in-law and trusted underboss, who flipped in 2003. Vitale, already imprisoned, was finally swayed when federal agents informed him that Massino put a contract out to have him murdered.

By 2004, convicted on multiple murder and racketeering counts, facing a likely death-penalty prosecution, Massino made a historic decision, agreeing to cooperate with the federal government, and even wear a wire.

As a family boss, Massino offered unprecedented access to the inner-workings of the Mafia. His cooperation helped put away dozens of gangsters, most notably the acting boss of his own family, Vincent "Vinny Gorgeous" Basciano, convicted in 2011.

During his testimony, Massino uttered, "I am hoping to see a light at the end of the tunnel."

After numerous trials, on July 10, 2013, citing Massino's poor health and cooperation, a U.S. federal judge resentenced Massino to time served and granted supervised release for the remainder of his life.

Massino has since escaped into the witness protection program.

13
Gus Farace –
Wanted By the Mob

There's a reason why organized crime groups prohibit targeting law-enforcement officials.

It has less to do with morality and more with mortality.

It simply brings down a world of heat and life-sentences.

In 1989, Costabile "Gus" Farace, Jr., brought drew such attention in a BIG WAY when he gunned down a federal Drug Enforcement Agent.

Before that fateful night, Farace was a bit player in a tiny corner of Brooklyn's sprawling underworld.

Born in Bushwick in 1960, Farace's family found their way to Staten Island when he was a young boy. As an unruly teenager, he joined a gang of local hoods, "The Bay Boys," and was arrested on a gun charge and then again later for forgery.

Farace's first major brush with the law came in 1979 when he and a mob of his Staten Island goons traveled into Manhattan's Greenwich Village, where they were supposedly propositioned by two young male prostitutes.

Instead of shrugging it off, Farace and his punk friends kidnapped the two innocent young men, drove them to Wolfe's Pond Park back in Staten Island, and then viciously attacked them on the beach. One victim was beaten to death, the other escaped by swimming out into the bay. That survivor later fingered Farace in a police line-up. Farace accepted a plea deal and was convicted of first-degree manslaughter, and sentenced to seven-to-21 years in prison.

While imprisoned, Farace struck up jailhouse friendships with various Italian gangsters, including Bonanno soldier Jerry Chilli. Upon his release in 1985, Farace threw himself into drug dealing, first peddling marijuana, before moving on to cocaine. By 1988, he was partners in Brooklyn with Gregory Scarpa, Jr., son of Gregory "The Grim Reaper" Scarpa, Sr., an infamous Colombo gangster and longtime secret FBI informer.

Then came that fateful night in the winter of 1989. Farace arranged a cocaine deal with Everett Hatcher, an undercover federal DEA agent. Hatcher lost contact with his backup team. They later found his body in his unmarked Buick ditched under an overpass in Staten Island. Hatcher had been shot in the head three times.

Farace was unaware Hatcher was undercover DEA, but he would soon learn, as would the rest of the New York Mafia. As Hatcher was the first DEA officer to die in the line of duty since 1972, the murder made national headline news.

Added to the FBI's 10 Most Wanted list, Farace's face was plastered on every newspaper and nightly newscast coast to coast, bringing intense heat down on the entire New York Mafia in the aftermath of the murder. The pressure was especially intense on the Brooklyn Bonannos, who hollered for Farace's head.

On the run, Farace surprisingly survived, flitting from safe house to safe house, staying one step ahead of government raids and head-hunting goons, eluding capture for months.

Farace's luck lasted through the summer and fall, until the evening of November 17, 1989, when his bullet-ridden corpse was found by police responding to a 911 call, in a car parked on 81st Street in Bensonhurst. Alongside the vehicle lay the wounded body of Bonanno associate Joseph Sclafani, who died in the ambulance on the way to the hospital.

In the made-for-TV movie version of the incident, "Dead or Alive: The Race for Gus Farace," Brooklyn's own Tony Danza played Farace.

Years later, on September 17, 1997, Mafia street soldiers James "Froggy" Galione and Mario Gallo copped pleas in court and admitted to murdering Farace. Both men served time and have since been released from prison.

12
Anthony Salvatore Casso - Gaspipe

Where do I start? There are so many reasons to bump Anthony "Gaspipe" Casso to the top of this list.

You'd be hard pressed to find another Brooklyn gangster with a more fearsome reputation. Casso left a bloody trail in his rise to power as the underboss of the Lucchese crime family. He could have been the don, but opted to place someone else in the line of government fire.

Anthony Casso (right) and Vittorio Amuso 1980s FBI Photo

Casso personally murdered or ordered the killing of dozens, including high-ranking mobsters like Frank DeCicco, Roy DeMeo, and Vladimir Reznikov. Casso engineered multiple attempts on the life of bitter rival and Gambino boss John "The Teflon Don" Gotti, none of which succeeded.

Casso was also amongst the most-senior Mafia members to cooperate with the government, AND he was chucked out of the witness program.

Born and raised in South Brooklyn, Casso was a child of Italian immigrants from Campania, Italy, who arrived before the turn of the last century. The son of a dockworker, Casso became a longshoreman, though his waterfront activity was far from laborious or legitimate. From an early age, Casso was influenced by his real-life godfather, Sally Callinbrano, a Genovese captain involved in the Brooklyn rackets.

A leader of the violent South Brooklyn Boys gang, Casso found a mentor, Christopher "Christie Tick" Furnari, a notorious Lucchese captain who ran his crew from "The 19th Hole," a mob hangout on 86th Street and 14th Avenue in Bensonhurst.

As a young man, Casso had a hand in everything from drug dealing and extortion to gambling and armed robbery. He notched his first attempted-murder indictment in 1961, which fell apart when the frightened victim refused to identify his attacker.

Like Alphonse "Scarface" Capone and Benjamin "Bugsy" Siegel before him, Casso was a criminal who hated his nickname. Gaspipe was a name he inherited from his father, who either used to carry a lead pipe for intimidation or to connect gas pipes as part of his occupation. Casso's father was not a career criminal, though Michael Casso had friends in the rackets. Throughout his life, the younger Casso loathed the nickname. But it was embraced by a mainstream media.

In 1974, the Lucchese Family inducted Casso into the organization, assigning him to crew captain Vincent "Vinnie Beans" Foceri, though Gaspipe would later transfer to Furnari's Brooklyn faction. During this period, Casso struck up a close partnership with Lucchese solider Vic Amuso. The two would rise together through the ranks of the Family.

When Furnari was tapped to step up to consigliere, or family counselor, he gave Casso the nod to take over his 19th Hole crew. In a surprising move, Casso declined the offer, instead pushing forward Amuso for the spot. Casso continued reporting directly to Furnari.

In 1985, Frank DeCicco of the Gambinos secretly contacted Casso. DeCicco reached out on behalf of John Gotti who was fermenting a plot to murder Paul Castellano, the family's boss.

Casso demurred, warning of the consequences of taking out a seated boss without permission from the ruling Mafia Commission. Subsequent to Castellano's assassination, when several members of the Gambino palace coup were gunned down, Gotti survived to assume the throne as one of the highest profile mob bosses in history.

In 1986, in the wake of the epic Commission Trial that landed life sentences for most of the leadership of the five New York Mafia families, Lucchese boss Anthony "Tony Ducks" Corallo knew his case was hopeless. Seeking a smooth transition of leadership to keep the family intact, Corallo tapped Casso for the acting-street-boss slot.

For the second time, Casso declined a leadership post, knowing that becoming the boss would make him a priority target for law enforcement. Also for the second time, he proposed Amuso in his stead. Amuso accepted the post in 1987. Casso served as Amuso's consigliere, and later underboss.

For all practical purposes, though, on the streets Casso answered to no one.

Casso lived the life of a gangster. While not as much of a media-magnet as Gotti, he was still under constant surveillance for much of his career. And while he may not have been loved by his underlings, he and Amuso were smart enough to spread the wealth and not impose overly harsh family taxes.

Meanwhile, Casso paved major inroads with other criminal organizations, including a crew of Greek gangsters operating in Brooklyn and Astoria. And, tapping into a massive gas tax scheme run by the Russian Mafia in Brighton Beach was among his most lucrative side projects.

In 1991, when Amuso was arrested on racketeering charges, Casso reluctantly accepted the bump up to street boss. With the feds on his tail, Casso masterminded multiple gangland homicides over the next couple of years, while conspiring with Mafia lion Vincent "the Chin" Gigante to assassinate Gotti. It was payback for Gotti's murder of Castellano without Commission permission. However, with Gotti under the FBI microscope, Casso's assassins could never get close enough to take him out.

Throughout the early 1990s the FBI's offensive against the Lucchese family resulted in round-ups of scores of gangsters, many who agreed to cooperate, quickly closing in on Casso and Amuso.

When Casso was arrested, a dramatic escape attempt was foiled. Then, Amuso banished him from the Lucchese family. Abandoned, alone, with former underlings tripping over themselves to testify against him, Casso accepted the previously unacceptable and decided to cooperate.

In March 1994, Casso pled guilty to the 72 counts on his indictment, including 15 murder charges.

Casso also revealed that he had two corrupt NYPD detectives working for him. The murderous, conniving Louis Eppolito and Stephen Caracappa became known as the "Mafia Cops." Responsible for multiple gangland murders and other crimes, that despicable duo was sentence to life in prison, in part based on information supplied by Casso.

Repeatedly violating the terms of his agreement with the government, Casso was expelled from the witness protection program.

With government support rescinded, Casso was hit with a 455-year-sentence and is currently serving his hard time in an undisclosed prison under an assumed name.

11
Albert Anastasia - The Lord High Executioner

In terms of piling up body counts, Albert Anastasia should top this list as the leader of Murder, Incorporated, the infamous hit squad operating out of a candy store in Brownsville, Brooklyn.

Depending on which crime historian you ask, within his 10-year-reign, The Lord High Executioner's "Brownsville Boys" are credited with 400 murders, though could have amassed as many as 1,000 cold-blooded killings.

Albert Anastasia
Mugshot 1930

Yet Anastasia wasn't always Brooklyn's maestro of murder,

"The Mad Hatter" was born Umberto Anastasio in a small village in Calabria, Italy. Orphaned at a young age, Albert jumped ship in 1919, sneaking into America with three of his nine brothers. He found work as a longshoreman along the rough Brooklyn docks.

By 1921 Anastasia was on trial for murder, stemming from a dispute where he beat to death fellow longshoreman George Turino. Sentenced to death and packed off to Sing Sing, Anastasia was saved by a technicality that sent him back for a second trial. When the primary witnesses refused to attend the trial, Anastasia was unleashed back onto the streets by 1922.

The witnesses just … disappeared.

Anastasia's liberty didn't last long. Convicted of possessing an illegal firearm in 1923, he was sent away for two more years.

Upon his release, now a seasoned criminal and bloodied murderer, Anastasia barreled headlong into the Brooklyn rackets, targeting the International Longshoremen's Association (ILA) until he had six chapters of the union under his thumb.

Remember, Anastasia cut his teeth in Brooklyn in the mob during the era of the Sicilian gang bosses, aligning himself with a powerful faction led by Giuseppe "Joe the Boss" Masseria.

As a young criminal, Anastasia befriended the young Turks in the mob, including the charismatic Charles "Lucky" Luciano, Benjamin "Bugsy" Siegel, Frank Costello, Meyer Lansky, Vito Genovese and others who became underworld giants. Anastasia joined forces with Luciano in the palace coup to unseat the old guard and install the modern-day Mafia, or La Cosa Nostra ("This thing of ours").

In a cunning ploy, the young guns pretended to side with Masseria-rival Salvatore Maranzano. Luciano requested a sit-down with Masseria in a seaside restaurant out in Coney Island. After Luciano excused himself to use the restroom, four gunman burst into the restaurant and opened fire, assassinating Masseria. Anastasia was one of the hitmen, joined by Genovese, Siegel, and Joe Adonis.

Maranzano was then eliminated in September 1931, paving the way for Luciano and his partners in crime to create the National Syndicate that included The Five Families in New York, and other satellite crime groups in many major US cities and regions. For his role in the rubout that won the war, Anastasia was named underboss of the Mangano crime family, a forerunner to the Gambinos.

To further reward Anastasia's loyalty, Luciano placed him and Louis "Lepke" Buchalter, a major leading labor racketeer, in control of what would become the Syndicate's enforcement arm, Murder, Inc.

The troop of mostly Jewish and Italian killers operated out of the back room of Midnight Rose's, a candy store owned by mobster Louis Capone in the Brownsville neighborhood of Brooklyn. Anastasia became known as the Lord High Executioner, the most feared hitman in the underworld.

Anastasia was dragged in by police many times on suspicion of murder, though investigators never made anything stick, usually due to the unwillingness of witnesses. And while many other members of Murder, Inc. were convicted and electrocuted, Anastasia escaped prosecution.

Luciano exited the picture in 1936, convicted on 62 counts of prostitution, jailed and then deported to Italy upon release.

As the body count rose, Murder, Inc. became a victim of its own success, a sinister cabal of killers drawing mainstream media and law enforcement. By 1941, investigators flipped Murder, Inc. member Abe "Kid Twist" Reles. Reles sold out his criminal associates to avoid the death penalty. The defection spelled certain doom for Murder, Inc., with everyone running for cover, including Anastasia.

As the indictments of his underlings piled up, Anastasia put out a $100,000 contract on Reles, though he was near-impossible to find, carefully stashed away by law enforcement between trial appearances.

In took until November of 1941 to track down the rat, when Reles was holed up in the Half Moon Hotel in Coney Island.

They say Reles fell to his death trying to escape out a sixth floor window.

Sure he did.

Once again, Anastasia escaped prosecution due to a lack of witnesses.

Anastasia was also noteworthy for helping to broker a deal between Luciano and law enforcement to help win the mob boss an early release in exchange for vital intelligence and assistance along the New York waterfront during World War II. At the time, acts of terrorism and sabotage were a real threat to American ports. Anastasia even joined the U.S. army and trained soldiers to go undercover and pose as longshoremen. He was granted citizenship during his stint in the army, receiving his honorable discharge in 1944.

Yet despite his wartime patriotism, Anastasia was a cold-blooded killer and ruthless gangster. His high-profile position in the mob prompted a subpoena to appear before the 1951 U.S. Senate Kefauver Hearings on organized crime.

In true mob fashion he pled the fifth, refusing to comment.

Anastasia orchestrated the murders of the upper echelon of the Mangano family, brothers Vincent and Philip. While never admitting the murders, he smoothed things over with the Commission, with the help of Frank Costello, and he ascended to lead the renamed Anastasia Crime Family.

In another interesting side story, Anastasia ordered the murder of Arnold Schuster, the man who fingered bank robber Willie Sutton. Anastasia did not have direct involvement with either men. But when he saw Schuster interviewed in the media, Anastasia supposedly said, "I can't stand squealers. Hit that guy." Sure enough, in March 1952, Schuster was found shot dead on the streets of Borough Park, Brooklyn, by none other than infamous mob rat Joseph Valachi, who went on the become the first Mafia inductee to publicly acknowledge the existence of the Mafia and the Commission.

Vying for control of the Luciano Family, Vito Genovese set his sights on eliminating Frank Costello, which also meant taking out Anastasia. In his campaign to undermine Anastasia and align support, Costello drew in Carlo Gambino, then a capo in Anastasia's family.

In 1957, a young thug named Vincent "The Chin" Gigante ambushed Anastasia outside his apartment, but only succeeded in wounding him. The murder attempted convinced Anastasia it was time to cede his power to Genovese. Yet Anastasia would not go quiet into that good night.

In one of the most epic mob-murder crime-scene pics, we see a lifeless Anastasia, slumped in the barber chair in 1957 October at the Park Sheraton, the shaving towel still covering his face.

Today his grave is a stop on the historic tour at Greenwood Cemetery in Brooklyn.

10
Roy DeMeo –
The Murder Machine

Roy Albert DeMeo never understood why he couldn't get ahead in the Brooklyn Mafia.

After all, throughout the 1970s and 80s, DeMeo was a virtual cash register for the Gambinos, funneling millions of dollars into the family from drug trafficking, loan sharking, car theft, gambling and extortion.

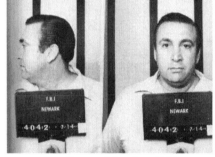
Roy Demeo Mugshot 1981

DeMeo assembled a hit squad the likes of which the Brooklyn underworld has not seen since the   days of Murder, Incorporated. DeMeo's cadre of killers was so prolific, notching upwards of 200 victims, the investigation was classified the longest serial-killer case ever worked by New York City law enforcement.

Cornering the Mafia market on creating cadavers, DeMeo's fiendish work was the focus of an exceptional best-seller by *New York Daily News* reporters Gene Mustain and Jerry Capeci, appropriately named "Murder Machine."

"Murder Machine" is a superb piece of crime reporting. It chronicled DeMeo's crew and their refined expertise "disappearing" a body, skills that earned them widespread recognition in the underworld, not to mention a steady stream of lucrative contracts.

Yet despite this success, the detestable DeMeo was despised by the upper echelon of the Gambinos.

Born in the Bath Beach section of Brooklyn in 1942, DeMeo was a chubby Italian kid with a head for getting ahead. Still in his teens, DeMeo launched his first criminal caper as a low-level loan shark, with a knack for numbers he spun into a prolific criminal career. DeMeo's ability to generate revenue for his bosses drew attention. As he built up a sizable loansharking book, he branched off into other crimes, such as orchestrating a highly profitable stolen-car ring.

DeMeo leapt into the arms of local Gambino hood Nino Gaggi, who rose to the position of *capo*, or captain, under the regime of boss Paul Castellano. As DeMeo's criminal portfolio expanded, he recruited young toughs from the neighborhood, forming a formidable crew of car thieves and killers.

One of the first murders orchestrated by DeMeo was a hit on Andrei Katz, a Brooklyn auto-body shop owner who ran afoul of the gang. (In Brooklyn at the time, auto theft was a rampant problem, with thieves stealing cars they disassembled, or "chopped," selling off the parts to shop owners like Katz.)

When DeMeo learned that Katz ran to the police, he marked him for murder. Katz was stabbed, shot and dismembered – a pattern DeMeo's murder machine perfected over time. Two DeMeo underlings were acquitted at trial of "disappearing" Katz.

In the years that followed, DeMeo's crew carried out scores of contract killings for other gang bosses. Their M.O. became known as "The Gemini Method," so-called for the Gemini Lounge, a Brooklyn bar that was the gang's de-facto clubhouse. Dozens of victims were killed and dismembered in an apartment attached to the bar.

The unsuspecting victim was drawn into the back room of the apartment, shot in the head with a gun equipped with a silencer. The head wound was covered immediately, and the heart stabbed to limit blood flow, making clean-up easier. The body was then stripped, drained of blood in the shower, then dismembered on plastic tarps. Many of the remains were buried in the Fountain Avenue dump, out by Pennsylvania Avenue off the Belt Parkway on your way out to JFK International Airport.

Investigators later abandoned a plan to excavate the remains, considering it too costly to dig up the dump.

DeMeo expanded his criminal portfolio into pornography, prostitution, drug dealing, gambling and more. Still, despite the flood of money DeMeo channeled upstairs, Castellano refused to induct him into the family, personally despising the chubby crew chief. DeMeo's whining became a constant source of frustration for Gaggi.

In 1976, Gaggi took over Castellano's Brooklyn crew when Big Paulie ascended the throne in the wake of the death of mob giant Carlo Gambino. DeMeo pushed even harder for membership, but Castellano held fast, considering DeMeo more of a street-level thug, and not mob management material.

Yet it was an alliance DeMeo brokered with the Westies, an Irish gang from Manhattan's Hell's Kitchen, which earned him his button. With the Gambinos drawing the Irish gang under their wing, including a 10 percent cut of all proceeds, Castellano relented and DeMeo was "Made." By then, DeMeo was deep into drug dealing, formally prohibited by Castellano, even as he accepted the large sacks of cash DeMeo's trafficking produced.

By the early 1980s, the FBI had a massive investigation underway to take down DeMeo and his crew of killers, throwing off more unwanted heat onto the Gambinos. That made DeMeo a paranoid mess. In fact, the feds learned that Paul Castellano had issued a contract on DeMeo, but there were no takers. That included John Gotti, who demurred, mainly because DeMeo was surrounded by a crew of homicidal maniacs.

Ultimately, someone did take the contract, likely someone in DeMeo's own crew.

Roy DeMeo was last seen heading to the home of crew member Patty Testa. Testa and Anthony Senter, the so-called Gemini Twins, probably assassinated DeMeo, though some say it was Richard Kuklinski, the infamous Ice Man, a prolific mob killer and frequent co-conspirator with DeMeo.

In the end, DeMeo was granted the same brutal treatment he and his henchmen doled out to so many of their victims. In January 1993 he was caught by surprise, shot and stuffed into the trunk of his car.

He was not found for a week.

The rest of the DeMeo crew was either murdered or indicted. To make matters worse, Dominick Montiglio, nephew of Nino Gaggi and a Gambino solider that worked closely with DeMeo, flipped and agreed to testify against the *family*. Montiglio was the main source of information for "Murder Machine," and his exploits make for a thrilling read.

Also a good read is "For the Sins of My Father," written by the murderer's son, Albert DeMeo, who thankfully did not follow in footsteps of his old man.

Most crime bosses shun the spotlight, for obvious reasons. Thumbing the eye of law enforcement motivates investigators to make examples.

It also justifies redirecting more resources to take you down.

Someone should have explained that to mob-boss Joe Colombo.

In the late 1960s and early 1970s, at a time when federal law enforcement was lobbying for more funding to attack organized crime, specifically to target anything-Mafia, Colombo should have practiced *Omerta*, or the ancient gangster code of silence.

But that's not what he did.

Not only did Joe Colombo dispute the existence of "The Mafia," at a time when he was the boss of one of the Five Families, but he mounted a high-profile counter-offensive, accusing law enforcement of discriminating against Italians and Italian Americans.

Then, in a disastrous misstep, he founded the Italian-American Civil Rights League and from this bully pulpit amplified his accusations again law enforcement.

Now, no one should dispute that Italians and Italian Americans have been the victims of discrimination and ugly typecasting, as have other ethnic groups in this country. But for a people looking to shed the stereotype that all Italians are somehow associated with the mob, having an actual mobster leading the charge is not really in their best interests.

Yet Colombo's movement took off, to the point that on June 29, 1970, more than 150,000 supporters swarmed Manhattan's

Columbus Circle to cheer on the League's first public rally.

Did I mention that, at the time, Colombo was a top crime boss?

Leading one of the largest criminal enterprises in America.

One of the so-called Five Mafia families in New York, that he renamed the Colombo Family after he took control.

Yes, this really happened.

Colombo even tried to shut down the filming of *"The Godfather."* In the early 1970s during Paramount's production of the film, Colombo not only staged Italian League rallies across NYC protesting the film, further behind the scenes his goons busted up the automobile of producer Al Ruddy, made threatening phone calls to Paramount executive Robert Evans, and called in multiple bomb threats to the studio's New York location.

You could say Joe Colombo was born into *the life*. His father, Anthony Colombo, was a soldier in the Profaci Family, the precursor to the Colombo Family.

Unlike the son, the father was not a significant gangster, and was murdered when Joe was a teenager growing up in Bensonhurst, Brooklyn. They found his father in his car, strangled to death, along with his mistress.

After two years at New Utrecht High School on 16th Avenue and 79th Street in Brooklyn, like many young toughs in the neighborhood, Joe dropped out of school. Instead of hanging out on the corners, Joe enlisted in the U.S. Coast Guard. He received a medical discharge in 1945 after being diagnosed with neurosis.

Returning to Brooklyn, Joe lived in a home in Dyker Heights, Brooklyn, a bit more affluent than neighboring Bensonhurst, as he embarked on a life of crime in the Profaci Family.

Rising to become a Capo in the Family, Colombo was among the family's leaders kidnapped by Crazy Joe Gallo when an internal rebellion broke out in the 1960s. Both sides came to an agreement and Colombo was released, but a double-cross sparked the first Colombo Family War.

When Profaci died in 1962, Joseph Magliocco became boss, but the overly ambitious Magliocco plotted against other bosses. Colombo revealed the scheme. When Magliocco was forced out in 1963, Colombo was awarded the remnants of the Profacis, stepping in as boss in the renamed Colombo Family. With his appointment, Colombo holds the distinction of being the first Mafia boss to be born on American soil.

Unlike many of his contemporaries, Colombo avoided significant prison time. He was jailed once for contempt of court, refusing to answer questions to a grand jury in 1966.

Chances are Colombo would have served much more time down the road. However, an assassin's bullet ended his criminal career at a rally for the Italian-American Civil Rights League.

Paralyzed and mentally incapacitated by the shooting, Joe Colombo lingered for seven years before passing away in 1978.

8
Louis Eppolito and Stephen Caracappa – The Mafia Cops

There is a special circle of hell reserved for corrupt police officers.

Forever branded "the Mafia Cops," Louis Eppolito and Stephen Caracappa are two such badge-traitors of the public trust who for years did the bidding of their Lucchese Mafia Family overlords.

I combined Louis Eppolito and Stephen Caracappa into one listing, because there is no discerning their despicable behavior. Just how filthy were these dirty cops?

Let's just say they did more than run license plates.

Following three decades on the streets of Brooklyn, this dastardly duo was convicted on numerous counts, from racketeering and narcotics trafficking, to gambling, extortion, conspiracy and more. Most disturbing were the eight murders involving these buddy-cop-bad-guys-with-badges, committed between 1986 and 1990. Two of those death warrants were personally executed by the Mafia Cops.

Eppolito and Caracappa must have felt they got away with their crimes. They got out, but were dragged back in, old men ensconced in comfortable retirement far out west, living large off their ill-gotten gains, supplemented by taxpayer-funded pensions.

Of the diabolical duet, it is less surprising that Eppolito betrayed the public trust. Growing up in Brooklyn he was around *the life*. His father, Ralph Eppolito, was a member of the Gambino crime family, and constantly railed against law enforcement. Eppolito later wrote: "My father hated cops with a passion, had no respect whatever for them. I guess that stemmed from the days when he was buying them off for nickels and dimes."

His father once told young Louis that FBI stood for "Forever Bother Italians."

An uncle and cousin on Eppolito's father's side were also gangsters, Gambinos assigned to the Bath Beach-based arm of the Family. They were later killed by crew captain Nino Gaggi and one of his top henchmen, the infamous Roy DeMeo. Those rub-outs made an impact on young Louis.

A year following the death of his father, Eppolito stunned his family by joining the New York City Police Department. However, on his application submitted in 1969, Eppolito conveniently omitted his familial relations to organized crime. But there were other signs of the betrayal to come, such as when Eppolito was cleared of a corruption charge in 1983, suspected of passing along NYPD reports to gangster Rosario Gambino.

Later, when not moonlighting for the mob, he had yet a third career, as a bit player in several movies, including the mob classic "*Goodfellas*." (In the famous mob roll-call scene introducing the various gangsters, he plays "Fat Andy, Moe Black's brother.")

In what now looks like near psychopathic ambivalence (or was it arrogance?), in 1992, Eppolito had the audacity to author, "Mafia Cop: The Story of an Honest Cop Whose Family Was the Mob," about his struggle to stay on the straight and narrow. That title would come back to haunt him years later.

Regardless of what he wrote, by then Eppolito was neck-deep doing dirt for the Mafia, so it boggles the mind why he would tempt fate and draw such attention by publishing a book of lies.

For his part, Stephen Caracappa, born in Brooklyn in 1942, joined the police force in 1969. He landed in the department's organized crime bureau in Brooklyn by the late 1970s. He later cashed out early on a disability pension in 1992, yet not before years of corrupt policing.

When the streets became too hot, both corrupt detectives retired, picked up stakes and headed west for Las Vegas in the mid-1990s. Caracappa set up shop as a private investigator. Eppolito became a corrections officer at the Las Vegas Women's Correctional Facility.

They thought they'd made it out, leaving the Brooklyn mob behind for good.

They were wrong.

As early as 1985, investigators were on their trail.

By 1985, law enforcement strongly suspected Eppolito and Caracappa were working for the New York Mafia. Yet it took nearly a decade of investigation for the full details of their criminal activities to emerge.

Anthony "Gaspipe" Casso, underboss of the Luccheses, dropped dime on the two double-dealing dirtbags, revealing enough damning details to drag the retired detectives back to Brooklyn to answer for their crimes.

In 1994, Casso, by then in federal witness protection, revealed how he paid the Mafia Cops nearly $400,000 for services rendered, including cashing in murder contracts, and sharing NYPD intelligence on investigations going as far back as 1985.

This wasn't just fixing parking tickets, but actual involvement as accessories and perpetrators of murder, such as the murder-for-hire killings of James Hydell (Gambino associate), Edward Lino (Gambino captain), Israel Kaplan (crooked diamond merchant), and five others. When they murdered suspected mob-informant Bruno Facciolo, he was found with a canary stuffed in his mouth, a nice touch the media rewarded with widespread coverage. Later it was discovered Facciolo was not an informant.

Perhaps the most high-profile contract the two picked up was the mark on Gambino Captain Eddie Lino. Casso put the hit out on Lino as a favor to Genovese Don Vincent "The Chin" Gigante. It was a retaliatory strike against rival John Gotti, revenge for taking out Gambino boss Paul Castellano without permission. More contract murders followed.

Following the epic Mafia Commission case, the Mafia Cops decided to pack it in, submitted their retirement papers. In the ensuing years, they'd periodically come out of retirement to moonlight for the mob, including stalking Sammy "The Bull" Gravano, when the notorious Gambino Family turncoat surfaced in Arizona.

Based on the testimony of various mobsters-turned-government-informants, Eppolito and Caracappa were arrested in March 2005 and hit with multiple counts, including racketeering, extortion and the eight murders. The government prosecution had more than enough to make all charges stick and in 2006 the Mafia Cops were both handed life sentences.

Initially thrown out of court on a technicality, the convictions were later upheld and in 2009 they were sentenced again, this time Caracappa receive life-plus-80 years, Eppolito, life-plus-100 years.

Today, Eppolito is doing time Arizona, while Caracappa is in a federal prison in Florida.

Both are in protective custody.

For more details on this deadly duo that did the bidding of the Lucchese Family, I highly recommend reading "Friends of the Family: The Inside Story of the Mafia Cops Case," written by Tommy Dades, Mike Vecchione and David Fisher. Dades is the highly decorated NYPD Detective and Vecchione the District Attorney, who brought them down.

7
Henry Hill - The Goodfella

Henry Hill Mugshot 1980

If you're reading this book, you've probably seen Martin Scorsese's "*Goodfellas.*"

If not, please put down my book and go watch that classic. Right. Now.

If they made a movie about your life, ever think who would play you?

Lucchese Family hanger-on Henry Hill, the career hench-man at the heart of "*Goodfel-*

las," could have done worse than handsome Hollywood-upstart Ray Liotta.

Thanks to Hill's snitching, federal investigators blew a massive hole in the side of the Lucchese leviathan, toppling family kingpin Paul Vario and scattering scores of gangsters to correctional facilities across the country. Hill's testimony helped convict more than 50 hoods, including James Burke, who was the very model for the modern master criminal Jimmy Conway, played so delightfully menacingly by Robert De Niro.

Because of the movie, the dozens of trials, as well as Hill's involvement in high-profile crimes (i.e., the multi-million-dollar Lufthansa cargo, the Boston College shaving scandal of the late 1970s), he more than earns his notch on this list.

Before "*Goodfellas*" was adapted for the screen, crime-journalist Nicholas Pileggi mined the mountain of testimony Hill provided as an FBI informant to write the bestseller, "*Wiseguy: Life in a Mafia Family.*"

Born in 1943 in Brooklyn, the son of a Sicilian mother, Hill was never officially inducted into the Mafia, as his father was Irish. But that wouldn't stop him from decades of criminal activity as an associate of the Lucchese Crime Family.

Hill grew up in Brownsville, East New York, one of nine siblings. His father had a hard time making ends meet on an electrician's salary. Hill, like most young boys in the neighborhood, was enamored by the local gangsters. Soon young Henry was running errands for the wiseguys. He shined shoes, served drinks, and before long was a regular presence at the cab stand and social club run by Paul Vario and his Lucchese crew.

By the late 1950s, Hill left school, and was granted a no-show job by Vario as a bricklayer, complete with union card. In actuality, Hill was a bag man for the mob, graduating to sidelines in arson, armed robbery, hijacking, stolen credit cards, and more.

Hill took his first collar at 16, and despite being roughed up by police, he did not provide any information to authorities. That left a strong impression on his mob mentors, so effectively captured in the movie. Though characters like Hill and Conway could never be made, solid earners are always welcomed by the mob.

Omitted in the movie are three relatively uneventful years Hill spent in the U.S. Army, stationed with the 82nd Airborne Division, far from Brooklyn in Fort Bragg, North Carolina. Throughout his stay in the military, Hill did a steady black market trade in illegal contraband and loansharking among the enlisted soldiers.

By the mid-1960s, Hill was back in Brooklyn and fully immersed in the criminal rackets, from hijacking trucks, many out of Idlewild Airport (later renamed John F. Kennedy International Airport), to arson, extortion, car theft and, proving disastrous, narcotics trafficking.

Hill was involved in the December 11, 1978 theft from the Lufthansa terminal at JFK airport, the largest such robbery in history, netting $6 million in cash and nearly $1 million in jewelry. But it was the combination of Hill's drug activity and association with Paul Vario that drew investigators from multiple law-enforcement agencies.

Arrested on April 27, 1980, a degenerate drug addict, paranoid he would be killed by his mob associates who were afraid he would flip on them, Hill switched teams. Hill's cooperation doomed Vario to die in prison, nearly capsized the Lucchese Family, and damaged other Mafia families as his testimony triggered the trials of more than 50 "Goodfellas."

Burke was handed a 20-year sentence just on the Boston College scam alone. He would die in prison. Vario was initially slapped with four years for the no-show job he gave Hill, followed up by more successful prosecution that assured the gang boss would never again see the light of day. He also died in prison.

Hill and his wife, Karen, and their two children, entered the federal witness protection program, shuttling around to various locations. Yet Hill was tossed out of the program for recklessly revealing his identity, among other indiscretions. Hill continued his drug abuse, and was jailed for a time for possession of methamphetamine, later divorcing from wife Karen after 25 eventful years.

Over the years, from Charlie Rose to Howard Stern, Hill made many guest appearances in the media and was the subject of numerous documentaries and articles. He even opened up a restaurant called Wiseguys in 2007 in West Haven, Connecticut.

Considering the massive number of dangerous criminals he sent away, it is a surprise that Hill did not die of unnatural causes, especially after his expulsion from federal protection. He died in 2012, at the age of 69, suffering from various ailments brought on by a wild life of excess.

6
Colin Ferguson - The Long Island Railroad Massacre

There are dangerous places we know to avoid, the dark alleys, the desolate side streets, the empty parking garages.

We halfway expect to be set upon when we wander to these places.

But when the unthinkable is committed where we feel safe, we become truly unhinged.

The events of December 7, 1993, aboard a Long Island Rail Road commuter train as it drew into the sleepy Merillon Avenue station in Garden City, Long Island, drew one of these collective gasps.

It wasn't just the horrific events of that evening, moments of insanity when a deranged gunman opened fire on riders, murdering six and injuring nineteen. In the early 1990s, mass murderers – those who kill many at once, not the spread-out staccato of a serial murderer – were not the frequent headliners we see today.

That wasn't *the story*.

Like the three heroic straphangers who disarmed the gunman – Kevin Blum, Mark McEntee, and Mike O'Connor – the events of that day were only part of the narrative.

The Long Island Rail Road Massacre, as it became known, was the story of a man from Brooklyn, Colin Ferguson, and his rage. Not any rage. They coined a name for Ferguson's special blend of anger.

"Black Rage."

Ferguson's "Black Rage" was long simmering, a constant theme in his life, percolating well before he boarded the commuter train.

While Ferguson studied business administration at Adelphi University in Garden City in the early 1990s, school officials reported several outbursts when Ferguson accused classmates of racism. During one episode in 1991, when Ferguson attended a lecture on South Africa, he became incensed, shouting "Kill everybody white...the black revolution will get you." He was suspended for this eruption.

This was the year Ferguson arrived in Brooklyn, renting a room in Flatbush, a vibrant area of West Indian influence. In the aftermath of the massacre, reporters descended on the neighborhood scavenging for soundbites from local residents crowded outside his cordoned-off residence. Those who could recall Ferguson remembered a strange man, anxious, suspicious, less than friendly.

Neighbors said if you passed Ferguson on the street, he never looked you in the eye. His Flatbush landlord, Patrick Denis, recalled one chilling conversation when Ferguson lamented, "I'm such a great person. There must be only one thing holding me back. It must be white people."

In February 1992, police arrested Ferguson following an incident on a Brooklyn subway, where a woman attempted to sit next to the future mass murderer. She asked him to move over to make room. Ferguson exploded, shouting and physically pressing against her, before police intervened, actually tackling and restraining him. Afterwards, Ferguson wrote rants he sent to the New York City Police Commissioner and other city officials complaining of his treatment, but nothing ever came of these missives.

In April 1993, Ferguson relocated to California for a fresh start, but failed again. The height of his humiliation in California came when he was turned away at a car wash where he sought employment.

During this Californian sojourn, two more pivotal events occurred. First, Ferguson bought a Ruger P89 9×19mm pistol at a Turner's Outdoorsman, following the requisite 15-day waiting period in California. For the purchase, all he needed was the California driver's license he'd procured two months earlier. He used the address of the motel where he stayed.

Soon after, Ferguson was violently mugged. Apparently, he did not have the weapon on his person at the time of the robbery.

In May 1993, Ferguson slinked back to Brooklyn, defeated, demoralized, renting the same room in Flatbush. The landlord testified later that upon Ferguson's return he was even more unstable, now prone to rants decrying his racially motivated oppression.

Neighbors reported hearing him chant: "All the black people killing all the white people."

The landlord asked Ferguson to leave by the end of that month. Ferguson did leave, but not by his own volition.

Ferguson's "Black Rage" burned to full boil the evening of

December 7, 1993, when he boarded the third car on an east-bound LIRR train at the Atlantic Terminal in Brooklyn. He pulled out that gun he picked up in California and took the lives of six, wounding three, before three brave riders disarmed him, launching months of intense media coverage.

The body count should have been much higher. The train held 80 passengers that night and Ferguson carried multiple firearms and 160 rounds of ammo. *The New York Times*, interviewing witnesses, reported how Ferguson moved through the car firing calmly, repeating over and over, "I'm going to get you. I'm going to get you."

None of the victims were black.

The investigation revealed that Ferguson planned the mass murder for weeks. During pre-trial proceedings, Ferguson appeared remote and calm, never speaking during his arraignment and not entering a plea.

Famed attorneys William Kunstler and Ron Kuby defended Ferguson, pro bono. The legal team conceived the "Black Rage" defense, arguing that racial prejudice drove Ferguson insane and he should not be held legally accountable for his crimes. They likened his mindset to that of victims of so-called Battered Woman Syndrome.

Ferguson didn't help his legal matters. He denied he was the shooter. He refused to cooperate with a psychiatrist the defense team brought in to bolster the Black Rage defense. Kunstler and Kuby filed a motion to pursue their insanity defense, in spite of their client's objection. Ferguson fired his attorneys and represented himself in what devolved into truly bizarre proceedings, resulting in obvious results.

On February 17, 1995, a jury convicted Ferguson on six counts of murder and 19 counts of attempted murder, among other offenses. He received a 315-years-and-eight-months-to-life sentence in prison and is incarcerated in the Upstate Correctional Facility in Franklin County, New York.

The massacre and trial tapped into a new national fear that an attack on a commuter train could happen at any moment.

And it gave us all a new reason to not nod off on the way home from work.

5
Salvatore Gravano – Sammy the Bull

What Benedict Arnold is to America, Salvatore "Sammy the Bull" Gravano is to the Mafia – the ultimate turncoat.

Make no mistake. There is no honor among thieves, drug dealers and murderers. But when Gravano agreed to cooperate with the federal government and violate Omerta, the Mafia code of silence, shockwaves shot out throughout organized crime.

Gravano wasn't the first "Made" member of the Italian Mafia to snitch, nor will he be the last. Gravano isn't even the highest-ranking gangster to save himself by tattling, though he was until 2004 when Joseph Massino, the Bonanno chieftain, became the first sitting boss of a Mafia Family to testify for the government.

Today, turning state's witness is more of an exit strategy for young mobsters, but that escape hatch became far more popular since Gravano took down his skipper.

As trusted underboss in the Gambino crime family, Gravano played the pivotal role in helping convict the previously untouchable Gambino Family boss, John Gotti. Until Gravano flipped, Gotti rode a succession of victories over criminal prosecutions that earned him the moniker "The Teflon Don." Because of Gravano, the feds finally made the charges stick.

Before Gravano became the poster-boy for boss betrayal, he was a highly successful and ruthless gangster, intimately involved in the high-stakes plot to murder seated Gambino boss Paul Castellano. That assassination was orchestrated by Gotti to seize power, conspiring with confederates Angelo Ruggiero, Frank DeCicco, and Joseph Armone.

Gravano grew up a tough hood on the streets of Bensonhurst, Brooklyn, the third of three children, with two older sisters. Yet Gravano did not come from a family of criminals. His father operated a small dress manufacturer, providing a comfortable middle-class lifestyle for his family. His son *chose* a life of crime.

Growing up in the Italian-American enclave of Bensonhurst, the wiseguys were everywhere in the neighborhood corners, cafes and social clubs. Gravano began his criminal career as a member of the Rampers, a local street gang. While in his early teens, he confronted the thieves who stole his bicycle and attacked them, much to the amusement of neighborhood gangsters watching from nearby. One of them commented how young Sammy "fought like a bull" and the nickname stuck.

Stymied in school by undiagnosed dyslexia, Gravano underperformed and acted out, dropping out at the age of 16. Drafted into the United States Army in 1964, he served stateside for two years as a cook, and left the service in 1968 with an honorable discharge, returning to Brooklyn.

Originally aligned with the Colombo family, jealousy from a rival gangster prompted Gravano's reassignment to the Gambinos to keep the peace. He reported to capo Salvatore "Toddo" Aurello.

Gravano proved a spectacular earner for the Gambinos, and he amassed interests in dozens illegal and legitimate enterprises, including several construction companies. Ruthless and cunning, Gravano muscled aside or murdered anyone in his path, drawing him into the orbit of upstart John Gotti.

Following decades of loyalty at Gotti's side, including numerous murders, Gravano fell out of favor with the boss. On November 11, 1991, federal investigators announced the stunning news that Gravano was cooperating with the government, instantly making him the most notorious gangster in the underworld.

Though Gravano admitted to 19 murders and decades of criminal activity, he received a reduced sentence for testimony that finally made charges sick to the "Teflon Don" John Gotti and assisted in the prosecution of dozens of wiseguys. Gotti was sentenced to life in a maximum security prison, where he died of cancer.

For his sins, Gravano received a pittance penalty of five years in prison, infuriating the families of his many victims. Imprisoned for four years by the time of his sentencing, Gravano was released after one more year of incarceration.

Upon his exit from prison, Gravano chafed in seclusion as a regular Joe, or in his case, a regular Jimmy. After only a year in hiding as "Jimmy Moran," Gravano exited the Witness Protection Program in 1995 and decamped for Arizona. Embracing his notoriety, Gravano soon started giving magazine and television interviews.

Gravano wrote a best-seller with acclaimed author Peter Maas in 1997, "Underboss," where he blasted the Mafia code of honor and explained that he turned on Gotti and his goombahs because they marked him for murder. Upon publication of the tome, New York State and many of the family members of his victims brought legal action pursuing profits from the book.

Unable to stay out of trouble, Gravano became embroiled in an Ecstasy ring in Arizona, when his son Gerard was involved with the "Devil Dogs," a drug gang of mostly white teens from middle-class families. Arrested in 2000 in a sweep in Phoenix that netted 35 co-conspirators, Gravano helped build and finance the gang's narcotics trafficking operation up to the point it was grossing a half-million dollars per week.

Sentenced to 20 years in an Arizona court, as well as 19 years on federal charges back in New York, Gravano is currently incarcerated in a prison in Arizona in protective custody. His son Gerard was handed a nine-year sentence. His wife, Debra, and daughter, Karen, pled guilty and received probation for their roles in the drug ring.

Karen Gravano later traded on her father's notoriety to land a spot on the VH1 reality series, "Mob Wives."

The confirmed murderer of 19 people is eligible for parole as early as 2019.

4
Rashid Baz - Terror Attack on The Brooklyn Bridge

Since its opening in 1883, the Brooklyn Bridge has become the most iconic image associated with the County of the Kings.

Yet on one after noon in March of 1994, the historic landmark became synonymous with something far more sinister.

Terror.

The first suspension span ever built, originally constructed for slow-moving horsedrawn carriages, has a narrow roadway bed barely wide enough to accomdate two cars whizzing by each other. It's challenging enough to navigate the bridge, let alone having to do it while being fired upon from another vehicle.

On the afternoon of March 1, 1994, a van of 15 Chabad-Lubavitch Orthodox Jewish students was traveling Brooklyn-bound on the bridge when livery-cab-driver Rashid Baz opened fired. First raking the van with a Cobray MAC-11 automatic, Baz then took aim with a Glock 17 9mm semi-automatic. For good meaure, he was also armed with a 12-gauge Armsel Striker shotgun.

Baz struck four targets. Ari Halberstam, a sixteen-year-old yeshiva student, shot in the head, would die from his wound five days later.

Amir Abudaif, an auto mechanic, reported the incident to police, leading to the capture of Baz. In a search of Baz' property, police found anti-Semitic literature, firearms, ammunition and a bullet-proof vest.

When Baz claimed he opened fire in a fit of anger after being cut off, the Federal Bureau of Investigation tagged the case an incident of road rage. The true motive ran much deeper.

Baz was an illegal immigrant from Lebanon and a Druze-Muslim, though religious fantacism was not his primary driver. At trial the defense entered a plea of insanity for the defendant, explaining how Baz was incensed over the Hebron Massacre that occurred February 25, just days before the incident on the Brooklyn Bridge. In the Hebron Massacre, 29 Palestinians were killed by an Israeli. The defense argued that Baz suffered from Post-Traumatic Stress Disorder (PTSD) from his violent childhood living through the Lebanese Civil War.

The U.S. Justice Department upgraded the charges, labelling the crime a terrorist attack, attracting an avalanche of media coverage. The case emerged as the latest flashpoint in the ancient animosity between Jews and Palestinians in the Middle East. Yet this one hit close to home in Brooklyn. Images of young yeshiva students, memorials, stock photography from the roiling Middle East, and horrified Brooklyn residents mingled in the media coverage.

The public outcry in the Jewish community was height
the Halberstam family's status in the ultra-Orthodox
Lubavitch movement. In fact, on the day of the
Halberstam had visited with Lubavitcher Reb
Mendel Schneerson, at the Manhattan Eye.

Hospital, and was returning to Brooklyn.

More than 10,000 mourners turned out for the funeral, staffed by hundreds of New York City police officers and scrums of media crews.

At trial, the jury disregarded the insanity defense and on December 1, 1994, convicted Baz of second-degree murder, along with 14 counts of attempted murder.

On January 18, 1995, Baz was sentenced to 141 years to life in prison and is currently incarcerated at the Auburn Correctional Facility in upstate New York State.

Today, if you look closely on the Manhattan side of the Brooklyn Bridge, you can see the "Ari Halberstam Memorial Ramp" plaque commemorating the innocent life lost that tragic day.

3
Crazy Joe Gallo - The Gang that Couldn't Shoot Straight

In Brooklyn gangster lore, Joseph "Crazy Joe" Gallo is unique. He was a ruthless murderer and mob rebel who ignited a family war.

Yet he was also a poet, who palled around with pop stars of his day. When famed rock-and-roll critic Lester Bangs reviewed Bob Dylan's "Joey," an 11-minute ballad of Gallo's life, he called it "one of the most mindlessly amoral pieces of romanticist bullshit ever recorded."

Born in Brooklyn April 7, 1929, Gallo would become one of he most feared and unpredictable gangsters of his age. Most ngsters don't want their children to follow in their footsteps. t Crazy Joe's Dad. The senior Gallo was a Mafia bootlegger from the Prohibition era that brought his work home with him, inspiring his three boys – Larry, Joey and Albert – to pursue lives of crime they fully embraced.

From a young age, Gallo fashioned himself a gangster, in the mold of Hollywood heavies like Jimmy Cagney. Less than physically imposing at just five foot six inches, Gallo made up for it with a violent temper masking deep-seeded psychological issues. In his early 20s, he was diagnosed schizophrenic by medical professionals at Kings County Hospital.

Gallo raised his profile in 1957 when he was part of the hit team that took out Albert Anastasia at Grasso's Barber Shop in the Park Sheraton Hotel in New York City. Following that major hit, Gallo felt entitled to a larger share of the family spoils. His boss, Joe Profaci, disagreed.

Gallo gained national notoriety in the mainstream media when he testified at the Robert Kennedy Senate hearings on organized crime in 1958 in Washington, D.C., taking the fifth from behind dark sunglasses, of course decked out all in black.

Back in Brooklyn, Gallo and his brothers had their hands in many of the local rackets. He called his gang "The Mod Squad" and they ran a lucrative jukebox extortion scheme throwing off a steady stream of cash.

Gallo wanted more out of mob life and he chafed under the thumb of Mafia Don Joseph Profaci, a throwback boss notoriously cheap with his underlings. When Gallo attempted to cede from the Profacis, it meant war. The first shot fired across the bow was the Profacis' botched assassination attempt of Joe's older brother Larry Gallo, foiled when police wandered across the crime scene (Larry later died of cancer while Joe was imprisoned).

Crazy Joe gathered his gang to hit the mattresses holed up in a safehouse on President Street, where it was rumored he kept a pet lion in the basement to scare delinquent creditors.

By the time Joe was sent away to federal prison on extortion charges, bodies had dropped on both sides, and the media was having a field day romanticizing the Gallos brothers in their underdog quest to take down the miserly old Profaci. When Profaci died due to cancer on June 6, 1962, successor Joseph Magliocco carried on the war, which subsided when Joe Gallo headed to prison on extortion charges.

Gallo was a creature of his age, and was one of the few Italian mobsters that embraced other criminal groups, especially African American gangsters. The 10 years he spent in prison helped him cement his relationships with these other criminal groups, including a tie with Harlem drug kingpin Leroy "Nicky" Barnes.

When Gallo was released from prison in 1971, Joe Colombo was the new boss. Colombo was one of the hostages Gallo took at the outset of the war, and despite a peace offering of $1,000 and offer to accept a solider position, Gallo reignited hostilities, vowing to take down Colombo.

When Colombo was shot in Manhattan in 1971 by an African-American assassin, Jerome Johnson, the rumor was that Gallo had ordered the hit and used his uptown connections. We'll never know, as Johnson was immediately killed by a Colombo bodyguard.

When not engaged in a running street war with Italian rivals, Gallo was pursued by the Paparazzi who snapped his pics alongside starlets and artists in the Greenwich Village artsy joints he frequented.

Gallo's notoriety was fed by creatives and celebrities who were enamored with a walk on the wild side. He was not only featured by Dylan in a song, but his crew's exploits were profiled in a Jimmy Breslin book and subsequent film, "The Gang That Couldn't Shoot Straight." Gallo also struck up a friendship with famed New York actor, and later Law & Order television detective, Jerry Orbach, who played Gallo in the film version of Breslin's book.

Despite these dalliances, Gallo was engaged in serious mob business, but his career came to a screeching halt on April 7, 1972. Celebrating his birthday with friends and family at Umberto's Clam House in Little Italy, Gallo was gunned down in one of the most dramatic gangland murders in mob history.

In true dramatic fashion, Gallo stumbled from the restaurant and died in the middle of the street.

2

David Berkowitz – The Son of Sam

Brooklyn was just bad luck for David Berkowitz.

Long before he was the infamous serial killer "Son of Sam," even before he was David Berkowitz, he was Richard Falco, an abandoned bastard from Brooklyn.

That's a pretty harsh way of putting it, but accurate.

Berkowitz' mother, Betty Broder, came from a poor Jewish family and married outside her faith, to Anthony Falco, an Italian-American merchant. The young couple ran a

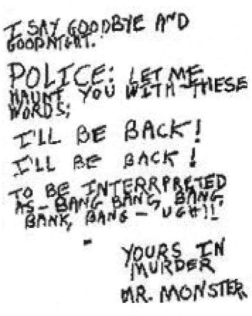

1st Son of Sam Letter

fish market in Brooklyn and had a daughter, but Falco abandoned Broder to raise the child by herself.

Broder was not yet divorced when she engaged in an affair with Joseph Kleinman, a married man who sold real estate in Brooklyn. When she became pregnant, Kleinman demanded that she get rid of the baby or he would leave her. This was years before New York State Governor Nelson Rockefeller signed into law a measure legalizing abortions in 1970. Broder had the baby in June of 1953, naming him Richard David Falco.

Days later Broder put him up for adoption.

It would be years before Berkowitz came to terms with the circumstances of his birth.

Pearl and Nathan Berkowitz, a Jewish-American couple in the Bronx that owned a hardware store, adopted the infant, transposing his first and middle name, and adding their last name. David Richard Berkowitz grew up an only child in a middle-class family.

While he was intelligent, young David did not excel in school and was a troubled child. He was a loner, a bully, started fires, picked fights, stole, yet nothing that resulted in trouble with the law. His adoptive parents tried intervening with a psychotherapist, with no discernable effect.

Many accounts of Berkowitz' upbringing cite the severe psychological trauma he suffered in 1967 when his adoptive mother, Pearl, succumbed to breast cancer. Berkowitz was 14 years of age. David exhibited signs of alienation and depression. His remaining teenage years were unpleasant, and he did not mix well with a new stepmother. His adopted father relocated to Florida leaving a damaged young man twisting in the wind.

Like many a disaffected youth short on prospects, David enlisted in the United States Army when he turned 18 years old. He served stateside as well as overseas, stationed in South Korea. While in the service, he did distinguish himself in one area: as a marksman. Otherwise, his time in the military was uneventful, though he did contract a venereal disease from a prostitute, his first sexual encounter.

Honorably discharged in 1974, Berkowitz returned to Brooklyn to seek out his birth mother. After several meetings, Betty Falco revealed the background story of his birth and subsequent adoption, as well as the painful news that his biological father had died years earlier. Berkowitz later claimed his biological mother's rejection fueled his inner rage.

Cycling through several failed employment stints he finally settled in as a sorter at the United States Postal Service. Outside work hours, Berkowitz re-embraced an old childhood hobby, as a prolific arsonist.

It was not until the summer of 1976, the bicentennial of the nation, that Berkowitz launched his campaign of terror. The "Son of Sam" moniker would come later, as he was first known by police and media as the unimaginative moniker "The .44 Caliber Killer," as he perpetrated a series of shooting attacks with the same .44 caliber Bulldog revolver.

Unlike a mass murderer that kills all of his victims in one encounter, a serial killer murders a series of victims over the course of time, often according to a pattern rooted in a need to satisfy some disturbed psychological craving.

By the time he ran into a bit of bad luck in Brooklyn in July 1977, leading to his capture, Berkowitz had killed six and wounded seven.

From the public's perspective, the murders were disturbing enough, but it was the discovery of a pattern and the anticipation of where the serial murderer will strike next, that got people so on edge. Speak to any adult in Brooklyn that lived during that period and they'll likely have a story or two of how the "Son of Sam" spree affected them in some way.

Berkowitz mocked the authorities with letters, signing some as the Son of Sam, warning of future attacks, chronicled in New York's tabloids, ratcheting up the fear factor.

As the body count climbed and bizarre messages continued to hit the local papers, Berkowitz achieved international notoriety. The people of New York were panicking, changing their behavior. No one wanted to be the next victim. News that Berkowitz set his .44-caliber sights on young, attractive, long-haired brunettes sent thousands of women throughout New York scrambling into hair salons to trim and dye their locks. Many more stayed home to ride out the reign of the Son of Sam.

Berkowitz' return to Brooklyn proved his undoing. The final murder that tripped him up took place in Bath Beach along a tree-lined lovers' lane, nearly a year after his first crime took place.

With police focusing on Queens and the Bronx, sites of other attacks, Berkowitz stalked a quiet street that rims the shore of Brooklyn just beyond the Verrazano Narrows. It was 2:30 a.m. the early morning hours of July 31, 1977, and Stacy Moskowitz and Robert Violante were parked in a car, doing what two 20-somethings do in such situations.

Distracted, the young lovers never noticed Berkowitz approach and pump four bullets into the car, killing Moskowitz and maiming Violante. Nineteen-year-old Tommy Zaino was a few cars away with his own date, and witnessed the shooting. Berkowitz was well-illuminated in an eerie glow cast by the mix of faded yellow streetlights and the moon.

Another witness provided police with a partial license plate number. Other witnesses provided bits and pieces of what they saw, yet it was local resident Cecilia Davis, out walking her dog, who days later tipped off cops that she passed a suspicious stranger shortly before the shooting, near the crime scene. She revealed that his car had been ticketed.

Sure enough, Berkowitz' illegally parked 1970 Ford Galaxie had been ticketed near the crime scene, and that led to his capture.

When confronted by police storming his Yonkers apartment, Berkowitz meekly surrendered, asking "What took you so long?"

In custody, Berkowitz confessed, spewing his bizarre tale. He explained how he was ordered to commit the crimes by a demon who inhabited a black Labrador retriever named Harvey owned by his neighbor.

The neighbor's name was *Sam* Carr.

In Berkowitz' apartment, police found satanic scrawlings and incriminating evidence, including the murder weapon. Aside from evidence related to the murders, police uncovered detailed notebooks chronicling the more than 1,400 arson fires Berkowitz set throughout New York.

Though clearly unbalanced, Berkowitz was found mentally competent to stand trial in court proceedings that became a media circus. Berkowitz has been a serial-killer superstar ever since.

The Son of Sam was slammed with 25-years-to-life for each murder, with the sentences to be served consecutively, not concurrently. He has since discovered religion, is periodically profiled in the media, and continues to serve his time in the Attica Correctional Facility in upstate New York.

Due to the intense coverage of his crimes, lucrative production deals started to pour in for books and movies. As a result, the New York State passed the so-called "Son of Sam Laws" to prevent criminals from profiting from their crimes, and instead channeling proceeds to survivors and victims' families. Since then, similar legislation has been enacted in other U.S. states.

1
Albert Fish – The Brooklyn Vampire

Even in the most depraved works of horror fiction, you'll be hard pressed to find a villain as heinous as Albert Fish – a living, breathing nightmare who preyed on the children of Brooklyn and beyond.

Albert Fish Mugshot 1903

In the annals of crime in the County of the Kings there is no one more sinister than the ferocious Fish. At trial, attorney James Dempsey stated, "Nowhere in legal or medical records was there another individual who possessed so many sexual abnormalities."

Dempsey was the counsel for the defense.

This violent, sadomasochistic sexual deviant went by many names, known as the Gray Man, the Werewolf of Wysteria, the Moon Maniac, and The Boogey Man. Yet none was more chilling for the children of the Depression than that of the Brooklyn Vampire. For years stressed-out Brooklyn housewives scared their naughty children into obedience with the specter of Albert Fish and his awful deeds.

It was a chilly morning in Brooklyn on February 11, 1927. America was in the midst of Prohibition as the Roaring 20s unwound into the age of consumerism, a time when America's wealth more than doubled. In Brooklyn people still left their doors unlocked, their children unwatched.

Gentle three-year old Billy Beaton was playing in the hallway of his Brooklyn apartment building with his 12-year-old brother and a friend, four-year-old Billy Gaffney.

Then the shadow cast by Albert Fish came across the boys.

The sequence of events is clouded, as it tends to be when trusting the recollections of the pre-pubescent. But a few things were clear. At some point the older boy left the hallway, and that was when the younger boys disappeared.

As reported in *The Brooklyn Eagle*, Billy Gaffney's mother said her child was a precocious scamp. Billy, she said, talked freely to people, and was trusting. She told a reporter Billy was out of her sight for no more than five minutes that afternoon.

As Beaton's father came up the stairs of the apartment house, arriving home from work, Gaffney's mother poked her head out the doorway. "Where are the wee Billies?" she asked in her Scottish lilt.

After a frantic search, young Beaton was discovered on the black-tarred roof of the building.

He was alone.

When questioned, Beaton's answer chilled investigators, uttered in a small, frightened voice: "Billy went away with a big man ... The bogeyman took him."

Billy Gaffney was never seen alive again.

A desperate manhunt ensued. Authorities scooped up Peter Kudzinowski, a Polish-born railroad worker, who was released after questioning. Kudzinowski was later convicted of a serial-killing spree throughout New Jersey and Pennsylvania, but Billy Gaffney was not among his victims.

The crime remained unsolved for years. The trail grew cold.

The break in the case came after Fish was arrested in 1934 on suspicion of murdering a young girl, Grace Bud. That murder occurred in 1928. The ghoulish Fish sent a taunting letter to Grace's mother, and investigators were able to track it back to him.

When Fish's gaunt image splashed throughout newspapers nationwide, the depraved details of his crimes drew many to take a closer look, including Joseph Meehan. The Brooklyn trolley operator recognized Fish' distinctively haunting face, though it was seven years. Meehan recalled Fish boarded his trolley on the day of Billy's disappearance in the company of a young boy. Meehan remembered the episode clearly, because the boy was without a jacket, unusual for a bitter cold Brooklyn windswept day in February. The episode was further memorable as the boy was incessantly whining for his mother, forcing an exasperated Fish to drag him from the trolley. That face, it stayed with Meehan.

Meehan thought little of it then, until he saw Fish's photo in the newspaper and the memory came back to him.

Detectives from the Manhattan Missing Persons Bureau jumped at the lead, discovering that Fish had the opportunity to abduct Gaffney. Fish worked as a house painter for a Brooklyn real-estate company at the time of the disappearance and was assigned to a job located nearby Billy's home.

Little did investigators know what horrors awaited when Fish confessed, in the form of a gruesome letter he wrote to his attorney. Here is an excerpt. WARNING, these contents are disturbing:

I brought him to the Riker Ave. dumps. There is a house that stands alone, not far from where I took him ... I took the G boy there. Stripped him naked and tied his hands and feet and gagged him with a piece of dirty rag I picked out of the dump. Then I burned his clothes. Threw his shoes in the dump. Then I walked back and took a trolley to 59 Street at 2 a.m. and walked home from there.

Next day about 2 p.m., I took tools, a good heavy cat-of-nine tails. Homemade. Short handle. Cut one of my belts in half, slit these halves in six strips about 8 in. long. I whipped his bare behind till the blood ran from his legs. I cut off his ears – nose – slit his mouth from ear to ear. Gouged out his eyes. He was dead then.

I stuck the knife in his belly and held my mouth to his body and drank his blood. I picked up four old potato sacks and gathered a pile of stones. Then I cut him up. I had a grip with me. I put his nose, ears and a few slices of his belly in the grip. Then I cut him thru the middle of his body. Just below his belly button. Then thru his legs about 2 inches below his behind. I put this in my grip with a lot of paper. I cut off the head – feet – arms – hands and the legs below the knee. This I put in sacks weighed with stones, tied the ends and threw them into the pools of slimy water you will see all along the road going to North Beach. Water is 3 to 4 feet deep. They sank at once.

I came home with my meat. I had the front of his body I liked best. His monkey and pee wees and a nice little fat behind to roast in the oven and eat. I made a stew out of his ears – nose – pieces of his face and belly. I put onions, carrots, turnips, celery, salt and pepper. It was good.

As the trial proceeded, it became apparent that Billy Gaffney was one in a long line of this monster's many young victims.

Born in 1870 to a family of minor historical note (politician Hamilton Fish was a distant relation) mixed with mental illness, Fish was placed in an orphanage at the age of five when his riverboat-captain father passed away. There Fish was raped and beaten for four years, developing sadomasochistic tendencies. By the age of 12, Fish was a serial rapist and practicing cannibal. Fish boasted at trial that he "had children in every state."

Fish arrived in Brooklyn at the age of 20, working as a male prostitute, a cover he used to lure and rape young boys. Three decades of sexual perversion of the most debased nature followed, as Fish became fascinated with sexual mutilation, paraphilia (perversions involving human excrement) and cannibalism. He selected children less likely to be missed, such as children of the poor, minorities and the mentally disabled.

Before investigators, Fish protested that God commanded him to torture and mutilate the children of Brooklyn. Fish placed the count of his victims at 100, though did not specify if these were rapes and/or murders.

Following a 10-day trial, covered by the mainstream media of the day, Fish was convicted of the murder of Grace Bud.

On January 16, 1936, the Brooklyn Vampire was executed by electric chair at Sing Sing.

Before his execution, Fish handed his attorney Dempsey his last words on pages he'd written. Dempsey refused to share those pages.

"I will never show it to anyone," he told reporters. "It was the most filthy string of obscenities that I have ever read."

ACKNOWLEDGEMENTS

This work would not have been possible without the tremendous support of the following people.

My mother, Marie McGuire, a New York City school teacher in some of the roughest neighborhoods in Brooklyn, who taught me strength, humility and integrity, sacrificed so much for us and never let me give up. My father, Francis X. McGuire. I regret deeply that you were not part of this latest caper, though your long shadow continues to drive me.

My publisher, WildBlue Press, for taking a chance on my work and nurturing it during the long march to market, especially Ashley Butler, Steve Jackson, Michael Cordova, Amanda Luedeke, and Ian Dickerson. There is something special going on at WildBlue Press, a publisher that truly supports its authors.

Those guilty of aiding and abetting on this latest racket, especially Ivan Avelancio, Christopher Bayer, Heath Berg, Rob Bolstad, Mike Deliso, Greg Janvier, Amy Kovar, Sean Lawler, Colleen McGuire, Andy Petery, Robert Sales, Christi Shingara, Artie and Dierdre Silva, David Troiano, Erin and the rest of Team Tupper, and Cindy Wen.

Retired NYPD Detective Tommy Dades, for inspiring me and selflessly spending time to help me at many points along this winding road, especially when I was in over my head.

Former Brooklyn Borough Historian and my first editor, John Manbeck, for seeing something in me no one else saw and giving me a chance when it really counted.

My co-conspirators at Brooklyn Creative, Ron Valdes and Bill Donnelly, I cannot thank you enough for all you do, my brothers.

Special thanks to Tony and Maria Deliso. Everyone should be blessed with such amazing in-laws, and the world would be a much better place. Also, my original partner-in-crime Susan McGuire, Barbara and John Ambre, Mary Ellen and Robert McGuire, and Carol and Dennis O'Connor.

Finally, my favorite accomplice, Anna my love, nothing I do is possible without your love, hustle and support, and the rest of our little crime ring, Frank, Fiona and Antonio, who keep me honest and inspire me in their own specials ways.

FURTHER REFERENCE

ABBANDANDO, FRANK "THE DASHER"

"Frank The Dasher Abbandano," By Robert Grey Reynolds Jr., *Amazon Digital Services LLC*, May 27, 2016 (eBook)

"Murder, Inc.: The Story Of The Syndicate," By Burton B. Turkus, *Da Capo Press*, July 29, 2003 (Book)

AGRON, EVSEI

"Red Mafiya: How the Russian Mob Has Invaded America," By Robert I. Friedman, *Little, Brown*, 2000 (Book)

"Family Business - the Russian Mob in New York," By Robert I. Friedman, *The Moscow Times*, March 19, 1993 (Newspaper Article)

"The Mafia Encyclopedia," Carl Sifakis, *Da Capo Press*, 2005 (Book)

AMBERG LOUIS "PRETTY"– INVENTOR OF THE "SACK MURDER"

"The Book of American Jewish Gangsters," By Maxmillian Zellner, *CreateSpace*, January 29, 2013 (Book)

"Our Gang : Jewish Crime and the New York Jewish Community, 1900-1940," By Jenna Weissman Joselit, *Indiana University Press*, November 22, 1983 (Book)

ANASTASIA, ALBERT "THE LORD HIGH EXECUTIONER"

"Albert Anastasia Biography," *A&E Network* (Television Program)

"Murder Inc.," By by Christian Cipollini, Strategic Media Books, February 1, 2015 (Book)

ARON, LEVI "BUTCHER OF BROOKLYN"

"Levi Aron Gets 40 Years to Life for Killing and Dismembering 8-year-old Brooklyn Boy Leiby Kletzky," By Oren Yaniv, *The New York Daily News*, August 29, 2012 (Newspaper Article)

"Amateur Sleuth Yaakov German Helps Cops Catch Levi Aron and Solve Murder of Leiby Kletzky," By Barry Paddock, *The New York*

Daily News, July 15, 2011 (Newspaper Article)

ASHBURN, YASSAR "SUPA SWERVE 6"

"The Leader and Two Members of Folk Nation Gang Operating in the Ebbets Field Houses in Brooklyn Convicted of Racketeering and Murder," U.S. Federal Bureau of Investigation, U.S. Attorney's Office, Eastern District of New York, March 18, 2015 (Press Release)

"Man Who Dodged Murder Rap as Teen Gets Life Sentence for Different Slay, By Selim Algar, *The New York Post*, March 18, 2016

BALAGULA, MARAT "THE RUSSIAN TONY SOPRANO"

"Red Mafiya: How the Russian Mob Has Invaded America," By Robert I. Friedman, *Little, Brown*, 2000 (Book)

"The Russian Mafia – A New Crime Menace Grows in Brooklyn," By Daniel Burstein, *New York Magazine*, Novmber 24, 1986 (Magazine Article)

BARRON, VICTOR

"Ex-Brooklyn Judge to Serve at Least 3 Years for Bribe," By William Glaberson, *The New York Times*, October 29, 2002 (Newspaper Article)

"Bag-Boy Barron: Crooked Judge's Dress-Shop Job," By Denise Buffa, *The New York Post*, October 16, 2004 (Newspaper Article)

BARRY, PHILIP "THE BERNIE MADOFF OF BAY RIDGE"

"'Bernie Madoff of Bay Ridge' Victims Sue Banks for $36 Million," By Lia Eustachewich, *The New York Post*, June 4, 2015 (Newspaper Article)

"American Greed: Brooklyn's Madoff / Corrupted Software," *CNBC*, May 2013 (Television Program)

BAZ, RASHID

"Killer: Jews My Target," By Larry Celona, *The New York Post*, March 26, 2012 (Newspaper Article)

"Brooklyn Bridge Shooting: Suspect Arrested in Shooting of Hasidim," By Francis X. Clines, *The New York* Times, March 3, 1994 (Newspaper Article)

"U.S. Decides '94 Attack On Hasidim Was Lone Act," By Shaila

K. Dewan, *The New York Times*, December 6, 2000 (Newspaper Article)

"Bridge Gunman Gets 141-Year Term Bridge Gunman Gets 141-Year Term," By George James, *The New York Times*, January 19, 1995 (Newspaper Article)

BERKOWITZ, DAVID "THE SON OF SAM"

"Confessions of Son of Sam," By David Abrahamsen, Columbia University Press, 1985 (Book)

"Son of Sam: Based on the Authorized Transcription of the Tapes, Official Documents and Diaries of David Berkowitz," By Lawrence D. Klausner, *McGraw-Hill*, 1981 (Book)

BERNSTEIN, JULIUS "THE LAST JEWISH GANGSTER"

"Julius Bernstein Was the Last Jewish Mobster and He Never Went to Jail," By Greg B. Smith, *The New York Daily News*, February 25, 2012 (Newspaper Article)

"The Last Jewish Gangster: Julius Bernstein's Once-secret FBI File Revealed," *The Daily Mail*,

February 2012 (Newspaper Article)

BLANCO, LUIS "KING HUMBLE"

"14 Brooklyn Thugs from Latin Kings Arrested for Allegedly Planning Attacks on Victims who Insulted their Gang," By Oren Yaniv, *The New York Daily News*, November 6, 2014 (Newspaper Article)

"14 Bushwick Latin King Members Were Arrested for Brutal Attacks," By Katarina Hybenova, *The Bushwick Daily*, November 7, 2014 (Web Article)

BONNEY, WILLIAM "BILLY THE KID"

"The Authentic Life of Billy, the Kid: The Noted Desperado of the Southwest, Whose Deeds of Daring and Blood Made His Name a Terror in New Mexico, Arizona and Northern Mexico," By Pat Floyd Garrett, *New Mexican Print and Publishing Company*, 1882 (Book)

"Billy the Kid: A Short and Violent Life," By Robert Marshall Utley, *Tauris Parke Paperbacks*, 2000 (Books)

BOOTH, JOHN WILKES

"The Fight to Find John Wilkes Booth's Diary in a Forgotten Subway Tunnel," By Joe Kloc, *Newsweek*, June 10, 2014 (Magazine Article)

"Why An 1830s Locomotive Appears To Be Trapped Under Brooklyn Streets," By Jen Carlson, *The Gothamist*, March 23, 2015

BORIELLO, BARTHOLOMEW

"Gotti's Driver Shot to Death Outside Home," By George James, *The New York Times*, April 15, 1991 (Newspaper Article)

"Wiseguys Breaking Mob Laws," By Jerry Capeci, *The New York Sun*, July 14, 2005 (Newspaper Article)

"Mob Cops' Role in Hit on Gotti's Chauffer," By Murray Weiss, *The New York Post*, June 13, 2006 (Newspaper Article)

BOVA, GINO

"Jurors Find Slaying of Black in Brooklyn Was Manslaughter," By Joseph P. Fried, *The New York Times,* March 9, 1983 (Newspaper Article)

"Teen Sentenced for Man's Death," *Observer-Reporter* (Washington,PA), April 1, 1983 (Newspaper Article)

"All Eyes are Upon Us: Race and Politics from Boston to Brooklyn," By Jason Sokol, *Basic Books*, December 2, 2014 (Book)

BOYLAND, WILLIAM JR.

"Assemblyman Is Convicted in Second Corruption Trial," By Mosi Secret, *The New York Times*, March 6, 2014 (Newspaper Article)

"William Boyland Jr., Ex-New York Assemblyman, Gets 14-Year Sentence for Corruption," By Nicholas Casey, *The New York Times*, September 17, 2015 (Newspaper Article)

BRINSELY, ISMAAIYL ABDULLAH

"Cop Killer Ismaaiyl Brinsley had a Long Criminal Record, Was Violent and Suicidal, and Frightened his Mom: Police," By Barry Paddock, *The New York Daily News*, December 22, 2014 (Newspaper Article)

"Police Combing Through Shooting Suspect's Arrest History and Violent Day," By J. David Goodman, *The New York* Times, December 20, 2014 (Newspaper Article)

Brooks, Shamar "Brooklyn's Most Wanted"

"NYPD Smashes Brooklyn's Most Wanted Gang, Called BMW, With Nine Arrests," By Thomas Tracy, *The New York Daily News*, December 2013 (Newspaper Article)

"Another Crew Cut: NYPD Gang Unit Puts Brakes on Violent BMWs," By Thomas Tracey, *The New York Daily News: The Shack*, December 13, 2013 (Blog)

Buchalter, Louis "Lepke"

The Life and Times of Lepke Buchalter: America's Most Ruthless Labor Racketeer," By Paul R. Kavieff, *Barricade Books*, January 26, 2006 (Book)

"The Rise and Fall of the Jewish Gangster in America," By Albert Fried, *Holt, Rinehart, and Winston*, 1980 (Book)

Cacace, Joel "Joe Waverly"

"11 Years After Officer's Slaying, Reputed Mob Figures Are Indicted," By Michale Wilson, *The New York Times*, December 18, 2008 (Newspaper Article)

"Mobster Joel Cacace Acquitted of Ordering NYPD Cop Killed in Murder Trial," By John Marzulli, *The New York Daily News*, November 26, 2013 (Newspaper Article)

"Jerry Capeci's Gang Land," By Jerry Capeci, *Penguin*, 2003 (Book)

"Gangland New York: The Places and Faces of Mob History," By Anthony M. DeStefano, *Rowman & Littlefield*, July 1, 2015 (Book)

"The Mafia Encyclopedia," By Carl Sifakis, *Infobase Publishing*, 2006 (Book)

Capone, Alphonse "Scarface"

"Mr. Capone: The Real - and Complete - Story of Al Capone," by Robert J. Schoenberg, *William Morrow Paperbacks*, September 30, 1993 (Book)

"Capone: The Life and World of Al Capone," By John Kobler, *Da Capo Press*, 1971 (Book)

Caracappa, Stephen "The Mafia Cops"

"Friends of the Family: The Inside Story of the Mafia Cops Case,"

By Tommy Dades, Mike Vecchione, David Fisher, *Harper Collins*, May 2009 (Book)

"Mob Cops: The Shocking Rise and Fall of New York's "Mafia Cops"," By Greg B. Smith, *Berkley Books*, 2006 (Book)

CASSO, ANTHONY "GASPIPE"

"Gaspipe: Confessions of a Mafia Boss," By Philip Carlo, *HarperCollins Publishers*, June 2009 (Book)

"The Brotherhoods: The True Story of Two Cops Who Murdered for the Mafia," By Guy Lawson, William Oldham, *Simon and Schuster*, November 2006 (Book)

CASTELLANO, PAUL "BIG PAULIE"

"Boss of Bosses: The Fall of the Godfather: The FBI and Paul Castellano," By Joseph F. O'Brien, Laurence Shames, Andris Kurins, *Random House Publishing Group*, May 1992 (Book)

"Five Families: The Rise, Decline, and Resurgence of America's Most Powerful Mafia Empires," By Selwyn Raab, *Macmillan*, May 2014 (Book)

CHEN, MING DON "THE SUNSET PARK MASSACRE"

"Mother, 4 Children Stabbed To Death in Brooklyn," *CBS News*, October 27, 2013 (Television / Web)

"Jealous Butcher Killed Mom, 4 Kids Because They Had Too Much," By Jamie Schram, Larry Celona, Kirstan Conley, Bruce Golding, *The New York Post,* October 27, 2013 (Newspaper Article)

COHEN, MICKEY

"Mickey Cohen: The Life and Crimes of L.A.'s Notorious Mobster," By Tere Tereba, *ECW Press*, 2012 (Book)

"Hollywood's Celebrity Gangster: The Incredible Life and Times of Mickey Cohen," By Brad Lewis, *Createspace Independent Pub*, 2009 (Book)

"Gangster Squad," Directed by Ruben Fleischer, *Warner Brothers*, January 11, 2013 (Theatrical Film)

COLOMBO, JOSEPH "COLOMBO FAMILY BOSS"

"Colombo: The New Look in the Mafia," By Nicholas Gage, *The New York Times*, May 3, 1971 (Newspaper Article)

"Joseph A. Colombo, Sr,. Paralyzed in Shooting at 1971 Rally, Dies." *The New York Times*, May 24, 1978 (Newspaper Article)

"Five Families: The Rise, Decline, and Resurgence of America's Most Powerful Mafia Empires," By Selwyn Raab, *St. Martin's Press*, September 5, 2006 (Book)

CUTOLO, WILLIAM "WILD BILL"

"Union Inquiry Looks at Charity's Tie to Reputed Mobster," By Kevin Flynn, *The New York Times*, December 12, 1998 (Newspaper Article)

"Body Identified as Missing Mobster's," *The New York Times*, October 7, 2008 (Newspaper Article)

"The Complete Idiot's Guide to the Mafia," By Jerry Capeci, *Alpha Books*, 2002 (Book)

DEFEO, RONALD JR. "THE AMITYVILLE HORROR"

"Couple and 4 children killed in 'Amityville Horror' Murders," By Jerry Schmetterer and Daniel Driscoll, *The New York Daily News*, November 14, 1974 (Newspaper Article)

"The Amityville Horror: A True Story," By Jay Anson, *Prentice Hall*, August 1977 (Book)

"New Evidence Raises Questions In Decades-Old Amityville Horror Murders: Did Ronald DeFeo Jr. Act Alone?," CBS News, February 27, 2012 (Web Article)

DEMEO, ROY "MURDER MACHINE"

"Murder Machine: A True Story of Murder, Madness, and the Mafia, By Gene Mustain, Jerry Capeci, *Penguin Publishing Group*, July 1993 (Book)

"For the Sins of My Father," By Albert DeMeo, Broadway Books, September 2003 (Book)

"The Westies: Inside New York's Irish Mob," By T. J. English, *G.P. Putnam's Sons*, 1990 (Book)

DOWD, MICHAEL "THE SEVEN FIVE"

"Good Cop, Bad Cop: Detective Joe Trimboli's heroic pursuit of NYPD Officer Michael Dowd," By Mike McAlary, *Pocket Books*, November 1994 (Book)

"The Seven Five," Directed by Tiller Russell, *All3Media America*, May 2015 (Documentary Film)

DWYER, MARY ANN

"Two Insane Women – Kate Stoddard and Mary Ann Dywer," *The New York* Times, July 14, 1874 (Newspaper Articles)

"The Three Graces of Raymond Street: Murder, Madness, Sex, and Politics in 1870s Brooklyn," Robert E. Murphy, SUNY Press, December 9, 2014 (Book)

EDWARDS, DELROY "UZI"

"A Drug Dealer Gets a Sentence Of 7 Life Terms," By Leonard Buder, *The New York* Times,

December 2, 1989 (Newspaper Article)

"Crack's Destructive Sprint Across America," By Michael Massing, *The New York Times,* October 1, 1989 (Newspaper Article)

ELSON, MONYA "ELSON'S BRIGADE"

"Red Mafiya: How the Russian Mob Has Invaded America," By Robert I. Friedman, *Little, Brown*, 2000 (Book)

"The Organizatsiya," By Robert I. Friedman, *New York Magazine*, November 7, 1994 (Magazine Article)

EPPOLITO, LOUIS "THE MAFIA COPS"

"Friends of the Family: The Inside Story of the Mafia Cops Case," By Tommy Dades, Mike Vecchione, David Fisher, *Harper Collins*, May 2009 (Book)

"Mafia Cop," By Lou Eppolito, Bob Drury, *Simon and Schuster*, August 2005 (Book)

EPSTEIN, MENDEL "THE PRODFATHER"

"Brooklyn Rabbi Gets 10 Years for Leading a Gang of Men Who Beat up Jewish Husbands Reluctant to Divorce Their Unhappy Wives," By Reuven Blau, *The New York Daily News*, December 15, 2015 (Newspaper Article)

"The Orthodox Hit Squad," By Matthew Shaer, *GQ*, September 2, 2014 (Magazine Article)

EREZ, SEAN "HOLY ROLLERS"

"Holy Rollers," By Ted B. Kissell, *The Miami New* Times, September 30, 1999 (Newspaper Article)

"Holy Rollers," Directed by Kevin Asch, *Deerjen Films, Lookbook Films, Safehouse Pictures*, December 23, 2010 (Theatrical Film)

"The Incredible History of Jewish Smuggling," By Gabe Friedman, August 21, 2014 (Newspaper Article)

FAMA, JOSEPH

"What Really Happened in Bensonhurst: How a Petty Neighborhood Feud, Stirred by Rumor, Posturing, And Racism, Led to A Senseless Killing," By Michael Stone, *New York Magazine*, November 6, 1989 (Magazine Article)

"For the Color of His Skin: The Murder of Yusuf Hawkins and the Trial of Bensonhurst," By John DeSantis, *St Martins Press*, 1991 (Book)

FARACE, COSTABILE "GUS"

"Dead and Alive: The Race for Gus Farace," Directed By Peter Markle, *Katie Face Productions, Patchett Kaufman Entertainment, World International Network*, November 24, 1991 (Theatrical Film)

"Death of a Hood," By Eric Pooley, *New York Magazine*, January 29, 1990 (Magazine Article)

"Suspect in Drug Agent's Slaying Found Shot to Death," By Howard W. Frech, *The New York Times*, November 19, 1989

FERRARO, ROMANO "PREDATOR PRIEST"

"Diocese Pays $1.2 Million In Sex Lawsuit," By Greg winter, *The New York Times*, April 2, 2002 (Newspaper Article)

"Rev. Romano J. Ferraro—Assignment Record," *BishopAccountability.org* (Website)

"Trying to Kill Santa? An Apology for a Priest's Zeal," *The Associated Press*, December 10, 1986 (Newswire Service)

FERGUSON, COLIN, "THE LONG ISLAND RAILROAD MASSACRE"

"The Long Island Railroad Massacre: 20 Years Later," Directed By Charlie Minn, *J&M Productions*, December 7, 2013 (Documentary Film)

"Great Crimes and Trials: The Long Island Railroad Massacre,"

Nugus/Martin Productions LTD, May 2011 (Television Series)

FISH, ALBERT "THE VAMPIRE OF BROOKLYN"

"Albert Fish: The Lying Cannibal," By Chloe Castleden, *Little, Brown Book Group*, April 2011 (Book)

"Albert Fish in His Own Words: The Shocking Confessions of the Child Killing Cannibal," By John Borowski, *Waterfront Productions*, September 2014 (Book)

FOGLIETTA, PHIL

"A Pedophile in Plain Sight," By Eric L. Lewis, *The New York Times*, January 13, 2013 (Newspaper Article)

"Poly Prep Football Players Warned Freshmen of Coach Phil Foglietta's Sex Abuse, School Threatened Discipline Against Reports: Lawsuit," By Michael O'Keefe, *The New York Daily News*, December 7, 2011 (Newspaper Article)

"Poly Shocker: Dyker Prep School Rocked by Allegations of Administrator, Kids Boozing With Hookers in Cuba," By Max Jaeger, *The Brooklyn Paper*, June 4, 2015 (Newspaper Article)

FURNARI, CHRISTOPHER "CHRISTIE TICK"

"U.S. Jury Convicts Eight as Members of Mob Commission," By Arnold Lubasch, *The New York Times*, November 20, 1986

"The Mafia Encyclopedia: Second Edition", By Carl Sifakis, *Checkmark Books*, 1999 (Book)

"The Complete Idiots Guide to the Mafia," By Jerry Capeci, *Alpha Books*, 2002

GALANTE, CARMINE "THE CIGAR"

"Five Families: The Rise, Decline, and Resurgence of America's Most Powerful Mafia Empires," By Selwyn Raab, *St. Martin's Press*, September 5, 2006 (Book)

"Galante and 2 Shot to Death in Brooklyn Restaurant," By Robert D. McFadden, *The New York Times*, July 13, 1979 (Newspaper Article)

"The Coffey Files: One Cop's War Against the Mob," by Joseph J. Coffey, Jerry Schmetterer, *St. Martin's Press*, February, 1992 (Book)

GALLO, JOSEPH "CRAZY JOE"

"The Gang that Couldn't Shoot Straight," By Jimmy Breslin, *Viking Press*, 1969 (Book)

"The Mad Ones: Crazy Joe Gallo and the Revolution at the Edge of the Underworld," By Tom Folsom, *Weinstein Books*, May 2009 (Book)

GARSON, GERALD PHILLIP

"Crooked Brooklyn: Taking Down Corrupt Judges, Dirty Politicians, Killers and Body Snatchers," By Michael Vecchione and Jerry Schmetterer, *Macmillan*, November 17, 2015 (Book)

"Brooklyn Noir 3: Nothing But the Truth," By Tim McLoughlin and Thomas Adcock, *Akashic Books*, June 1, 2008 (Book)

"Former Judge is Convicted of Bribery in Divorce Court," By Michael Brick, *The New York Times*, April 20, 2007 (Newspaper Article)

GOLDSTEIN, MARTIN "BUGGSY"

"New York City Gangland," By Arthur Nash, *Arcadia Publishing*, 2010 (Book)

"The Canary Sang But Couldn't Fly: The Fatal Fall of Abe Reles, the Mobster Who Shattered Murder, Inc.'s Code of Silence," By Edmund Elmaleh, *Sterling Publishing Company, Inc.*, 2009 (Book)

"The Mammoth Book of Gangs," By James Morton, Little, *Brown Book Group*, April 19, 2012 (Book)

GRAVANO, SALVATORE "SAMMY THE BULL"

"Underboss: Sammy the Bull Gravano's Story of Life in the Mafia," By Peter Maas, *Harper Perennial*, January 1999 (Book)

"Mob Daughter: The Mafia, Sammy "The Bull" Gravano, and Me!" By Karen Gravano, Lisa Pulitzer, *Macmillan*, February 2012 (Book)

HARDY, DAMION "WORLD"

"Lil' Kim's Ex Damion (World) Hardy Gets Life Prison Sentence for 6 Murders," By John Marzulli, *The New York Daily News,* May 11, 2015 (Newspaper Article)

"Emotions Run High as Damion Hardy Is Sentenced to Life Term for Killings," By Stephanie Clifford, *The New York Times*, May 11,

2015 (Newspaper Article)

HATCHER, JOHN "THE BLOODY HATCHET"

"B'KLYN Kingpin's Reign of Carnage," By Murray Weiss, *The New York Post*, March 5, 2007 (Newspaper Article)

"Crack King Admits 30 Murders," By Tim Reid, *The Australian*, March 6, 2007 (Newspaper Article)

HENDRIX, TROY

"Local College Student Slain," By Charles Roghers, Canarsie Courier, May 15, 2003 (Newspaper Article)

"Trial No. 2 in Torture, Rape & Slay," By Hugh Son, *The New York Daily* News, February 23, 2006 (Newspaper Article)

"College Student's Killers Are Sentenced to Life in Prison," By Michael Brick, *The New York Times*, April 12, 2006 (Newspaper Article)

"EXCLUSIVE: Judge nixes claim of racial bias in search for missing woman found dead in 2003," By John Marzulli, *The New York Daily News*, August 4, 2014 (Newspaper Article)

HERRON, RONALD "RA DIGGS"

"Ronald Herron, Brooklyn Rapper Known as Ra Diggs, Gets 12 Life Prison Terms," *The New York Times*, April 2, 2015 (Newspaper Article)

"EXCLUSIVE: Brooklyn Drug Kingpin Gets 3 Life Terms in Colorado's Supermax Prison," By John Marzulli, *The New York Daily News*, April 24, 2016 (Newspaper Article)

HILL, HENRY "GOODFELLAS"

"Wise Guy, By Nicholas Pileggi, *Simon & Schuster*, January 1995 (Book)

"Goodfellas," Directed By Martin Scorsese, *Warner Brothers*, September 1990 (Theatrical Film)

IVANKOV, VYACHESLAV "LITTLE JAPANESE"

"Infamous from Moscow to N.Y.," By Gene Mustain and Jerry Capeci, *The New York Daily News,* April 21, 1997 (Newspaper Article)

"Red Mafiya: How the Russian Mob Has Invaded America," By Robert I. Friedman, *Little, Brown*, 2000 (Book)

"For a Departed Mobster, Some Roses but No Tears," By Michael Schwirtz, The New York Times, October 13, 2009 (Newspaper Article)

KAPELIOUJNYJ, OSTAP "THE GREENPOINT CREW"

"Twenty-one Members of an East European Organized Crime Ring Indicted by a Federal Grand Jury in Brooklyn," U.S. Attorney's Office, Eastern District of New York, March 08, 2006 (Press Release)

"Racket Busters – Feds Nab 15 Brooklyn Gang Thugs," By Cynthia R. Fagen, *The New York Post*, March 9, 2006 (Newspaper Article)

"The Stringfellas. Cops Bust Euro Gang in Drug and Violin Capers," By John Marzulli, *The New York Daily News*, Thursday, March 9, 2006 (Newspaper Article)

KING, ELIZABETH "LIZZIE" LLOYD

"Two Insane Women – Kate Stoddard and Mary Ann Dywer," *The New York* Times, July 14, 1874 (Newspaper Articles)

"The Three Graces of Raymond Street: Murder, Madness, Sex, and Politics in 1870s Brooklyn," Robert E. Murphy, SUNY Press, December 9, 2014 (Book)

"The Goodrich Murder: The Mystery Solved. Confession of the Murderess; Findings of the Pistol and Other Articles Belonging to the Deceased," *The New York Times*, July 12, 1873 (Newspaper Article)

"Kate Stoddard Finally Disposed Of," *The New York Times*, July 16, 1874 (Newspaper Article)

KOSLOW, JACK "THE KILL FOR THRILLS GANG"

"The Brooklyn Thrill-Kill Gang and the Great Comic Book Scare of the 1950s," By Mariah Adin, ABC-CLIO, December 9, 2014 (Book)

"When Good Kids Kill," By Michael D. Kelleher, *Turtleback Books*, 2000 (Book)

"Thrill Killers," Time Magazine, December 27, 1954 (Books)

KRUGER, CARL

"Former State Senator Is Sentenced to 7 Years in Vast Bribery Case," By Benjamin Weser, *The New York Times*, April 26, 2012 (Newspaper Article)

"King Carl of Canarsie: The Gothic Saga of Brooklyn Power Broker Carl Kruger," By Geoffrey Gray, *New York Magazine*, January 8, 2012 (Magazine Article)

LEE, LUDWIG

"Torso Parts Clues in Double Murder- New York Has Dual Murder Mystery as Women's Dismembered Bodies Are Found," *The Evening Independent* (St. Petersburgh, Florida), 1927 (Newspaper Article)

"The Mammoth Book of Bizarre Crimes," By Robin Odell, *Running Press*, May 18, 2010 (Book)

LEGRAND, DEVERNON "THE REVEREND"

"Back to Brooklyn House of Evil," By Brad Hamilton, *The New York Post*, August 1, 2010 (Newspaper Article)

"Angel Dust Sex, Kids in Cages, Other Horrors Remembered in '70s Brooklyn Nun Cult," By Joe Coscarelli, *The Village Voice*, August 1, 2010 (Newspaper Article)

LITTLEJOHN, DARRYL

"Imette Slay Suspect Linked to Abduct Try," *The New York Daily News*, August 9, 2007 (Newspaper Article)

"Imette St. Guillen Murder Suspect Claims 'Frame Up' Involving Rudy Giuliani," By Scott Shifrel, *The New York Daily News*, December 12, 2007 (Newspaper Article)

"Bouncer Darryl Littlejohn Found Guilty of Murdering of Imette St. Guillen," By Scott Shifrel, *The New York Daily News*, June 3, 2009 (Newspaper Article)

"Secrets Can be Murder: What America's Most Sensational Crimes Tell Us about Ourselves," By Jane Velez-Mitchell and Nancy Grace, *Simon and Schuster*, June 10, 2008 (Book)

LONERGAN, RICHARD "PEG LEG"

"The Gangs of New York: An Informal History of the New York

Underworld (pg. 78)," By Herbert Asbury, *Alfred A. Knopf*, 1928 (Book)

"Paddy Whacked: The Untold Story of the Irish American Gangster (pg. 158-159)," By T.J. English, *HarperCollins*, 2005 (Book)

"An Unlikely Union: The Love-Hate Story of New York's Irish and Italians," By Paul Moses, *NYU Press*, July 3, 2015 (Book)

LOPEZ, VITO

"Vito Lopez Dead at 74: Disgraced NY Assemblyman and Brooklyn Powerbroker Succumbs to Leukemia," By Kenneth Lovett, *The New York Daily News*, November 11, 2015 (Newspaper Article)

"Vito Lopez is Dead," By David Seifman, *The New York Post*, November 10, 2015 (Newspaper Article)

LOVETT, WILLIAM "WILD BILL"

"Wild Bill Lovett Irish Gangster From Brooklyn," By Robert Grey Reynolds Jr., *Smashwords*, July 6, 2016 (Book)

"Gangster City: The History of the New York Underworld 1900-1935," By Patrick Downey, *Barricade Books*, 2004 (Book)

"Light of the Diddicoy," By Eamon Loingsigh, *Three Rooms Press*, March 25, 2014 (Book)

MASSINO, JOSEPH "THE LAST GODFATHER"

"King of the Godfathers: Joseph "Big Joey" Massino and the Fall of the Bonanno Crime Family," By Anthony M. DeStefano, *Kensington: Pinnacle True Crime Series*, June 2007 (Book)

"The Last Godfather: The Rise and Fall of Joey Massino," By Simon Crittle, *Penguin*, March 2006 (Book)

MASTROMARINO, MICHAEL "THE BROOKLYN BODY SNATCHER"

"Michael Mastromarino, Dentist Guilty in Organ Scheme, Dies at 49 (Obituary," By Daniel E. Slotnik, *The New York* Times, July 8, 2013

"The Organ Grinder: The Living Need the Dead Like Never Before, and Michael Mastromarino Had a Dickensian Scheme for Supplying the Parts," By Randall Patterson, *New York Magazine*, October 16, 2006 (Magazine Article)

MCFARLAND, THOMAS "THE SEX KILLER OF BROOKLYN"

"The Sex Killer of Brooklyn, 1935: Originally published: "Snaring Brooklyn's Lust Killer," By Harvey Henderson, Front Page Detective, December 1936 (Magazine Article)

MILLER, WILLIAM "520 PERCENT"

"Anatomy of a Ponzi Scheme: Scams Past and Present," By Colleen Cross, *Slice Publishing*, March 16, 2016 (Book)

"Beggars, Cheats and Forgers: A History of Frauds Throughout the Ages," By David Thomas,

Wharncliffe, June 30, 2014 (Book)

NAPOLITANO, DOMINICK "SONNY BLACK"

"Donnie Brasco: My Undercover Life in the Mafia," By Joseph Pistone (assisted by Richard Woodley), *Dutton Books*, 1988 (Book)

"Donnie Brasco," Directed By Mike Newell, *Mandalay Entertainment, Baltimore Pictures*

Mark Johnson Productions, February 1997 (Theatrical Film)

NARVAEZ, ISRAEL

"Second Chance: The Israel Narvaez Story," By Darla Milne, *Living Books*, February, 1980 (Book)

"Vampires, Dragons, and Egyptian Kings: Youth Gangs in Postwar New York," By Eric C. Schneider, *Princeton University Press*, 2001 (Book)

NAYFELD, BORIS

"Influx of Russian Gangsters Troubles F.B.I. in Brooklyn," By Selwyn Raab, *The New York Times*, August 23, 1994 (Newspaper Article)

"Red Mafiya: How the Russian Mob Has Invaded America," By Robert I. Friedman, *Little, Brown*, 2000 (Book)

"Russian Mafia in America: Immigration, Culture, and Crime," James O. Finckenauer, Elin J. Waring, *UPNE*, 1998

NELSON, LEMRICK "CROWN HEIGHTS RIOTS"

"Lemrick Nelson Stabbed in the Head with Ice Pick, 19 Years After Knifing Student to Death in Riots," By Barry Paddock, *The New York Daily News*, September 12, 2010 (Newspaper Article)

"Lemrick Nelson Jr. is Acquitted of the Murder of Yankel Rosenbaum," By Frances McMorris, *The New York Daily News*, October 30, 1992 (Newspaper Article)

"Crown Heights: Blacks, Jews, and the 1991 Brooklyn Riot," By Edward S. Shapiro, *UPNE*, 2006 (Book)

NITZBERG, IRVING "KNADLES"

"Gang Killer Tells Why He 'Reformed'; Became Disgusted With Way of Life That Required 11 Murders," *The New York Times*, May 17, 1941 (Newspaper Article)

"Murder Inc.: Mysteries of the Mob's Most Deadly Hit Squad,"By Chris Cippolini, *Strategic Media Books*, 2015 (Book)

NORMAN, CLARENCE JR.

"Former Democratic Leader in Brooklyn Is Convicted," By Anemona Hartocollis, *The New York Times*, February 24, 2007 (Newspaper Article)

"Crooked Brooklyn: Taking Down Corrupt Judges, Dirty Politicians, Killers and Body Snatchers," By Michael Vecchione, Jerry Schmetterer, *Macmillan*, November 17, 2015 (Book)

O'DONNELL, ALICE

"Nurse Kills Her Charge: Horrified Mother the First to Discover the Tragedy," *The New York Times*, December 8, 1900 (Newspaper Article)

"10 Creepy Murders in Old New York: No. 9 – The Nurse Girl Murder," By Nene Adams, *Listverse.com*, November 20, 2012 (Web Article)

O'MALLEY, WALTER

"Forever Blue: The True Story of Walter O'Malley, Baseball's Most Controversial Owner, and the Dodgers of Brooklyn and Los Angeles," By Michael D'Antonio, *Penguin Publishing Group*, March 2, 2010 (Book)

"Mover and Shaker: Walter O'Malley, the Dodgers, and Baseball's Westward Expansion," By Andy McCue, *University of Nebraska Press*, May 1, 2014 (Book)

PAPPA, JOHN

"Life Without Honor," By Jerry Capeci, *Gangland*, May 17, 1999 (Web Article)

"Colombo Hit Man John Pappa Makes the Most of His Time Cooking and Cheering on the Yankees as He's Holed up in High-Security Prison," By John Marzulli, *The New York Daily News*, June 27, 2012 (Newspaper Article)

PARKER, GEORGE

"For You, Half Price," By Gabriel Cohennov, *The New York* Times, November 27, 2005 (Newspaper Article)

"The Modern Con Man: How to Get Something for Nothing," By Todd Robbins, *Bloomsbury Publishing USA*, December 8, 2008 (Book)

PARKER, JAMES

"Coercive Control: The Entrapment of Women in Personal Life," By Evan Stark, *Oxford University Press*, Mar 1, 2009 (Book)

"Girl Drawn Into Angry Man's World," By Randy Kennedy, *The New York* Times, September 17, 1996 (Newspaper Article)

"Goodbye Danielle, Many Cry for Victim," By James Rutenberg, *The New York Daily News*, September 24, 1996, (Newspaper Article)

PEARSON, KAYSON

"Local College Student Slain," By Charles Rogers, Canarsie Courier, May 15, 2003 (Newspaper Article)

"Trial No. 2 in Torture, Rape & Slay," By Hugh Son, *The New York Daily* News, February 23, 2006 (Newspaper Article)

"College Student's Killers Are Sentenced to Life in Prison," By Michael Brick, *The New York Times*, April 12, 2006 (Newspaper Article)

"EXCLUSIVE: Judge nixes claim of racial bias in search for missing woman found dead in 2003," By John Marzulli, *The New York Daily News*, August 4, 2014 (Newspaper Article)

PERRONE, SALVATORE "SON OF SAL"

"'Son of Sal' Serial Killer Salvatore Perrone, Who Gunned Down Three Shopkeepers in Brooklyn, Gets 75 Years to Life in Prison,"

By Christina Carrega-Woodby, *The New York Daily News,* March 4, 2016 (Newspaper Article)

"Convicted Triple Murderer Salvatore Perrone Sentenced to 75 Years to Life," By Thomas MacMillan, *The Wall Street Journal,* March 4, 2016 (Newspaper Article)

PERSICO, CARMINE "THE SNAKE"

"Persico Convicted in Colombo Trial," By Arnold Lubasch, *The New York Times,* June 14, 1986 (Newspaper Article)

"Persico, His Son and 6 Others Get Long Terms as Colombo Gangsters," By Arnold Lubasch, *The New York Times,* November 18, 1986 (Newspaper Article)

Persico (Carmine) v. U.S. U.S. Supreme Court Transcript of Record with Supporting Pleadings," By Abraham Glasser, *Gale, U.S. Supreme Court Records,* October 30, 2011 (Book)

PIMENTEL, JOANNA "LA MADRINA"

"18 Held as Members of Gangs That Sold Weapons and Drugs," By William K. Rashbaum, *The New York Times,* April 6, 2000 (Newspaper Article)

"Godmother Fights Rap: Calls Her Conviction in Gang Slay a Setup," By Mike Claffey, *The New York Daily News,* May 29, 2001 (Newspaper Article)

"United States of America, Appellee, v. Joanna Pimentel, Also Known As "la Madrina," George Viruet, Defendants-appellants, Elvin Cruz; Jorge Aponte, Also Known As "cano," Also Known As "john Doe," Defendants, 346 F.3d 285 (2d Cir. 2003)", *U.S. Court of Appeals for the Second Circuit - 346 F.3d 285 (2d Cir. 2003),* Argued: June 10, 2003 / Decided: October 8, 2003 (Court Document)

PITERA, THOMAS "TOMMY KARATE"

"The Butcher: Anatomy of a Mafia Psychopath," By Philip Carlo, *William Morrow Paperbacks,* October 19, 2010 (Book)

"Reputed Mobster Guilty In Six Narcotics Murders," By Arnold H. Lubasch, *The New York Times,* June 26, 1992 (Newspaper Article)

"Life Prison Term in 6 Drug-Case Murders," *The New York Times,* October 25, 1992 (Newspaper Article)

Profaci, Joseph "Don Peppino"

"The Mafia At War," Nicholas Gage, *New York Magazine*, July 17, 1972 (Magazine Article)

"Profaci Dies of Cancer; Led Feuding Brooklyn Mob," *The New York Times*, June 8, 1962 (Newspaper Article)

"Sixty-two Top Mafia Leaders Were Seized in the Apalachin Meeting in 1957," By Howard Wantuch and Sidney Kline, *The New York Daily News*, November 15, 1957 (Newspaper Article)

Reles, Abe "The Canary Who Couldn't Fly"

"The Canary Sang But Couldn't Fly: The Fatal Fall of Abe Reles, the Mobster Who Shattered Murder, Inc.'s Code of Silence," By Edmund Elmaleh, *Union Square Press*, April 7, 2009 (Book)

"Tough Jews: Fathers, Sons, and Gangster Dreams," By Rich Cohen, *Vintage*, April 20, 1999 (Book)

Seda, Herbieto "The Brooklyn Sniper"

"Suspect Is Charged in 4 Zodiac Cases in Queens," By Lynda Richardson, *The New York Times,* June 22, 1996 (Book)

"Herbieto Seda," *Murderpedia*

Scarpa, Greg "The Grim Reaper"

"Deal with the Devil: The FBI's Secret Thirty-Year Relationship with a Mafia Killer," By Peter Lance, *Harper Collins*, July 2, 2013 (Book)

"Who Handled Who?" By John Connolly, *New York Magazine: Cityside section*, December 2, 1996 (Magazine Article)

Shapiro Brothers

"Gangster City: The History of the New York Underworld 1900–1935," By Patrick Downey, *Barricade Books*, 2004 (Books)

"Tough Jews: Fathers, Sons, and Gangster Dreams," By Rich Cohen, *Vintage*, April 20, 1999 (Book)

Shkreli, Martin

"Everything You Know About Martin Shkreli Is Wrong – Or Is It?" By Bethany McLean, *Vanity Fair*, February 2016 (Magazine Article)

"Pharma Bro Is the Face of U.S. Health Care: Martin Shkreli is a symptom of a dangerous system," By James Hamblin, *The Atlantic*, September 23, 2015 (Magazine Article)

"Martin Shkreli, the Bad Boy of Pharmaceuticals, Hits Back," By Julie Creswell and Andrew Pollack, *The New York Times*, December 5, 2015 (Newspaper Article)

SIEGEL, BENJAMIN "BUGSY"

"Bugsy," Directed By Barry Levinson, *TriStar Pictures, Mulholland Productions*, December 20, 1991 (Theatrical Film)

"When the Mob Ran Vegas: Stories of Money, Mayhem and Murder Paperback," By Steve Fischer, *Berkline Press*, July 7, 2005 (Book)

"Bugsy: The Bloodthirsty, Lusty Life of Benjamin "Bugsy" Siegel," By George Carpozi, *Spi Books*, July 1992 (Book)

"Little Man: Meyer Lansky and the Gangster Life," By Robert Lacey, *Little Brown & Co.*, September, 1991 (Book)

SPERO, ANTHONY "THE OLD MAN"

"Anthony Spero, a Name in the Bonanno Crime Family, Is Dead at 79," By Bruce Weber, *The New York Times,* October 2, 2008 (Newspaper Article)

"Spero Guilty of Racketeering," By Michael Claffey, *The New York Daily News*, April 6, 2001 (Newspaper Article)

"Old-Style Mob Trial for a Murder Case in Brooklyn," By Alan Feuer, *The New York Times*, March 7, 2001 (Newspaper Article)

STRAUSS, HARRY "PITTSBURGH PHIL"

"Mafia Hits: 100 Murders that changed the Mob," By M. A. Frasca, *Arcturus Publishing*, November 25, 2015 (Book)

"Tough Jews," By Rich Cohen, *Vintage Books*, 1999 (Books)

SUTTON, WILLIE "WHERE THE MONEY WAS"

"Where the Money Was: The Memoirs of a Bank Robber," By Willie Sutton, Edward Linn, Ballantine Books, May 12, 1977 (Book)

"I, Willie Sutton," By Quentin Reynolds, Macmillan, December 19, 1953 (Book)

"Sutton," by J.R. Moehringer, *Hachette Books*, May 7, 2013 (Book)

THOMAS, CHRISTOPHER "THE PALM SUNDAY MASSACRE"

"Mass Killer Eyes Freedom," By John Doyle, *The New York Post*, February 16, 2009 (Newspaper Article)

"Ex-Convict Held In 'Palm Sunday' Massacre of Ten," By Margot Hornblower, Dody Tsiantar, *The Washington Post*, June 21, 1984 (Newspaper Article)

VARIO, PAUL "BIG PAULIE"

"Vario and 4 Held in Hijacking Case," By James Markham, *The New York Times*, October 26, 1972

"Obituary in New York Times: Paul Vario, 73; Called a Leader Of Crime Group," By Mark A. Uhlig, *The New York Times*, May 5, 1988

"The Lufthansa Heist: Behind the Six-Million-Dollar Cash Haul That Shook the World," By Henry Hill an Daniel Simone, *Rowman & Littlefield*, August 1, 2015 (Book)

VOLPE, JUSTIN "ABNER LOUIMA POLICE BRUTALITY"

"An Officer and an Atrocity: The barbaric brutalization of Abner Louima and the tragic fate of a handful of flawed Brooklyn cops," By Craig Horowitz, *New York Magazine*, October 1999

"Louima Says His Attackers Did Not Yell 'Giuliani Time'," By John Kifner, *The New York Times*, January 15, 1998 (Newspaper Article)

WEINER, ANTHONY "CARLOS DANGER"

"Weiner," Directed by Josh Kriegman and Elyse Steinberg, *Edgeline Films, Motto Pictures*, May 26, 2016 (Documentary Film)

"The Rapid Rise and Spectacular Fall of Anthony Weiner – War Room," By Steve Kornacki, *Salon.com*, June 16, 2011 (Web Article)

WOJTOWICZ, JOHN STANLEY

"The Boys in the Bank," By P. F. Kluge, *Life Magazine*, September 22, 1972 (Magazine Article)

"Ernest Aron Became Elizabeth Eden: AIDS Kills Woman Behind 'Dog Day'," *The Los Angeles Times*, September 30, 1987 (Newspaper Article)

"The Bank Robbery That Would Become 'Dog Day Afternoon,'" By Tony Ortega, *The Village Voice Blogs*, March 11, 2011 (Web

Article)

"Dog Day Afternoon," Directed By Sidney Lumet, *Warner Brother*, September 21, 1975 (Theatrical Film)

WOLFSON, BARNEY

"Chronicles of Historic Brooklyn," By John B. Manbeck, *The History Press*, April 30, 2013 (Book)

"Four N.Y. Gunmen Tell police They Killed Wrong Man," *The Chicago Tribune,* August 30, 1931 (Newspaper Article)

YALE, FRANKIE

"American Mafia: A History of Its Rise to Power," By Thomas Reppetto, *Holt, Henry & Company*, January 2, 2005 (Book)

"Get Capone: The Secret Plot That Captured America's Most Wante," By Jonathan Eig, *Simon and Schuster*, April 27, 2010 (Book)

For More News About Craig McGuire and Future Releases, Signup For Our Newsletter:

http://wbp.bz/newsletter

Word-of-mouth is critical to an author's long-term success. If you appreciated this book please leave a review on the Amazon sales page:

http://wbp.bz/brooklynsmostwanteda

WILDBLUE
PRESS

Available Now From WildBlue Press:

BETRAYAL IN BLUE by BURL BARER, FRANK C. GIRARDOT JR., and KEN EURELL

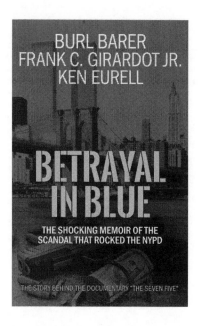

**They Had No Fear Of The Cops
Because They Were The Cops**

NYPD officers Mike Dowd and Kenny Eurell knew there were two ways to get rich quick in Brooklyn's Lower East Side. You either became drug dealers, or you robbed drug dealers. They decided to do both.

Read More: **http://wbp.bz/bib**

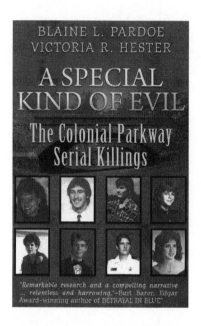

See even more at:
http://wbp.bz/tc

More True Crime You'll Love From WildBlue Press

BOGEYMAN: He Was Every Parent's Nightmare by Steve Jackson
"A master class in true crime reporting. He writes with both muscle and heart." (Gregg Olsen, New York Time bestselling author). A national true crime bestseller about the efforts of tenacious Texas lawmen to solve the cold case murders of three little girls and hold their killer accountable for his horrific crimes by New York Times bestselling author Steve Jackson. *"Absorbing and haunting!"*(Ron Franscell, national bestselling author and journalist)

wbp.bz/bogeyman

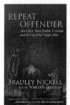

REPEAT OFFENDER by Bradley Nickell
"Best True Crime Book of 2015" (Suspense Magazine) A "Sin City" cop recounts his efforts to catch one of the most prolific criminals to ever walk the neon-lit streets of Las Vegas. *"If you like mayhem, madness, and suspense, Repeat Offender is the book to read."*(Aphrodite Jones, New York Times bestselling author)

wbp.bz/ro

DADDY'S LITTLE SECRET by Denise Wallace
"An engrossing true story." (John Ferak, bestselling author of Failure Of Justice, Body Of Proof, and Dixie's Last Stand) Daddy's Little Secret is the poignant true crime story about a daughter who, upon her father's murder, learns of his secret double-life. She had looked the other way about other hidden facets of his life - deadly secrets that could help his killer escape the death penalty, should she come forward.

wbp.bz/dls

BODY OF PROOF by John Ferak
"A superbly crafted tale of murder and mystery." – (Jim Hollock, author of award-winning BORN TO LOSE) When Jessica O'Grady, a tall, starry-eyed Omaha co-ed, disappeared in May 2006, leaving behind only a blood-stained mattress, her "Mr. Right," Christopher Edwards, became the suspect. Forensic evidence gathered by CSI stalwart Dave Kofoed, a man driven to solve high-profile murders, was used to convict Edwards. But was the evidence tainted? A true crime thriller written by bestselling author and award-winning journalist John Ferak.

wbp.bz/bop